"For all those, with an interest in our field, this book provides a welcome and much-needed account, in English, of the 'Portuguese model'. In articulating this distinctive approach, against the broader historical background of Group Analysis, the authors remind us of its vital international character."

David Glyn, president of the group,
Group Analytic Society International

"This book is not only the long-missed history of the Portuguese school of group analysis. It's also a comprehensive and thorough description of its present conceptional understanding of theory, methods and clinical use of group analysis and the requirements in training, which are probably the most demanding in Europe. An engaging and inspiring reading."

Kristian Valbak, PhD,
group analyst and former president of EGATIN

"This is a most interesting book about the different identity of Portuguese school of 'groupanalysis'. Cortesao, its founder, conceptualized a fascinating framework of three times a week group analysis, which is considered 'a psychoanalytic treatment of the individual in and through the group'. This book will be an important step into a fertile international dialogue between different approaches of group analytic therapy."

Robi Friedman,
group analyst, former president of the
International Group Analytic Society,
former chair of the Israeli Institute for Group Analysis

"The book seeks to integrate theory, clinical wisdom and research and generously offers clinical examples and references to illustrate and support the text. I am happy to recommend this comprehensive, ambitious and well-written book, which addresses and reflects upon questions that are highly important and urgently need answers."

Steinar Lorentzen,
Professor of Psychiatry at the
University of Oslo, psychoanalyst, group analyst

The Portuguese School of Group Analysis

At the time group analysis was emerging in the United Kingdom through the ideas of S. H. Foulkes, one of his followers, Eduardo Luís Cortesão, returned to Portugal and founded the Portuguese Society of Groupanalysis, with the first group-analytic Symposium taking place in Estoril, Portugal, in 1970. In this vital new book, an impressive collection of contributors demonstrate how group analysis in Portugal has always embraced the relational paradigm that has become central to contemporary psychoanalysis.

The Portuguese school of groupanalysis, through several of its senior members, has contributed to many of the organizations responsible for the development of group analysis, such as EGATIN, IAGP and GASi. Nevertheless some of the concepts and variations of the Portuguese school of groupanalysis tend to be unknown to the English speaker. Their focus is on the "pattern," allowing transformation of each patient's personal matrix, working through primitive relational failures and paving the way to new beginnings, always in a transgenerational group context.

This book will be of tremendous importance to psychotherapists working in group analysis around the world.

Isaura Manso Neto, MD, is a training and supervisor member, and current president of the Portuguese Society of Groupanalysis and Analytic Group Psychotherapy, a GASi full-member, a member of the Portuguese Society of Psychoanalysis and of the Portuguese Association of Relational Psychoanalysis. She is currently working in private practice as a psychoanalytic psychotherapist, supervisor and group analyst, conducting four group-analytic groups.

Margarida França is a specialist in clinical psychology, community psychology and psychotherapy. She is a member of the Portuguese Society of Groupanalysis and Analytic Group Psychotherapy, and an associate member of GASi. She is currently working as a psychotherapist in private practice in Lisbon, with adults, young children and adolescents.

The New International Library of Group Analysis (NILGA)
Series Editor: Earl Hopper

Drawing on the seminal ideas of British, European, and American group analysts, psychoanalysts, social psychologists and social scientists, the books in this series focus on the study of small and large groups, organisations and other social systems, and on the study of the transpersonal and transgenerational sociality of human nature. NILGA books will be required reading for the members of professional organisations in the field of group analysis, psychoanalysis, and related social sciences. They will be indispensable for the "formation" of students of psychotherapy, whether they are mainly interested in clinical work with patients or in consultancy to teams and organisational clients within the private and public sectors.

Recent titles in the series include:

The Social Unconscious in Persons, Groups, and Societies:
Volume 3: The Foundation Matrix Extended and Re-configured
Edited by Earl Hopper

Fairy Tales and the Social Unconscious: The Hidden Language
By Ravit Raufman and Haim Weinberg

Group Analysis in the Land of Milk and Honey
Edited by Yael Doron

The Linked Self in Psychoanalysis: The Pioneering Work
of Enrique Pichon Riviere
Edited by Roberto Losso, Lea S. de Setton and David E. Scharff

On Group Analysis and Beyond: Group Analysis as Meta-Theory,
Clinical Social Practice, and Art
By Anastassios Koukis

Applications of Group Analysis for the Twenty-First Century:
Applications
Edited by Jason Maratos

The Portuguese School of Group Analysis

Towards a Unified and Integrated Approach to Theory Research and Clinical Work

Edited by
Isaura Manso Neto
and Margarida França

LONDON AND NEW YORK

First published 2021
by Routledge
2 Park Square, Milton Park, Abingdon, Oxon OX14 4RN

and by Routledge
52 Vanderbilt Avenue, New York, NY 10017

Routledge is an imprint of the Taylor & Francis Group, an informa business

© 2021 selection and editorial matter, Isaura Manso Neto and Margarida França; individual chapters, the contributors

The right of Isaura Manso Neto and Margarida França to be identified as the authors of the editorial material, and of the authors for their individual chapters, has been asserted in accordance with sections 77 and 78 of the Copyright, Designs and Patents Act 1988.

All rights reserved. No part of this book may be reprinted or reproduced or utilised in any form or by any electronic, mechanical, or other means, now known or hereafter invented, including photocopying and recording, or in any information storage or retrieval system, without permission in writing from the publishers.

Trademark notice: Product or corporate names may be trademarks or registered trademarks, and are used only for identification and explanation without intent to infringe.

British Library Cataloguing-in-Publication Data
A catalogue record for this book is available from the British Library

Library of Congress Cataloging-in-Publication Data
A catalog record has been requested for this book

ISBN: 978-0-367-68372-6 (hbk)
ISBN: 978-0-367-37074-9 (pbk)
ISBN: 978-1-003-13723-8 (ebk)

Typeset in Times New Roman
by KnowledgeWorks Global Ltd.

Contents

List of tables x
List of contributors xi
Foreword xiv
Acknowledgements xviii
List of abbreviations xx

Introduction 1
ISAURA MANSO NETO AND MARGARIDA FRANÇA

1 **History of group psychotherapy, group analysis, and the contributions of the Portuguese school of groupanalysis** 9
ANTÓNIO GUILHERME FERREIRA

The historical, socio-political, economic, philosophical, and scientific context 9
The evolution of psychoanalytic theory 12
Group psychotherapies, the psychoanalytic approach, and Trigant Burrow 15
Group analysis. Its history. Foulkes and the British group, Cortesão and the Portuguese school of groupanalysis 18

2 **Group analysis: A cluster identity. Redefining/rethinking Group Analysis** 28
ISAURA MANSO NETO AND MARIA JOÃO CENTENO

Introduction 28
The 'Crisis' in psychoanalysis and group analysis 30
Controversies and ambiguities within group analysis 32
The group-analytic cluster—a kind of brand 41
The group-analytic cluster/brand—the tables 41
Concluding remarks 52

3 **The Portuguese school of groupanalysis: The integration of psychoanalytic concepts in groupanalysis** 53
   SARA FERRO AND MARGARIDA FRANÇA

   Preliminary considerations 53
   Cortesão's legacy 54
   Other concepts in groupanalysis 60
   Specificities in groupanalysis 64
   Other contributions 68
   Training 69
   Concluding remarks 71

4 **The concepts of groupanalytic matrix and personal group matrix** 73
   PAULO MOTTA MARQUES AND JOÃO CARLOS MELO

   Theoretical framework: historic and evolutive perspectives 73
   The groupanalytic matrix 77
   Personal group matrix 80
   Other contributions by Portuguese authors 83
   Clinical practice 86
   Concluding remarks 88

5 **The pattern** 90
   ISAURA MANSO NETO AND CÉSAR VIEIRA DINIS

   Introduction 90
   The concept—history, controversies, and debate 91
   Pattern—current definition (Portuguese school
      of groupanalysis) 94
   Beginning of the 21st century: is "pattern" still
      a useful concept? 112

6 **Foulkes, Cortesão, and beyond: Other specific concepts of the Portuguese school of groupanalysis** 113
   JOÃO CARLOS MELO AND PAULO MOTTA MARQUES

   Introduction 113
   Main differences between group analysis
      (Foulkes) and groupanalysis (Cortesão) 113
   The groupanalytic process 117
   Interchangeable levels of communication and interpretation 120
   Empathic resonance box 122

Inner space of optional doubt and metadramatic communication 124
Concluding remarks 125

7 **Transference and countertransference in the Portuguese school of groupanalysis**   126
CÉSAR VIEIRA DINIS AND JOSÉ DE ABREU-AFONSO

Introduction 126
The complexity of transference neurosis in groups 126
The group transference neuroses 129
Groupanalysis and analytic group psychotherapy 133
The transference and other therapeutic factors in the group-analytic treatment 134

8 **Group analysis and group-analytic psychotherapy as favoured settings to deal with conflicts and difficult feelings**   137
ISAURA MANSO NETO AND ANA BIVAR

Introduction 137
Phenomenology and meaning 140
Triggers 145
Dealing with difficult situations in therapeutic groupanalysis 151
Concluding remarks 154

9 **The groupanalyst as a patient and related training issues**   155
MARGARIDA FRANÇA AND ISAURA MANSO NETO

Why talk about training? 155
Crisis in analytic societies? 155
Programme structure: theory, personal groupanalysis, and supervision 157
Discussing the theoretical programme 158
The importance of supervision 161
The group analyst as a patient 165
Concluding remarks 168

References	170
Bibliography	186
Index	188

Tables

2.1	Template	43
2.2	Group analysis: therapeutic group analysis, groupanalysis, operative groups (in the broader sense)	44
2.3	Group-analytic psychotherapy (short- and long-term groups)/institutional groups/operative groups (in the broader sense)	45
2.4	Multifamily group analysis/parents groups	46
2.5	Mentalization-based group therapy (MBT-G)	47
2.6	Internet groups	48
2.7	Group-analytic coaching	49
2.8	Experiential groups/T-groups/demo groups	50
2.9	Task-centred groups: operative groups (strict sense)/Supervision groups/Balint groups/Team work groups	51

Contributors

Editors

Isaura Manso Neto, MD, is a psychiatrist, training and supervisory member, and current president of the Portuguese Society of Groupanalysis and Analytic Group Psychotherapy (SPGPAG), a GASi full-member, and a member of the Portuguese Society of Psychoanalysis (SPP) and of the Portuguese Association of Relational Psychoanalysis (PsiRelacional). She worked in a psychiatric hospital applying group-analytic and psychoanalytic conceptualizations in the treatment framework of severe cases as well as teaching residents. She now works in private practice as a groupanalyst, psychoanalytic psychotherapist and supervisor. She currently conducts four groupanalytic groups and has organized international and national conferences on Group Analysis (GA) and Psychoanalytic Psychotherapy (PP). She has also written papers and contributed chapters to published books on GA and PP. E-mail: isauramansoneto@gmail.com

Margarida França is a clinical psychologist and specialist in clinical psychology, community psychology and psychotherapy; Master of Clinical Psychology (ISPA—Instituto Superior de Psicologia Aplicada); trainee member of the Portuguese Society of Groupanalysis and Analytic Group Psychotherapy (SPGPAG) and associate member of GASi. She worked in a social care institution with the homeless and other victims of social exclusion for several years and as a teacher in the context of vocational training courses for economically disadvantaged young people. She is currently working as a psychotherapist in private practice, in Lisbon, with adults, young children and adolescents. E-mail: margarida_mcf@hotmail.com

Contributing Authors

António Guilherme Ferreira MD, was a psychiatrist, training and supervisory member of the Portuguese Society of Groupanalysis and Analytic Group Psychotherapy (SPGPAG) and its former president (1983–1995); director (1987–1998) and clinical director (1988–1997) of Miguel Bombarda Hospital; the president of WASP (1971–1983) and chairman of its Board of Trustees (1992–1996); and member of the Standing Committee of Presidents of International Non-Governmental Organizations Concerned with Mental Health Issues (1990–1993). He retired after 50 years of private practice and, unfortunately, passed away while the book was being finished.

Maria João Centeno is an educational psychologist, Master of Educational Psychology (Instituto Superior de Psicologia Aplicada—ISPA); full member of the Portuguese Society of Groupanalysis and Analytic Group Psychotherapy (SPGPAG); associate member of GASi; specialist in clinical and health psychology and psychotherapy; and has a Europsy Certificate in Psychology (EFPA). She works as a psychotherapist in individual, group and multifamily settings, both at the Day Hospital and at the Outpatient Consultation Services in the Psychiatry and Mental Health Service of the Neuroscience Department of Santa Maria Hospital, in Lisbon. She provides health professionals' training and supervision as member of the Day Hospital Team. E-mail: maria.centeno@chln.min-saude.pt

Sara Ferro, MD, is a psychiatrist, training and supervisory member of the Portuguese Society of Groupanalysis and Analytic Group Psychotherapy (SPGPAG) and its former president (2009–2015) and a full member of GASi. She worked at the Clinical Psychiatric Service at the Santa Maria Hospital (a University Hospital in Lisbon) with care and teaching functions; and was a co-founder of the Day Hospital at the same institution. She currently works in private practice as a groupanalyst, a psychoanalytic psychotherapist and a supervisor. E-mail: saracferro@gmail.com

Paulo Motta Marques, PhD, is a clinical psychologist, groupanalyst and psychoanalytic psychotherapist; a full member and training and supervisory groupanalyst of the Portuguese Society of Groupanalysis and Analytic Group Psychotherapy (SPGPAG) and full member of the Group Analytic Society International (GASi); full member of the Portuguese Association of Relational Psychoanalysis (PsiRelacional); and member of the International Association for Relational Psychoanalysis and Psychotherapy (IARP). He currently works in private practice. E-mail: paulo.motta.m@portugalmail.pt

João Carlos Melo, MD, is a psychiatrist, training and supervisory member of the Portuguese Society of Groupanalysis and Analytic Group Psychotherapy (SPGPAG) and full member of the Group Analytic Society International (GASi). He works as a graduate assistant at Fernando da Fonseca Hospital and is the team leader of the Psychiatric Day Hospital Unit. He also works in private practice in Lisbon. E-mail: jcmelo@netcabo.pt

César Vieira Dinis, MD, is a psychiatrist, training and supervisory member of the Portuguese Society of Group Analysis and Analytic Group Psychotherapy (SPGPAG) and full member of the Group Analytic Society International (GASi). He is a consultant psychiatrist in the psychiatric department of a general hospital in Lisbon where he has worked for over thirty years and where he was one of the founder members of a Day Hospital with a group-analytic framework which he headed for ten years. He currently works in private practice as a groupanalyst and supervisor. His writings on group-analytic subjects have been published in Brazil, France, Germany and Portugal. E-mail: dinisenetopsi@clix.pt

José de Abreu-Afonso, PhD, is a training groupanalyst of the Portuguese Society of Groupanalysis and Analytic Group Psychotherapy (SPGPAG) and psychoanalyst of the Portuguese Society of Psychoanalysis (SPP) and International Psychoanalytic Association (IPA). He is a professor and researcher at *ISPA-Instituto Universitário*, teaching subjects related to groupanalysis and psychoanalysis where he is also the pedagogical coordinator of the internships in Clinical and Health Psychology. He currently works in private practice in Lisbon and is a supervisor of individual and group psychotherapies in institutions and private practice. E-mail: joseabreuafonso@netcabo.pt

Ana Bivar is a clinical psychologist and groupanalyst of the Portuguese Society of Groupanalysis and Analytic Group Psychotherapy (SPGPAG). She has worked at Santa Maria Hospital with teenagers and adults as a co-conductor in groups for young women with eating disorders and at the Hospital D. Estefânia with children and parental support, has written papers on eating disorders and presented a paper at the 16th European Symposium in Group Analysis, and has been working in private practice with adults and teenagers since 2003. E-mail: ana.bivar.marques@gmail.com

Foreword

Whether as a broad church or spectrum or range of interrelated orientations which have developed around several charismatic colleagues who were both innovative thinkers and passionate teachers and clinicians, what is known in Portugal as "groupanalysis" has hardly received the international recognition and appreciation that it has earned and deserves. There are many reasons for this, perhaps the most important being that we in the English-speaking world tend not to read the Portuguese literature, at least not outside the wine trade in which relations between Portugal and England have been established for several centuries. However, colleagues from Portugal have taken important, leading roles in various organizations in our field, such as the International Association for Group Psychotherapy and Group Process (IAGP), the Group Analytic Society International (GASi), and the European Group Analytic Training Institute Network (EGATIN). They have also presented their work at conferences and workshops, and this has been highly valued.

Following the 16th International Symposium of GASi in Lisbon in 2014, I asked Dr Isaura Manso Neto and Dr César Vieira Dinis, two of the leading figures in our profession in Portugal, to write and edit a book about groupanalysis, focusing on current work, but with an appreciation of its history and development. Perhaps not fully aware of the effort that this would involve, especially in the context of their active and fulfilling professional and family lives, they readily agreed to take on this important task. While gazing across the ocean towards Brazil and after a second round of coffee and Aguardente Bagaceira, we more or less outlined some of the main features of this project.

My expectations and their determination have been richly rewarded. Three of my own favourite contributions from Portuguese colleagues have been emphasized. The often-overlooked theory and concept of the pattern, as formulated by Eduardo Cortesão, has been re-introduced. The "pattern" is not unrelated to Bion's concept of group mentality, Ezriel's concept of common group tension, Stock-Whitaker's concept of focal group conflict, and to Foulkes' overarching theory of what has recently been called the tripartite matrix. The notion of pattern is also reminiscent of Ruth Benedict's ideas concerning "cultural patterns", which are at the foundation of the culture and personality school of thought in anthropology, to which Bronislaw Malinowski made core contributions, and from which Foulkes drew important insights. It is not generally appreciated how difficult it is to think about the so-called "collective transference" without using at least a modified conceptualization of the pattern.

The second contribution which has been very important to me is the theory and concept of the internal relational matrix developed by Maria Rita Sá Mendes Leal (David & Neto, 2019). I believe that Leal's ideas were an important influence on the early conceptualization of what Foulkes called the "personal matrix". Both concepts emphasize the unconscious intrapsychic relational and interpersonal lives of the participants in a clinical group. Without such concepts serious clinical group analysis is merely an economically efficient way of attempting to provide personal therapy for people in groups. Dr Leal also specialized in the development of group work with children and adolescents, and in the study of sub-symbolic processes. In 1971, Dr Leal was awarded the first Foulkes Prize for her work.

I would also like to mention Antonio Guilherme Ferreira's theorization of transference processes in groupanalysis. He presented his work in 2008 at the GASi Symposium in Dublin, where we shared a panel on the topic of transference. We agreed that the analysis of transference and countertransference processes was at the heart of clinical work (Hopper, 2006, 2007a, b). We should never have shifted away from our commitment to this, even though our thinking about transference and the interpretation of it had gone through important changes. The notion of a mutative interpretation was still valid, provided that it was offered with respect for interpersonal affect. We remained committed to an appreciation of psychoanalysis as one of the three roots of group analysis, along with those of sociology and the study of group dynamics.

I was very sad to have learned that Guilherme died just as this book was going into production. He was looking forward to its publication. Guilherme was a member of the Board of the IAGP, and was of great help to me when I was the President of this organization. On several occasions we listened to authentic fado in the back streets of Old Lisbon. We acknowledged that there was something of significance in the Foulkesian notion of the "music of the group". He said that fado might be the music of the foundation matrix of Portugal. If so, Guilherme had an ear for it. He also had a special sensitivity to the pains of trauma. I will miss him.

I want to express my appreciation to the co-editors of this book. Isaura and Margarida, the latter having taken on the role from César, have both contributed chapters and edited material from their colleagues, having also encouraged them to present their work. It is all too easy to overlook the efforts and even sacrifices of our female colleagues, who have many commitments to their families, partners, children, and grandchildren, as well as to their patients, students and colleagues. I asked Isaura and Margarida to tell me a little about themselves, beyond their professional accomplishments: what did they regard as important to their own identities, and how might they wish to be recognized? Accordingly, I quote from what they have written to me, lightly edited:

Isaura Manso Neto:

I have lived according to my personality traits, which are mainly unconformity and resilience towards reaching my main objectives, looking for pleasure in my family, profession, and hobbies—dance, swimming in the sea. I am married and I have two sons: the eldest, is an economist, and the youngest is a psychiatrist with psychoanalytic training. I have two teenage grand-daughters, beautiful, and intelligent. Being with them all is a real pleasure. I have always been strongly influenced by the psychoanalytic and group-analytic way of understanding and dealing with human beings, and, thus, with human suffering. In 2008, together with the Day Hospital team, I was awarded the Jane Abercrombie Prize. I have tried to make bridges between group-analytic cultures using different languages—English, Portuguese/Brazilian, Spanish and French, taking advantage of a good enough knowledge of each of them. Another passion is to teach residents and supervisees, from whom I have learned so much. And last but not the least: I love to be a psychotherapist, and a groupanalyst; moreover, I will take the risk to say that I love my patients.

Margarida França:

I am a mother of two boys, ten and eight years old. My husband is also a psychotherapist. I try to divide my day time with them, working mostly while the children are at school, and cooking (which I love) dinner every day. I think, family life is my recipe for keeping emotional balance. My two princes are also two very demanding savages, and I guess I take pleasure in being pushed around by them! Although I have always felt quite cosmopolitan, I really like the sun and the beach, and lately I have started to imagine myself, in a few years, living most of the time in a peaceful village in Algarve, by the sea.

While taking my psychology degree, I swiftly understood that before taking care of others, I needed to be taking care of my own mental health. So, I started psychotherapy with Isaura when I was 20 years old. After a while she suggested that I could be in a group. I feel very welcome in the Portuguese Society of Groupanalysis. I have been a member of the Local Organizing Committee of a Luso-Brazilian Congress, and I was a member of the LOC of the Lisbon GASi Symposium in 2014. Isaura and I continued to work together, and her invitation to be her co-editor for this book made me feel very proud of myself and very grateful to her for her trust in me.

As is the case for most books in the New International Library of Group Analysis (NILGA), this book is essential reading for colleagues who practice group analysis, whether called "group-analysis", "groupanalysis", or even "psychoanalytical group psychotherapy". This important contribution will be of value to our students. I look forward to wetting its head at our next International Symposium.

References

David, M. & Neto, I. (2019). Maria Rita Sá Mendes Leal. *Contexts.* June.

Hopper, E. (2006) Theoretical and conceptual notes concerning transference and countertransference processes in groups and by groups, and the social unconscious: part I. *Group Analysis*, 39(**4**): 549–559.

Hopper, E. (2007a, b) Theoretical and conceptual notes concerning transference and countertransference processes in groups and by groups, and the social unconscious: part II, *Group Analysis*, 40, 1, 21–34 and part III. *Group Analysis*, 40(**2**): 285–300.

Earl Hopper
Series Editor

Acknowledgements

First and foremost, we would like to acknowledge Earl Hopper, in his capacity as the editor of the New International Library of Group Analysis (NILGA) series, for having invited us to take up this stimulating challenge. As editors of this work, we assumed an enormous responsibility towards the Portuguese school of groupanalysis, a legacy of Eduardo Luís Cortesão and his immediate followers, to whom we pay tribute.

In addition to Cortesão's legacy, the Portuguese school of groupanalysis has been influenced very much by other perspectives on group analysis and psychoanalysis of colleagues from Europe, North America and Latin America, as well as by scientific contributions from other disciplines. We are grateful to them for the chance to learn and embrace a variety of perspectives, paving the way to making group analysis a useful, creative and democratic therapeutic setting with several applications.

We thank our editors at Routledge—Russell George and Alec Selwyn—for their encouragement and patience. A word for Rod Tweedy, initially at Karnac, when the adventure began.

This book would not have happened without the valuable cooperation of the contributing authors, all of whom are hard-working members of SPGPAG (the Portuguese Society of Groupanalysis and Analytic Group Psychotherapy) who entrusted us with their ideas about groupanalysis after having developed the themes that we suggested to them at the outset.

We regret that one of them is not amongst us anymore. Guilherme Ferreira died while this book was entering production. We will deeply miss his presence within the Groupanalytic Society.

We are grateful to our mentors, teachers, colleagues, and post-graduate psychotherapy and groupanalysis students from whom we have learnt so much, either in their presence or through their writings. It has been great to be stimulated by all of them, even those with whom we do not agree.

We acknowledge our original families with whom we lived both pleasurable and difficult experiences that gave rise to our need to better understand human and group dynamics.

We especially thank our current families for their tolerance, emotional support and confidence in our abilities.

Lastly, we would like to express our gratitude to our patients and group members for their trust and the possibility to learn so much.

We offer a warm thank-you to those who agreed to our inclusion of real clinical vignettes in which they are portrayed, and therefore contributed to making this book a more vivid and credible experience.

Isaura Manso Neto and Margarida França
Editors

Abbreviations

AGPA	American Group Psychotherapy Association
BSPA	British Society of Psychoanalysis
EFPP	European Federation for Psychoanalytic Psychotherapy
EGATIN	European Group Analytic Training Institutions Network
GAS	Group Analytic Society
GASi	GAS International, Group Analytic Society International
IGA	Institute of Group Analysis
IPA	International Psychoanalytical Association
MBT	Mentalization-based treatment, Mentalization-based Therapy
MBT-G	Mentalization-based Group Therapy
MFGA	Multifamily groupanalysis
PSG	Portuguese school of groupanalysis
SPG	Portuguese Society of Groupanalysis
SPGPAG	Sociedade Portuguesa de Grupanálise e Psicoterapia Analítica de Grupo
	Portuguese Society of Groupanalysis and Analytic Group Psychotherapy

Introduction

Isaura Manso Neto and Margarida França

In this book, we will argue that group analysis is used as a therapeutic way to access the unconscious, providing introspection, insight, and development of the self. It is a psychoanalytic treatment of the individual in and through the group. Its aims are similar to those of psychoanalysis. Nevertheless, it can also be used in other settings without therapy as its main purpose.

As Portuguese groupanalysts, we owe our groupanalytic tradition to Eduardo Luís Cortesão (1919–1991), and some of his immediate followers, who worked in Lisbon from the early 1950s onwards. Although Portugal was under a dictatorship, Cortesão and some others managed to start working with groups in psychiatric hospitals and other public institutions by means of the creation of a Study Group in 1958. In 1960, the first General Meeting was held, which led to the establishment in 1963 of the Groupanalytic Section of the Portuguese Society of Neurology and Psychiatry which worked under this designation until 1981 (Pinto & Salgado, 2001, 2002). This subsection gave birth to the Portuguese Society of Groupanalysis (SPG) in December 1981 (Pinto & Salgado, 2002). In 2012, the SPG changed its name to the 'Sociedade Portuguesa de Grupanálise e Psicoterapia Analítica de Grupo' [Portuguese Society of Groupanalysis and Analytic Group Psychotherapy] (SPGPAG) to reflect its activities more precisely.

We think that Cortesão's proposals were far ahead of his time in many aspects: he developed Foulkes's ideas from a deeper psychoanalytic perspective, integrated South American authors perspectives, gave great importance to the therapist's role in the process far away from the neutrality preconized by classical psychoanalysis and closer to the relational paradigm that has taken its place, among other things. Many chapters in this book will approach considerations on theory and technique that Cortesão and his followers had, and examine why those ideas are still useful. Although Cortesão was also an English speaker (as was his mother) he wrote only a few articles in English. His more important work, a book called "Grupanálise—Teoria e Técnica" [Groupanalysis—Theory and Technique] (1989) has only ever been published in Portuguese. We believe this justifies the importance of this particular publication.

Since then, transformations have occurred in theory and practice in the SPG alongside international group-analytic perspectives and changes in society in general. The scope of this work is therefore not confined solely to Cortesão and his legacy.

Because transformations have occurred and because in the last 20 years both psychoanalysis and group analysis seem to have been suffering a crisis, with many probable internal and external causes, we felt we could not leave these issues aside. Therefore, some chapters of this book will address where group analysis stands now from our perspective, how SPGPAG is facing its most difficult clinical challenges and what our considerations on training are. We have been watching changes in society provoke psychoanalytic and group-analytic associations to redefine their rules and demands. But perhaps we do not question sufficiently the merits of some changes. We undoubtedly resist deeply acknowledging a certain lack of internal coherence in the functioning of societies and the acceptance of some practices. This does not mean we are rejecting changes at all! It is our perspective that mental health workers should try at all times to sustain an open attitude towards transformations in society and their implications in the individual's suffering. Analytic societies should evolve in order to comprehend and adequate to the environment surrounding them. This implies looking at our past theoretical and technical grounds and adapting (or not) our intervention techniques to prevent them from becoming obsolete or ineffective in the near future. Nevertheless, we do not see transformation as a value in itself. Changes must have a theoretical basis or principle, since leaving behind a theoretical or technical corpus cannot be faced lightly. This has been the perspective of Portuguese groupanalysts for more than 40 years.

Diversity in group analysis and group psychotherapy is likely to cause confusion with destructive consequences in individuals in general, but especially in group analysts or group conductors. Over the past years, we have felt compelled to look at group analysis from a systematic, critical point of view. We intend to share some of our main concerns and why it is important for group analysts to look deeply into certain issues. These issues include the group analyst's role, the variety of target groups and its implications, the depth of therapeutic group analysis as a way to transform the individual(s), including the therapist, and the training process to be a group analyst.

The 34th Group Analytic Society (GAS) Winter Workshop under the theme "Group Analysis today: Concepts and Preconceptions" was held in Lisbon in 2006. It seemed clear that most authors agreed that a crisis was affecting psychoanalysis, group analysis, and psychoanalytic/dynamic psychotherapies in general and that it would be important to look into it.

Fonagy (in Garza-Guerrero, 2002a) defines the crisis as the difficulty that psychoanalysis has in constructing a solid foundation of knowledge.

Wallerstein (2005) argues that it is possible for psychoanalysis to belong to the group of sciences, but in order for this to take place, it will have to be supported by a unified theoretical structure.

Other authors, such as André Green (2005), argue that psychoanalysis cannot be compared to other sciences, like physics; pluralism is possible, but he considers that the tendency nowadays is towards chaos, adding confusion to confusion, originating schools of thought that have frank similarities to religious, and sectarian methods of functioning. Green defends the need to establish and thoroughly discuss these differences in order to ascertain the theoretical principles that are the basis of contemporary psychoanalysis.

At the 43rd International Psychoanalytical Association (IPA) Congress in 2004, the theme of which was "Psychoanalysis—Method and Application", numerous prejudices that are prevalent in the psychoanalytic community were identified. Discussion centred on difficulties:

- in establishing therapeutic objectives,
- in evaluating the clinical process,
- in comparing psychoanalysis with other forms of psychotherapy, and
- in the notations of analytic treatments.

Should groupanalysis step away from this discussion? At the 43rd Foulkes Lecture, Juan Tubert-Oaklander (2019) renewed the discussion by saying that psychoanalysis as hermeneutics should not be underrated for being apart from the natural sciences. But if we do not accept, define, and evaluate group analysis as a form of psychotherapy, how can we expect to compete with other methods of treating psychic distress, and how can we demand professional certification and financial subsidies from health systems? This is an issue that needs to be discussed.

Other issues that relate only to groupanalysis and not to psychoanalytic therapies in general are also important to discuss. Is group analysis an analysis like psychoanalysis or is it psychotherapy? If we consider it an analysis, how can we argue in favour of one session a week? It is clear that the definition of the analytic process does not depend solely on the frequency of the sessions, yet frequency is necessary for transference to develop. Is it possible to talk about analysis of transference, when the group analyst is in a position of only formulating interpretations of the group's phantasies and movements as a whole? How do we conceive the transformation process that occurs whilst we work? May it exclude consciousness and rational comprehension, in line with António Damásio's (2019) remark that "without affective intelligence there would never have been life"? And so on. We believe that it is important to define precisely what group analysis is for the majority, what the main points of discordance are, and what group analysis is not. We need to redefine concepts to avoid preconceptions (Neto & Centeno,

2006). We believe we should define these concepts within each local society as well as at a multinational level.

An important research study promoted by the Group Analytic Society and conducted by the University of Sheffield in 2009—"A Systematic Review of the Efficacy and Clinical Effectiveness of Group Analysis and Analytic/Dynamic Group Psychotherapy" (Blackmore, Tantam, Parry & Chambers, 2012), recommended further research: "Specifically, we recommend the use of structured abstracts, clear definitions of different types of group intervention, and agreed keywords for use in titles and abstracts and consistent use of a set of outcome measures". During the presentation of this study in London in 2010, some concerns were highlighted about what Group Analysis and group analysts are all about.

In his essay for which he was awarded the first Dennis Brown Essay Prize, Douglas Young (2006, p. 477) declares:

> At present, if we ask ten different group analysts how Group Analysis works (or why it works), we are likely to obtain ten different answers. This goes beyond simple semantics, and reflects both the variable use of terms and lack of a robust and coherent theoretical underpinning which precludes us from answering 'how' it works in a consistent way. For the 'how' is predicated upon the 'why' and the 'why' demands a theoretical explanation which is robust, coherent, transparent, and acceptable to the questioner.

Based on our experience in Portugal and in numerous formal and informal contacts with various group analysts across Europe and some South American countries as well as in literature on these themes, we do feel that Group Analysis has not been sufficiently conceptualized.

It has become clear that group analysis is being used as a large umbrella term to cover almost every kind of group work. Groups are conducted by professionals trained in various ways but call themselves group analysts/group therapists/conductors, and are undifferentiated from others who have different ways of conducting and understanding groups as well as different objectives. As Harold Behr (2008, p. 55) puts it,

> The problem for Group Analysis is compounded by confusion in the public mind between the different forms of psychotherapy. There is a lack of definition which lends itself to the myth that group therapy, whether analytic or any other kind, is not a particularly specialized field of practice, that it can therefore be practiced by almost anybody who works in a clinical setting.

Moreover, group analysis is sometimes used to refer to a psychoanalytic psychotherapy of 3 sessions, or only 1 session, per week; continuous over time or attended in blocks; for working groups, small, medium, or large groups.

We may call this umbrella a "group-analytic spectrum" (Neto, 2006) constituted by several areas: therapeutic group analysis per se; analytic group psychotherapy including institutional analytic psychotherapeutic groups; other forms of group-analytic psychotherapy such as multifamily groups (Neto & Centeno et al., 2014), parents groups, mentalized-based treatment groups, internet groups, group-analytic coaching, and task-centred groups (team work; team supervision; Balint groups).

David Zimerman (Zimerman, Osório et al., 1997, p. 127, translated from the Portuguese), a Brazilian groupanalyst and psychoanalyst (who died in 2014), wrote:

> Can group therapy inspired and built on psychoanalytic grounds be considered 'true psychoanalysis'? Can it be called Group Analysis? The authors are not unanimous, ranging from group therapists that more discreetly support the name group therapy to those who, with confidence, consider themselves groupanalysts, as in the case of the highly competent and recognizable colleagues of the Lisbon Group Analytic Society.

This leads us to explore a little further the importance that the group conductor/groupanalyst has in the Portuguese school of groupanalysis.

A prevailing old prejudice among the group-analytic community seems to be the avoidance of calling the conductors of therapeutic groups "group analysts". We strongly suggest that the term "conductor" be used by those conducting working groups and large groups. We consider that the personality and training of the conductor/groupanalyst/psychoanalytic group psychotherapist roots the way he/she deals with each individual in a specific group—this implies the pattern of the groupanalyst. This concept, introduced by Eduardo Luís Cortesão (1967a), is fundamental in our practice because it influences the way each individual's transformation process will occur. It is not a way to be authoritarian, or intrusive, or any other way to block someone's freedom and autonomy. It is a way to facilitate psychoanalytic knowledge and process. Therefore, the concept of pattern may be useful in group analysis and psychoanalysis.

There has been a large discussion about what is more important in a group setting: the individual or the group, even in a therapeutic group setting. This discussion may have contributed to the ambiguity surrounding the therapeutic capacities of group analysis/group-analytic psychotherapy/psychoanalytic group psychotherapy.

The eternal debate about whether we should care more for the individual or the group will be discussed at various points in the book. When we treat patients, we must look at the individual, his/her life history, early object relations, "transgenerational inheritance" (Badaracco, 1986), transference, and countertransference. Historical interpretations are often needed. In our groupanalytic treatment practice, we usually keep each patient in a dyadic setting before bringing him/her to a therapeutic group. Of course there are moments when everybody in a group is sharing similar conflicts and emotions. Then we must interpret the group as a whole. From our perspective, Bion's most interesting contributions to group analysis were the ones he made as a psychoanalyst. Regarding groups, he mainly conceptualized several group defences, the "basic assumptions". As he said in 1978, in *The Four Discussions with W.R. Bion*, his main interest and investment was in individual analysis.

We should point out once more that groupanalysis is a form of treating the individual within a small or even medium-sized group that expands upon complementary perspectives of other works on group analysis such as Garland's (2010a) and Steinar Lorentzen's (2014) recent books and builds bridges between psychoanalysis and group analysis as Hopper (2008) defends.

But about the name: which one should we choose? Group analysis, analytic/dynamic group psychotherapy, or psychoanalytic group psychotherapy? Discussing these aspects will lead us to other matters, such as the training of the conductors/group analysts. Foulkes seemed ambivalent about this issue and used the terms group analysis and group psychotherapy in different periods. The question about what should be considered group analysis remains undiscussed within GAS International (GASi). Groupanalysis may be understood as a spectrum as we have mentioned above. In the beginning, EFPP (European Federation for Psychoanalytic Psychotherapy) called it group-analytic psychotherapy; some years later, it was changed to psychoanalytic group psychotherapy. The training needed to achieve this competence became mixed: individual psychotherapy complemented by a group-analytic training component or merely psychoanalytic group training on its own. On top of that, the qualification requirements have steadily become lower and lower, unlike the criteria to become an individual psychoanalytic psychotherapist. This situation has spread to other societies and federations, including EGATIN (European Group Analytic Training Institutions Network). Even GASi has progressively lowered the standards for one to become a full member.

Perhaps the names are important: beside the specificities related to training that we may infer from them, they carry the symbolism of how we conceptualize our work and what our aims really are.

What differentiates our practice and the theoretical points of view that support it has been recognized among the European societies, members of GASi, EGATIN, EFPP, and others. Nevertheless, it is necessary that these perspectives do not remain isolated and we hope this book will contribute to motivating discussion to promote the development of our societies. We have been expressing our points of view in international events, such as the most recent 16th European Symposium of GASi held in Lisbon in 2014 (Abreu-Afonso et al., 2015; Ferro et al., 2014) but we think this initiative deepens this purpose.

We believe that the characterization of groupanalysis made by the groupanalysts who participated in this book will be a helpful instrument to explain how groupanalysis and analytic group psychotherapy are very useful forms of psychoanalytic psychotherapy (Neto & Centeno, 2006). All the authors belong to the Portuguese Society of Groupanalysis and Analytic Group Psychotherapy, and have been greatly influenced by psychoanalysis.

The first chapter will address the historical background of group analysis before and after Foulkes and of the Portuguese Society of Groupanalysis. António Guilherme Ferreira will show how Cortesão's contributions give rise to complementary perspectives on group analysis.

In Chapter 2, Isaura Manso Neto and Maria João Centeno approach what they call the group-analytic cluster to be characterized according to several aspects of the setting and the group-analytic process. They consider the common ground of this cluster to be the omnipresence of unconscious Phenomena and processes by individuals in every kind of group. These phenomena may be understood and translated in a more or less explicit way according to the kind of setting being worked with.

The authors have done some research on the application of Group Analysis in psychiatric departments, with treatment and training aims (Centeno et al., 2014; Neto, 2010a, b). Other studies about multifamily group analysis, strongly influenced by "Psicoanálisis Multifamiliar" [Multifamily Psychoanalysis] (Badaracco, 2000) also deserve the authors' attention.

As groupanalysis is a psychoanalytic form of psychotherapy, we need to understand how the most important psychoanalytic tools and concepts are used in groupanalysis and how they appear and are named by groupanalytic authors. We stress that the Portuguese school of groupanalysis has been defending the importance of integrating recent authors from psychoanalysis, child development, neurosciences, and neuropsychoanalysis into groupanalytic theory and practice.

In Chapter 3, Sara Ferro and Margarida França will examine this issue further after they review some of the features that closely align groupanalysis as practiced in Portugal with psychoanalysis. Group analysis goes far beyond Foulkes and Bion and the rivalry conflicts among their followers that have closed group analysis institutes and group-analytic organizations, which have paved the way to weakening the impact of group analysis as a very useful kind of psychoanalytic treatment.

The specific way the internal relational objects of each individual appear in a group interacting with the others will be examined by Paulo Motta Marques and João Carlos Melo in Chapter 4, which deals with the matrix and the internal relational matrix (Leal, 1970; Pichon-Rivière, 1965).

In Chapter 5, Isaura Manso Neto and César Vieira Dinis will explain the importance of the "pattern" concept (Cortesão, 1967a, b/1989) in groupanalysis and psychoanalysis. Focus will be on highlighting the fundamental role of the groupanalyst and the complexities that role entails.

João Carlos Melo and Paulo Motta Marques, in Chapter 6, will approach other specific concepts of the Portuguese school of groupanalysis, such as the interchangeable levels of communication and interpretation (Cortesão, 1989), the group as an empathic resonance box (Dinis, 2001), the importance of creating an inner space of optional doubt and metadramatic communication (Silva, 1994). The main differences between Foulkesian group analysis and Portuguese groupanalysis will be explained.

Transference and countertransference in psychoanalytic therapeutic groups reach highly complex levels. They will be brought into focus by César Vieira Dinis and José Abreu Afonso in Chapter 7.

We think that group analysis is an excellent setting to work through difficult relational emotions and conflicts such as peer rivalry, jealousy and envy (Neto & David, 2017). Aggressive feelings and behaviour are seen more quickly in a group than in a dyadic setting. Therefore, if there is an adequate pattern, it can be worked through and overcome. We think that analysis must include the experience of such feelings and conflicts, sometimes denied in some psychoanalytic processes until the end. De-idealization is part of life; it is a turning point in human development. Therefore, we have included consideration of this issue in Chapter 8, by Isaura Manso Neto and Ana Bivar.

We will discuss our training, which is a major issue in our demanding work, and how it gives us the capacity to cope with new challenges. Margarida França and Isaura Neto will address the fundamental issue of training in Chapter 9. We believe that personal experience in a small therapeutic mixed group is the most important part of the training; this way of thinking runs counter too many psychoanalytic and group-analytic training organizations which progressively value theoretical courses and supervision. In 2008, a survey was conducted among the members of the SPG about their own groupanalytic experience (Carvalho, Galamba & Neto, 2008). The answers to the questionnaire reveal that personal groupanalysis is the part of groupanalytic training which is valued the most by Portuguese groupanalysts.

We suggest that therapeutic group analysis is a form of relational psychotherapy (Hopper, 2009) that is definitely useful in overcoming misinterpretations and conflicts based on primary relational experiences, opening doors to freedom and autonomy in current relationships, and paving the way to so-called cures.

We hope this book contributes to further discussion on group analysis and provides impetus for its development and research.

Chapter 1

History of group psychotherapy, group analysis, and the contributions of the Portuguese school of groupanalysis

António Guilherme Ferreira

The historical, socio-political, economic, philosophical, and scientific context

The end of the 18th century marked the development of important shifts in the paradigm of the existing State: The autocratic monarchies assumed the divine right of Kings. Although, in fact, the monarch represented civil power, he was perceived as deriving the right to rule directly from the will of God. Absolute monarchic rule was gradually succeeded by liberal regimes of a representative nature based on popular sovereignty.

The American Declaration of Independence in 1776 and the French Revolution in 1789, with their respective proclamations of the rights of the citizen and assertion of human right, embraced this idea of a sovereign people. The French Revolution saw the end of a society strictly regulated for centuries by a system of Orders, in which individuals were awarded the rights of its insertion in a certain social group, or Order.

Concurrently, the traditional dominance of agriculture in society changed rapidly with the rise of successive industrial revolutions across Europe, with rifts occurring in the social fabric of the communities wherever they took place. The emergence of social groups with great economic issues led to the development of Marxism as an economic theory, the proclamation of the Communist Manifesto by Marx and Engels, the creation of the communist and anarcho-syndicalist movements, with the consequent repercussions on the working masses and the development of violent actions with strikes and similar situations, and finally, the creation of coordinating entities of these masses, as were, successively, the 1st, 2nd, and 3rd Socialist Internationals and the counterpart, the Anarcho-Syndicalist International, that attempted (often successfully) to coordinate each of these movements.

To better understand the facts that led to the emergence of psychoanalysis and group psychotherapy, however, one cannot fail to mention that besides this social movement, the evolution of human knowledge over the last few centuries also played a contributory role.

From 1600, Francis Bacon (1560–1626) drew attention to the importance of the experimental methods for the development of sciences.

In 1639, Descartes (1596–1650) published his *Discourse on the Method*, culminating in the famous "Cogito ergo sum" (I think, therefore I am) which set out the principles of the deductive method, a concept that has most recently been opposed in *O erro de Descartes* by António Damásio (1995).

However, it was undoubtedly Immanuel Kant's (1724–1804) *Critique of Pure Reason* (1781) and *Critique of Practical Reason* (1788), in which he defended an idealistic view of philosophy with an active attitude of humankind in the development of thought, that most influenced Freudian thinking.

Likewise, Hegel (1770–1831), who in some respects at least, continued Kant's thinking and developed the study of a phenomenology which did much to centre this study as a whole.

Auguste Comte (1798–1857) reacted against such conceptions, defending the development of a philosophy, which he claimed to be positivist, in which he sought to explain human behaviour through phenomena that occurred in a certain situation and the relationships between them.

Husserl (1859–1938) developed a phenomenological conception of philosophy, which prevailed from the end of the 19th to the beginning of the 20th century. Jaspers (1883–1969) continued this development, which he applied to psychiatry (through his *General Psychology*, published in 1913).

Meanwhile, Bergson (1859–1941) explained the development of human thought through his concept of intuition. Some authors even feel that he strongly influenced the Freudian thinking, which Freud had always denied.

Returning to the rationalistic concepts, Bertrand Russell's (1872–1970) body of work in this field was vast. He studied the most important aspects of philosophy in works such as *Principia Mathematica* (1910, 1912, and 1913), *A History of Western Philosophy* (1945), and *Human Knowledge: Its Scope and Limits* (1948).

His student, and then contemporary, Ludwig Wittgenstein developed a logical analysis of world-thought-language in his *Tractatus Logico-Philosophicus* (1922) to find the limits of world, thought, and language. Also known as the picture theory of language, it postulates that statements are meaningful if they can be pictured or defined in the real world. His later work *Philosophical Investigations* (1953) is essentially a critique of his earlier work. He showed that philosophical thinking is the search for a way to untie the knots in language to reach an understanding of what is really being said. Wittgenstein's revised way of looking at language gave rise to the view of philosophy as therapy.

In France, three key names in recent times should be noted for their relationship with psychoanalysis.

Merleau-Ponty (1908–1961) developed phenomenological concepts in new terms, which challenged some aspects of Husserl's theory of knowledge and reduced Marxism to a simple heuristic methodology.

Michel Foucault (1926–1984) devoted himself to the study of societies through their behaviour and corresponding deviations within institutions such as prisons.

Finally, Jacques Derrida (1930–2004) used concepts from psychoanalysis, literature, and linguistics to explain philosophical points of view.

Particularly important was the action of the Austrian philosopher Karl Popper (1902–1994), author of works such as *The Poverty of Historicism* (1944) and *The Open Society and Its Enemies* (1945). An earlier work *The Logic of Scientific Discovery* is a treatise on scientific knowledge in which he defended the criterion of falsifiability. By applying this criterion, bodies of knowledge, such as astrology, metaphysics, Marxist history, and psychoanalysis, would not be considered sciences since it is impossible in principle to establish their theories as false. In *The Logic of Scientific Discovery*, Popper rejected inductive empiricism and developmental historicism. Nevertheless, Sulloway (1969) and Grunbaum (1984) were able to refute their postulations thanks to the extra-clinical and scientific arguments put forward by Freud, with whose work they were familiar.

It should be noted that throughout this period, great development in the social sciences (e.g., sociology, anthropology, and social psychology) and human sciences (e.g., psychology) occurred in areas that previous centuries had conceived of as being simply literary, or pre-scientific, concerns rather than matters pertaining to true science.

As far as human sciences, we will only provide a previously mentioned reference (psychology), that a purely rational conception, of philosophical nature, has transformed into a true science that led to Koch, in the '50s, to publish a seven-volume book, called *Psychology: A Study of Science*, where he studied the various perspectives through which it could be conceived.

Sociology studied the insertion of individuals in society and their organization. Having originated from Auguste Comte, it was, however, in Emile Dürkheim's work on suicide, that it had its first research paradigm at the end of the 19th century and beginning of the 20th century. Figures such as Gustave Le Bon, Gabriel Tarde, Wilfred Trotter, and William McDougall worked in this field, having all of them being referenced by Freud in his works.

Lastly, one should note the importance of new sociological research studies, centred on Darwinian designs and Mendelian inheritance.

As for anthropology, one should refer to the importance of society on the evolution of the individual that can be variously expressed:

- through the data on culture patterns (supported by Ralph Linton, Ruth Benedict, and Margaret Mead), that would determine the functioning of the individuals in the societies where they find themselves;
- through the culturalist, nowadays called interpersonalist, view which defends a psychoanalytical approach focused on the determination of

social behaviour that was developed by Alfred Adler (with his individual psychology) and further developed by Harry Stack Sullivan, Karen Horney and Abram Kardiner;
- in terms of the conditioning factors that determine social behaviour as seen through the lens of structuralism conceived by Claude Lévy-Strauss and Marcel Mauss and how this centred on the organizational structures in society; and
- through the complementary theses of Georges Devereux, who attempted to combine the structuralist point of view with psychoanalytical concepts.

Still within this approach, one must not forget the contributions to anthropology made by psychoanalysts such as Géza Róheim, Bronislaw Malinowski, and Erik Erikson.

Nowadays, anthropology is centred on biological and behavioural contributions, culminating in neo-Darwinian views based on ethology and behavioural ecology.

A final reference should be made regarding social psychology, focused on the studies of small groups, particularly relevant in the work of Kurt Lewin. Reference should also be made to the importance of Ludwig von Bertalanffy's general system theory, which behavioural scientist James G. Miller applied to his conceptual framework of living systems of which the levels of the group, organization, and society are of primary interest when considering social, group, interpersonal, and intrapersonal interaction.

The evolution of psychoanalytic theory

In 1896, in letters to Wilhelm Fliess, Freud supported the development of *The Project for a Scientific Psychology*, which transcended the classic concepts of psychology.

With the publication of his work, *The Interpretation of Dreams* (1900), *Formulations on the Two Principles of Mental Functioning* (1911), *Papers on Metapsychology* (1915), *Beyond the Pleasure Principle* (1920), *The Ego and the Id* (1923), and *An Outline of Psycho-Analysis* (1938), Freud was progressively giving shape to this aim.

Metapsychology. The first dissidents. The Freudian authors. The culturalists

The importance of metapsychology and the development of the structural theory, centred on the importance of the ego as a means of adaptation to the external environment, make it the centre of Freudian intervention. Such has found expression in the publication of Anna Freud's *Ego and the Mechanisms of Defence* (1937).

At the very start of the psychoanalytic movement, divisions occurred, first with Adler, creating the movement of individual psychology (giving great importance to social determination of behaviour) and with Jung, creating the movement of analytical psychology (with its notion of collective unconscious where determinant archetypes were found). Another split occurred with Otto Rank, S. Ferenczi, and W. Reich, creating body language techniques, among which ergonomics and bioenergy.

Individual psychology was particularly relevant to the evolution of the movement of group psychotherapy, which appears at the source of culturalist movement, also known today as interpersonalism. In the wake of Adler and thanks to the actions of Sullivan, K. Horney, and Kardiner (author of the basic personality concept) the idea of social determination of behaviour obtained a major importance regarding the libido theory.

Finally, attention should be drawn to the rapprochement of Jungians and Adlerians with Freudians and the integration of culturalists (or interpersonalists) in the main psychoanalytic conceptions, made by Hartmann.

The Kleinians and the British Middle Group

Leading on from the Freudian group is the Kleinian group, created around Klein (1952) and centred on the formation of a precocious Ego in the organization of the depressive and paranoid-schizoid positions, in the existence of partial and total objects, internalized object relations, and leaning on concepts such as envy and gratitude, and loss and reparation.

To these we should add the conceptions of the post-Kleinian theorists Meltzer et al. (1980), Bion (1961a, 1965, 1967a), and Money-Kyrle (1956). Particularly relevant in this field are Bion's contributions (basic assumptions established in groups; theory of thinking, centred in α and β elements; the study of links L, H, and K—and the corresponding grid; theory of change; and the structuring of container-contained relationships).

Similar to the Kleinian positions (group A of the British Psychoanalytical Society) are those of the so-called Middle Group situated between groups A and B, but supporters of the object relations theory (ORT) in terms of the former, although defenders of an objectivist position, and thus opposed to the subjectivist position of Melanie Klein and her followers.

This group was constituted by persons such as Fairbairn (1954), Guntrip (1975), Winnicott (1958) (holding theory, transitional objects and phenomena, and the good enough mother conception), and Balint (1968) (basic fault and new beginning).

Kohut's self psychology

Emerging from the latter, Kohut (1971, 1972) developed the concept of self and the study of primary narcissism (Kohut's "double" axis theory). It is based on the study of the importance of narcissism in the evolution of the individual, in the existence of normal and pathological narcissism, and in the establishment of external object relations that are vital for the interactions of the individual. The importance of empathy, necessary for the evolution of this therapy and for the assessment to narcissistic transferences, is also a fundamental issue in this intervention.

Ego psychology. The American perspective

Designed as a result of Freud's work and that of his daughter Anna regarding the relative autonomy of the ego, ego psychology focuses on the establishment of a general psychology, on the autonomy of the ego, and of other structures of primary and secondary autonomy and to its adaptability, also taking into account the psychosocial dimension of the external environment.

This last fact is also expressed by the integration made by these authors of culturalist concepts in mainstream psychoanalysis.

Hartmann centred his work on Freud's metapsychological positions, redesigned in terms of the structural theory, which will gather the genetic point of view (explaining the existence of the apparatuses of primary and secondary autonomy), and the adaptive and psychosocial conceptions, established by Rapaport who gave special importance to psychoanalytic social dimensions.

The criticism to this theory and the technique it developed was systematized by Greenson and linked to its biological basis and possibly inaccurate scientific grounds, in which are included the importance of the development of a general psychology and the study of child development.

Lacan

Although not particularly relevant in the field of group psychotherapies in general, but essential for the French institutional psychotherapeutic approach are the views of J. Lacan, centred on Ferdinand de Saussure's concepts of signifier and signified and on the importance of the ISR (imaginary—symbolic—real) system. Nevertheless, Michel Laxenaire and some others used this approach in group psychotherapy.

New developments

In recent times, efforts have been made to relate the data on psychoanalysis with the progresses made in anatomical-histological and physiological studies of the CNS (central nervous system) as well as in its physiopathology, leading to the development of a new scientific subject that has been named neuropsychoanalysis. In her tendency to develop empirical studies that could be experimentally confirmed, M. R. Leal (1994a) has often used this method.

Group psychotherapies, the psychoanalytic approach, and Trigant Burrow

The historical and economical evolution of society, the development in psychological and human and social sciences, and the evolution of psychoanalysis itself led to the emergence of group psychotherapies and particularly, of their psychoanalytic approaches.

In early 1905, the American psychosomatic society, under the direction of J. H. Pratt, used a group approach for the first time in the treatment of tuberculosis, as did Buch with patients suffering from hypertension, while Stephen, Chappel, Rogerson, and Pike used a group approach with patients with peptic ulcers. For these authors, group psychotherapy was seen as a psychopedagogical method. The patients were taught to live with their illnesses and to protect themselves from using adaptive means to defend themselves against them and preventive healthcare to avoid their dissemination.

Meanwhile, in Vienna, Austria, one should mention the action of J. L. Moreno, not yet from the perspective of psychodrama that he developed later, but merely in a group approach, centred on free discussion and in which he mainly worked with young people or children.

Groups can be used as treatment settings, either in support techniques which are aimed at individuals included in them, as direct intervention, as it is the case in the Palo Alto Group and the Mara Selvini Palazzoli School or in family therapy, as a vehicle for several techniques, such as psychodrama (whether in its Morenian, triadic, or analytic form, used by Lebovici), or verbal techniques, like psychoanalysis, that we will develop ahead and in cognitive behavioural, phenomenological, existential, non-directive models.

The first time that psychoanalytic techniques were used in group psychotherapies was by Louis Wender and Paul Schilder during the 1930s in the USA.

Nevertheless, according to Roth (1993), Freud was the first to lead a group of analytical inspiration, more precisely, the Vienna Group, in which he met with his followers and which included prominent figures of the psychoanalytical movement, such as Adler, Otto Rank, Karl Abraham, Stekel, and Ferenczi. The Vienna Group worked on the basis of discussing the points of view and concept of psychoanalytical theory using the free association method.

Naturally, there were internal conflicts, the inevitable emulation between them and with Freud in particular, with whom the majority had very incomplete analysis, in some cases, of only two months or less and with whom they had an ambivalent relationship of admiration and rivalry.

Also very important for the development of group therapy were Freud's works, which we usually designate as anthropological and which are, respectively, *Totem and Taboo*, written in 1913–1914; *Group Psychotherapy and the*

Analysis of the Ego, published in 1921, which some group psychotherapists consider his nuclear work in this field; and *Moses and Monotheism*, posthumously published in 1939.

If one wishes to find a common ground in these three works, we would note that in all of them, the leader of the group could be represented by the ego ideal, whether it takes the form of the primal father, dominant and aggressive, or of the totem, who replaced him after his murder, whether it is seen as the central element of the group he organized himself, or whether emerging as a liberator-emancipator, connecting his people to a destination of salvation.

Group psychotherapy was greatly developed in World War II, in the treatment of disorders resulting from the trauma of war during the so-called Northfield experience, driven primarily by Foulkes and Bion.

From then on, there was a great development of these techniques. So, in the 1950s and 1960s, many streams were developed, of which there are eight discussed below that we consider as being particularly important.

In the United States, Slavson used them systematically with children, adolescents and adults, delinquents, neurotic, psychotic, and borderline patients, never intending to carry out a true psychoanalysis, but always using the management of transference situations. Bach developed a technique in which he used a Lewinian approach with a later development of a psychoanalytic intervention in the final stages of the group. Eric Berne developed what he called a transactional analysis, where he carried out its intervention, focusing on the study that he called ego contradictory states. Klapman also used an approach centred on the group, through an analytical intervention.

Finally, I would refer to psychoanalytic group approaches followed in Latin American countries. Pichon-Rivière used Kleinian conceptions in his group psychotherapy; and the Brazilian authors centred their approaches on Bion's last psychoanalytic point of view, namely, his thought and transformations theories. We cannot forget Bion's influence in Brazilian psychoanalysts, through his "Brazilian papers" and the revision of his work, done by Zimerman.

Three different approaches which I consider being of particular importance and worth mentioning are as follows:

- "Psychoanalysis in groups", according to Wolf and Schwartz (1962)
- The intervention centred on the group used by Bion (1961a) and the Tavistock group
- Group analysis

Let's focus on these three approaches:

Psychoanalysis in groups was developed by Wolf and Schwartz (1962) in the United States of America, and Locke (1961) in the United Kingdom. It is centred on the study of the unconscious contents of communication and on dreams and fantasies (through countertransference and aims at working through); however, the systematic use of the so-called alternating sessions, i.e., without the therapist (strongly criticized by Foulkes and Cortesão), led these authors to limit the chances of working-through, creating two types of sessions that would affect the natural evolution of the therapeutic process. Creating this system they were promoting a real acting-out, though they consider it duly institutionalized.

In one of his last interviews, Wolf himself acknowledged the limits this situation raises. One must note, however, that Locke (1961) did not use these alternating sessions in such a systematic way as his American peers.

The Tavistock group (Sutherland, Ezriel, Bion) focuses on the group as a whole, seeking to find what Ezriel calls the common tension of the group (Kibel & Stein, 1981), which finds expression in Bion's basic assumptions (dependence, fight and flying, pairing).

One final word on the term group analysis. The first person to use this expression was Trigant Burrow (1949), a psychiatrist who worked with Adolf Meyer and who was analysed by Carl Jung, having also known Sigmund Freud. His approach focuses both on group community interventions and tests the individual's inadaptability to them. For Burrow, this intervention always has a biological dimension.

His contemporary, Lawrence K. Frank, thought differently, and saw intervention as being primarily social.

Burrow later abandoned the term group analysis and replaced it with philoanalysis. However, he always felt a certain ambiguity about that decision, which led Foulkes to assume that Burrow had already abandoned the expression "group analysis", and to choose the same expression for his therapy, regardless of the biological dimension of Burrow's approach. J. Campos (1992), who carefully studied the positions of this author, and worked with Alfreda Galt (and the Lifwynn Foundation for Laboratory Research in Analytic and Social Psychiatry that tried to keep Burrow's legacy) thinks that this, in fact, was not really the case.

Cortesão considered Burrow to be the founder of group analysis. Notwithstanding the above, my opinion is that, in essence, Foulkes is correct. The term to designate both techniques is, in fact, the same. But the concepts of group analysis as posited by Burrow and Foulkes respectively are different.

The basic principles that are common to these two different analytic approaches in group psychotherapy (including those we have mentioned above) are as follows:

1 Analysis of psychological behaviour
2 The importance of unconscious processes
3 Behaviour dynamic determination

4 The analysis of the functions and structures of psyche (id, ego, and super-ego)
5 The individual epigenetic development

Recently, some authors have advocated the use of more specific approaches related to recent developments in psychoanalytic therapy that are predominantly used in certain types of groups:

- Ego psychology and the importance given to the analysis of defence mechanisms.
- Yalom's existential evolution basically centres on this philosophical approach, though also making use of psychoanalytic and cognitive-behavioural conceptions.
- Therapy centred in the group itself and Bion's conceptions referred to above.
- ORT, minor phenomena and intervention focused within the group (H. Kibel [1993] based particularly on Margaret Mahler's and Edith Jacobson's conceptions).
- Self psychology—Kohut's contributions and the quest for reorganization through the development of specific structures (Baker, 1993; Stone, 2009).

Group analysis. Its history. Foulkes and the British group, Cortesão and the Portuguese school of groupanalysis

Foulkes

As we have acknowledged above, the concepts of Foulkes's group analysis (1964a) completely differ from Trigant Burrow's and are based on work in small groups, from six to eight people, which he considered the privileged agent of this therapeutic action; although later on, through Pat de Maré and Leonel Kreeger, large groups were also considered as vectors of this type of action. Foulkes conceived group analysis as an intervention, notably social, that aimed to act on individuals who compose the basic biological units of its intervention, through the group, the key psychological unit of this action. He gave, from the onset, great emphasis on the notion of matrix, developed from Ruesch and Bateson, who, in 1951, had published a paper, particularly relevant at the time, named *Communication: The Social Matrix of Psychiatry* (Ruesch & Bateson, 1951, 1987).

Moreover, when Foulkes was president of the Psychoanalytic Society of Frankfurt, he came in close contact with the Institute of Sociology, which was in the same building where figures such as Norbert Elias, well known for his social science research, Max Horkheimer, and Franz Bokeman also worked. One must not forget also his personal training in organismic theory, with his tutor, Goldstein, who always had a great influence on him.

This approach focused on social intervention does not mean that Foulkes set aside the importance of the psychoanalytic contribution. In addition to many articles where this importance was shown, although focused on social intervention, we notice, as a paradigm of this concept, the fact that Foulkes admitted in *Therapeutic Group Analysis*, in 1964(a), that in group-analytic therapy, one can develop a group transference neurosis, and working-through can even occur.

However, in his last work, *Group Analytic Psychotherapy: Method and Principles*, published in 1975(a), a year before his death, Foulkes (1975a) argued that the development of this situation would needlessly extend group-analytic therapy and considered, as he always had, the preferential importance of "ego training in action", which consists in the analysis of the several structures (id, ego, and super-ego) of the different members of the group in interaction and which would allow the study and analysis of the bond established between different group members and the structures that make up that bond.

Dennis Brown (1985) states that, although Foulkes has always shown some reservations regarding Bion's concept of basic assumptions, he seemed to accept that of common group tensions advanced by Ezriel, another member of the Tavistock group.

It is in fact, in this context of the global functioning of the group that Foulkes inserts the occurrence of phenomena that characterize the phenomenology of group analysis, such as the mirror phenomenon (that he, as did M. R. Leal, considered the basis of the group-analytical process, and with which the latter approaches the neurobiological evolution which occurs in toddlers and is fundamental for their maturing (Leal, 1994a)), resonance (that he linked to the interaction between different group members, with different regression levels, as opposed to what Bion claimed), and condenser phenomena (that allow the emergence of deep, repressed material, primitive in the following of polarization of ideas associated within the group). To this interaction paradigm, which Foulkes believed to be basic, one should add the importance of the work on dreams, highlighted by Malcom Pines (1994).

Despite Foulkes always maintaining that the group itself is a key factor in the therapeutic process, he considered that the action of the therapist is by no means negligible, whether as a group administrator, maintaining the organization of the therapy setting and regularity of the group process, or through the development of the translation movement, allowing its members to be aware of certain processes which can occur, or through the development of interpretative actions, which are, in fact, shared with other members of the group.

Foulkes (1975a) defines group analysis as a transference situation that he defines in terms of structure, process, and content. In Foulkes (1957a), he sought to find a meta-theory to group analysis, which, in addition to being based on sociological and philosophical concepts, seeks to be based on location, communication, and spheres of relationship (autocosmos, microsphere, and macrosphere), points of view obtained from Erikson (1951), which, in turn, were based on Wernicke's conceptions, formulated in the early 20th century.

Therefore, Foulkes established a conceptualization that approaches the theory of communication, at the time very much in vogue. Psychoanalysis itself accepted it as a means to explain how it worked. It was in this context that psychoanalysis came to be defined as a communication with a specific rule and proxemics, while it was also argued that it could be expressed through three communication channels (information, interpretation, and insight).

Therefore, it is no surprise that Foulkes resorted to this conceptualization to explain group analysis.

The British group, later on, International

Foulkes had always intended to develop group analysis and give it a solid background. Thus, he founded the Group Analytic Society (London), GAS. Despite its name, he tried to include members of several nationalities. Therefore, when Nuno Ribeiro and I proposed the organization of the First Symposium on Group Analysis in Estoril, Portugal, in 1970, he accepted the idea, because it corresponded to his own wish.

It was, however, the British group in general, and Malcolm Pines and Earl Hopper in particular, who gave great strength to this movement, organizing the European Symposia every three years, and especially hosting the yearly summer, autumn, and winter workshops that were a must for the training of group analysts from several different countries. Later, the Foulkes Lecture and the Foulkes Day, aimed at differentiated colleagues, completed this educational nucleus on a yearly basis.

It was thus that group analysis developed throughout Europe, where it became the most widespread analytical group psychotherapeutic technique. Besides the United Kingdom and Portugal, it developed greatly in Italy, Scandinavia (Denmark, Sweden, Norway, and Finland), Northern Europe (Germany, Austria, Belgium, Netherlands, and Luxembourg), Eastern Europe (Poland, Hungary, Czech Republic, Slovakia, Romania, Russia, Ukraine, and Bulgaria), and in Southern Europe (Greece, Croatia, Serbia, Bosnia and Herzegovina, Montenegro and Macedonia) and, most recently, in Spain. Only in France, where there is a close liaison between group psychotherapy and the psychoanalytical group, and even, in some cases to the Lacanian group (M. Laxenaire), has group analysis been slow to gain ground. Outside Europe, group analysis has spread to Argentina, Brazil, China, Egypt, Israel, South Africa, and the United States of America.

At an initial stage, this action seemed to have as its objectives the consolidation and standardization of the group-analytical movement in Europe and the provision of high standards of training, while the Society accepted the membership of the International Society of Group Psychotherapy, to whose Board of Directors many important group analysts belonged. Foulkes himself was the first vice president of GAS (Moreno was the then president and Lebovici the second vice president). Later, after GAS was given fresh impetus by Hadden, Battegay, and Malcolm Pines, Pines and Earl Hopper served as presidents. However, the predominance of other therapeutic approaches, such as psychodrama, family psychotherapy and the intervention on organizations, made it difficult to agree on common training standards because of the heterogeneous nature of the society, despite the creation of sections to cater to the various areas of interest. GAS was, therefore, forced to look for other solutions.

Our Greek colleague, Yannis Tsegos, played an important role in the creation of EGATIN (European Group Analytic Training Institutions Network). Our Portuguese colleague, Paula Carvalho (president 2014–2018) met with relative success in focusing attention on the need to organize and unify group-analytic training in the different countries.

The formation of the European Federation for Psychoanalytic Psychotherapy, or EFPP (which had Brian Martindale as its first president, and whose foundational meeting César Dinis attended as Portugal's representative), and its creation internally of a group section, raised the issue of protecting and regulating the identity of several groups of analytical psychotherapists in the public sector. The Portuguese Society of Groupanalysis and Analytic Group Psychotherapy has been a full member of the EFPP since 1999. Isaura Manso Neto, Antonieta Ferreira de Almeida, and Mário David are the Portuguese delegates who have been participating in the EFPP Group Section.

All these factors led to GAS—the Group Analytic Society (London)—renaming itself the Group Analytic Society International, or GASi, in an attempt to reflect that it has become a more European organization, with presidents not only from the United Kingdom but from other countries too: Werner Knauss (Germany), Luisa Brunori (Italy), Gerda Winther (Denmark), and Robi Friedman (Israel). Its Management Committee is also an international one. Thus, it sought to coordinate group-analytic activities at a European level. Our colleague Isaura Manso Neto served on this Committee between 2006 and 2014.

E. L. Cortesão

Although never questioning Foulkes's concepts, in their essential aspects, including the importance of their social components expressed in the concept of group-analytic matrix, E. L. Cortesão has a different approach regarding the concept of group analysis, based on the key position given to the psychoanalytic contribution, which he considers basic and fundamental and the importance given to the role of the group analyst which he believes to be crucial in the therapy development.

This different approach led him to replace the two words "group analysis" with the term "groupanalysis", the latter being used whenever reference is made to the Portuguese conceptualization of group analysis.

Cortesão claims in fact that psychoanalysis and groupanalysis are different research and therapy techniques, despite not being contradictory, with common theoretical bases but distinct operative procedures, clearly shying away, in this concept, from the Foulkesian paradigm.

Cortesão considered three key aspects in his concept of groupanalysis: the groupanalytic process, the pattern, and the matrix that determine the evolution of the therapy.

a The **groupanalytic process**—Cortesão defined the groupanalytic process in the same way Bibring defined the psychoanalytic one. However, he integrated four lines of thought found in psychoanalysis that he believed complement one another:

   i   The metapsychological approach, obtained directly from Freud.
   ii The object relations theory, mainly according to the positions of the British Middle Group and in particular with some of its most relevant members, such as Fairbairn, Guntrip, Balint, and Winnicott.
   iii Otto Kernberg's perspectives on borderline states and narcissistic personalities, as well as ego psychology, according to Hartmann's concepts and his integration in the main psychoanalytic chain of the culturalists' perspectives, and above all, Rapaport's adaptive and psychosocial points of view, which Cortesão believed to be the meeting point between metapsychological perspectives and the ORT concepts.
   iv The concepts of self psychology, with its perspectives of normal and pathological narcissism.

   Cortesão showed great plasticity, elegance and dexterity in synthesizing these various perspectives, which he did particularly well in our view.

b The **groupanalytic pattern**—The most important and controversial concept introduced by Cortesão is the groupanalytic pattern, which he linked to the father figure and defined as the nature of specific attitudes that the groupanalyst sustains and maintains within the groupanalytic matrix, with an interpretative function that boosts and develops the groupanalytic process.

   This process would lead to the development of working-through and reconstruction situations and the creation of common processes of origin of the structures and functions of the self, followed by the search of an individual meaning, as a result of the necessary and essential distinction of the selves.

Foulkes has always challenged the concept of pattern, which he considered overestimates the action of the therapist and consequently leads to the tendency of excessive intervention in the coordination of the group-analytic process. Leonardo Ancona (1992) objected to this point of view and instead associates it with Cortesão's need to create a meta-theory of groupanalytic situations. M. Etelvina de Brito (1992), and E. Cruz Filipe (1992) believed, as Cortesão did, that the actions of pattern are no more than the spark of the matrix activity and the core of the groupanalytic intervention.

It is our view that Cortesão drew attention to the action of the therapist sparking the development of the groupanalytic process within the groupanalytic matrix, and we agree with Ancona regarding his need to develop a meta-theory in groupanalysis.

c   The **groupanalytic matrix**—Cortesão did not undermine the basic idea of Foulkes's concept of group-analytic matrix, not even regarding its social dimension, but he did change it by taking into account the importance of groupanalytic pattern in its definition and organization. Thus, Cortesão defined groupanalytic matrix as a specific web of communication, relationship, and working-through, to which, by the integration of groupanalytic pattern, boosts the evolution of groupanalytic process within the theoretical and technical dimensions that compose it.

Cortesão, therefore, does not question Foulkes's concept of matrix, but considers essential for its organization the incorporation of the concept of pattern.

Unlike Foulkes, Cortesão did not believe the therapist is a simple group administrator, or conductor, of the transmission process and attender in the interpretative process.

The therapist is someone who moulds in the group a certain attitude of analytical listening that helps the development in it of an identical position allowing the working-through of the group transference neurosis of the different elements that compose it and the consequent individualization of the selves. However, it is this someone who, after being encouraged by the groupanalytic pattern, develops such a process. The matrix will be further discussed in another chapter.

d   The **evolution of the therapeutic action**—When starting groupanalysis, each individual has certain internalized representations within the family and socio-cultural matrices, or according to M. R. Leal (1968), a certain internal relationship matrix that was built throughout their life as they moved over from one group to the others (from the mother-child union through the oedipal family and extended family to study and leisure groups).

By working through the group transference neurosis, such representations are analysed in their metapsychological and object relations dimension. In this context, the groupanalytic process fosters the development of individual meaning and the differentiation of the selves of each group member with unique and specific features. The groupanalyst, however, takes on a specific layout and meaning through the transmission, induction and feeling of the groupanalytic pattern.

Cortesão also assigned great importance to the concept of aesthetic equilibrium which he initially linked to artistic accomplishment but ended up considering as inherent in the actual evolution of the therapeutic process and corresponding to the feeling of accomplishment and creativity developed by each individual within it and acquiring its completeness at the end of the analysis.

The Portuguese school of groupanalysis

When Guilherme Ferreira first used this expression back in the 1970s, referring to the group of individuals who worked around E. L. Cortesão and that he mentions in his book *Groupanalysis—Theory and Technique*, his close friend and companion during so many struggles, N. A. Ribeiro, told him that he was exaggerating in the development of this insight.

One can say that the Portuguese school of groupanalysis received recognition at the 1st European Symposium on Group Analysis held in Portugal in 1970, when Foulkes recognized its existence, noticing the divergence between the Portuguese authors' communications (E. L. Cortesão, J. A. Silva, N. A. Ribeiro, and A. G. Ferreira) all marked by a psychoanalytic approach (despite their differences and particularities) and his own, centred mainly on the social approach mentioned above, which he always endorsed (Foulkes, 1971). The Portuguese groupanalytic model was more clearly introduced internationally in 1989 at the first National Congress on Groupanalysis that took place in Lisbon.

Leading figures in the Group Analytic Society (GAS), such as Malcom Pines (UK), Karl König (Germany), Leonardo Ancona (Italy), and Juan Campos (Spain), as well as Anne Schützemberger, a prominent figure in the field of triadic psychodrama and of the International Association for Group Psychotherapy, took part. Distinguished members of the Brazilian group of São Paulo who participated were well prepared, particularly from the point of view of the psychoanalytic training Brazilian groups linked to group psychotherapy: Luis Miller de Paiva, Francisco Heládio Capisano, Manuel Muñoz, and Nelson Póci as well as Waldemar José Fernandes, already President of the Brazilian Association of Analytical Group Psychotherapy despite his relative youth.

Meetings between Portuguese groupanalysts and the European group analysts that occurred after the death of Cortesão in 1991 with the organization of the "E. L. Cortesão Seminars" involved successively Malcolm Pines (UK), Claude Pigott (France), and Earl Hopper (UK); this contact decreased for several reasons, including the economic ones. The interaction with the Brazilian colleagues pioneered a systematic cooperation, which progressively led to the inclusion of other Brazilian federated states and respective study groups, in analytic group psychotherapy, such as those in the cities of Rio de Janeiro, Porto Alegre, and Belém and to the organization of Luso-Brazilian meetings every two years, taking place alternately in Brazil and in Portugal. The XIV Luso-Brazilian Conference took place in Lisbon in 2019.

International cooperation has always been an important issue for the SPG with Guilherme Ferreira having played a role of some significance in establishing such cooperation, in the wake of E. L. Cortesão, having been twice a member of the board of directors of the International Association for Group Psychotherapy, from 1977 to 1986 and from 1995 to 2003.

This cooperation, especially at the European level, has been developed in recent years by César Vieira Dinis, and particularly by Isaura Manso Neto, who, as already mentioned, was a member of the Management Committee of GAS, from 2006 to 2014. In addition, she was the chairperson of three important international scientific events: the 3rd EFPP group section conference (2004), the 34th GAS Winter Workshop (2006), and the 16th European Symposium on Group Analysis (2014). At the latter event, Guilherme Ferreira served as President of the Scientific Committee.

However, it is, undoubtedly, in the scientific field that the action of the SPG has become more relevant. Cortesão became Full Professor of Psychiatry at the Faculty of Medicine of the Universidade Nova de Lisboa.

I would also like to mention the work done by M. R. Leal, marked by its specificity and creativity. She started by her work in analytic group psychotherapy, where innovative perspectives were presented on analytical psychotherapy in children and adolescents (1964). She developed the concept of the internal relational matrix, which is discussed in Chapter 4.

After the presentation of her doctoral thesis at the University of London entitled "Socialization processes in the young child", M. R. Leal developed a biological approach, focusing first on the work developed by Bowlby, Watson, and Lorenz, and later, on Fonagy, Gerjely, Jurist, Target, and Unoka, among others, and her research began to look for a way to explain the individual in evolution, through clinical action and therapy, giving particular emphasis to the process of mirroring. (Leal, 1994a, 2010).

João Azevedo e Silva tried to focus his position on the influence that the pioneers Foulkes, Bion, Zimerman, and others had on his work, and created such concepts as the "inner space of optional doubt" and meta-dramatic communication. César Dinis revised the conceptions of transference and group transference neurosis and their working-through and established the notion of the "empathic resonance box", while Isaura Neto, building on the conceptions of Zinkin's malignant mirroring and Nitsun's anti-group, drew attention to the importance of their use in therapy through the use of the mirror phenomenon and together with Maria João Centeno, she used the groupanalytical concepts in multifamily group analysis (Neto, 2014, 2015), based on Jorge Garcia Badaracco's *Psicoanalisis Multifamiliar. Los otros en nosotros y el descubrimiento del sí mismo.* [Multifamily Psychoanalysis: The others in us and the discovery of the self.].

In an essentially clinical perspective, the author reviewed the concepts of transference and transference neurosis, the notion of matrix and its evolution, and following Foulkes's proposal of the construction of a metatheory based on philosophical and sociological concepts developed in the first edition of his book *Group Psychotherapy: The Psychoanalytic Approach*, he proposed a new approach in this field, focused on the concepts of pattern, matrix, and internal relational matrix (Ferreira, 1988, 1992, 2004, 2006)

Lastly, mention should be made of the changes in groupanalytic technique, as a result of this psychoanalytic view of groupanalysis. It is a fact that the British group, under the influence of Earl Hopper (2008), had already considered it fundamental to the increase in the number of sessions to allow the analysis of more regressive and archaic levels of the individual's functioning.

In Portugal, we implemented the frequency of three to four sessions per week until 2014. Azevedo e Silva and I practised GA four times a week, the paradigm of psychoanalysis itself. I did so between September 1985 and December 2012, with promising results, as I explained and detailed at the 14th European Symposium on Group Analysis, which took place in Dublin, during a session chaired by Earl Hopper.

Aside from the importance of the frequency, other crucial variables are the number of members, their selection, and the groupanalytic pattern. Progressively, we have noticed that true groupanalytic processes could develop within groups with a lower frequency—two sessions per week, say—in the case of accurate selection and a smaller number of group members. For this reason, the SPGPAG has now settled on personal groupanalysis for candidates, with either three or two sessions per week.

The influence of groupanalysis in institutional therapy has been particularly significant. Inspired by Cortesão's conception of groupanalysis and Maxwell Jones's social therapy, Fernando Medina developed an institutional intervention in the early 1960s at the Miguel Bombarda Hospital that was continued after his death by J. A. e Silva, N. A. Ribeiro, and Guilherme Ferreira, when the latter transferred to Miguel Bombarda Hospital.

In 1965, the author developed a therapeutic community in the psychiatric day hospital (Ferreira, 1969) of the Santa Maria Hospital, the largest general hospital in Portugal. This intervention was abandoned after his transference to the Julio de Matos Hospital. After a gap in 1977, João França de Sousa, César Vieira Dinis, and Sara Ferro organized a groupanalytic framework in the day hospital. In 2008, Isaura Manso Neto and her team (Neto et al., 2010a, b) were given the Jane Abercombie Prize awarded by GAS, after she presented her and her team's work spanning 30 years (Neto, 2010b).

The influence of the groupanalytic training of doctors, nurses, social workers, occupational therapists, and even judges was important in other institutional interventions, and it was thus that Cortesão himself, H. Rodrigues da Silva, and A. Alves Gomes organized an intervention of this kind in forensic and custodial services.

Finally, the author would like to stress the importance of the groupanalytic movement in the development of community and social psychiatry, at least in the initial stages. The author played an important role in this field, first in Portugal and afterwards internationally, as WASP (World Association of Social Psychiatry) President.

In a general historico-political, socio-economical, and scientific framework, the intervention in groups (including group psychotherapy) appears to be one of the greatest achievements of the 20th century. Not only were they a means for the realization of some important psychotherapies (as was psychoanalysis itself, but also cognitive-behavioural, existential, transactional, psychodrama, short-term, couples, family, multiple-family therapies), but also a vehicle for institutional interventions (mental health, forensic, custodial), as well as for the organization of community and social psychiatry, though the use of counselling, self-help and, naturally, group therapy for mental health education. The interventions in health programs, in their general approaches and in education, were also strongly influenced by the developments in our knowledge of group process. Group analysis can also be seen as the basis for political, social, and cultural interventions in society.

In Portugal, groupanalysis, as we call it within SPGPAG circles, has made an important contribution to the treatment of mental disorders both directly and through the organization of teams and psychiatric units. It has also contributed to training programmes for healthcare students and residents.

Chapter 2

Group analysis
A cluster identity. Redefining/ rethinking Group Analysis

Isaura Manso Neto and Maria João Centeno

Introduction

We consider that the existing contradictions and ambiguities within the theory and practice of group analysis and psychoanalysis are some of the reasons why these disciplines have suffered a crisis over the last decades.

We have noticed that there are several group settings that despite their differences are called group analysis. Is there one or are there several types of group analysis? What are the main differences, similarities, connections, and boundaries between the several group analysis applications/group-analytic-based groups?

We think that those groups have specific common features which may shape a group-analytic cluster, a kind of brand, and perhaps a group-analytic spectrum.

After reflecting on the therapeutic group analysis and analytic-based groups' differences, we have set eight kinds of groups, including therapeutic group analysis; we will compare them according to their objectives as well as their processes.

In order to further visualize their main features and then compare their differences and commonalities, we have displayed them in individual tables.

There are several questions which need to be answered, such as those made by Steinar Lorentzen (2011, pp. 43–44), which we agree with:

> Does a 'main-stream' Group Analysis exist? [...] What is GA today? What necessary elements have to be present to call a therapy GA? How does Group Analysis differ from other psycho dynamic group approaches? How can they be distinguished? How may Group Analysis be modified working with different patient categories? Are longer therapies better than short-term interventions? What are the typical technical interventions in group analysis? Do we need or want a manual in group analysis? Would it be possible to develop a smaller 'core manual'

of group analysis, and open up for the possibilities of modifying this approach in different directions depending on which patient category one treats?

Similarly, Harold Behr (2008, p. 55) said:

> The problem for group analysis is compounded by confusion in the public mind between the different forms of psychotherapy. There is a lack of definition which lends itself to the myth that group therapy, whether analytic or any other kind, is not a particularly specialized field of practice, that it can therefore be practiced by almost anybody who works in a clinical setting, […].

Hutchinson (2010, p. 9) wonders if group analysis can adapt to changing times and if all group analyses are applied group analysis? In her view,

> Group analysis is an applied discipline—it is the application of certain principles and basic assumptions, using a methodology, (creating a group-analytic situation), that can be adapted according to the task and the context. The strength of group analysis is in its creative adaptability and its identity is protected by its clearly defined basic assumptions and method.

Valbak (2015, p. 519) argues that "group-analytic psychotherapy always—more or less deliberately—has been adapted and modified for attending patients." He thinks "it is artificial to distinguish so-called 'classical' group analysis from 'applied' group analysis equal to group-analytic psychotherapy (GAP)".

In 2009, the Institute of Group Analysis, London (IGA) and the Group Analytic Society (GAS) commissioned Sheffield University (Blackmore, Tantam, Parry & Chambers, 2012) to carry out a study. The study revealed what evidence suggests the reasons for the efficiency and effectiveness of that group analysis and analytic/dynamic group psychotherapy and described the factors that influence the outcome of group therapy. The study also drew attention to the need for further methodological quality studies, using outcome psychometric measures and more clearly defined terminology to describe therapeutic interventions. Concerning the clarification of terminology, we believe that for better therapeutic interventions and research, define and clarify concepts and practices, as we propose to do in this chapter, are imperative.

In this regard it also should be mentioned an important collective work—the GASi international dictionary of group analysis—which has been in progress since 2011—a long interactive process initiated by

Ankjær Olsen. Since then several authors have given and continue to give their contribution, suggesting terms that should or should not be included.

These issues are still prevalent in the group-analytic community as seen from the contributions made by many authors in recent years. One such example was the lecture by Farhad Dalal at the 2017 GASi Symposium in (...) Berlin, under the theme "One Group Analysis or many?" (Dalal, 2018).

In this chapter we would like to answer to some of the above questions and clarify what group analysis is about, thereby contributing to the explanation of some issues concerning therapeutic group analysis and other forms of applied group analysis/several kinds of group-analytic-based groups, paving the way to raise group-analytic credibility, and overcoming the crisis we believe groupanalysis is going through.

The 'Crisis' in psychoanalysis and group analysis

There have been several signs leading us to believe that psychoanalysis and group analysis are going through difficult times: fewer requests for treatment; fewer candidates for training; psychiatrist candidates are becoming scarce.

Based on a questionnaire applied to IPA members in 1997 (Ad Hoc Committee on 'The Crisis of Psychoanalysis—Challenges and Perspectives'—Welcome to the Crisis; Engelbrecht, 1997), Zimerman (1999) has divided the 'crisis' intervening factors into three groups: a) the crisis of psychoanalysis/group analysis as theory and technique; b) the crisis of the psychoanalytic and group-analytic institutions; and c) the crisis of the psychoanalysts/group analysts.

Another author, Garza-Guerrero (2002b), wrote a very critical article about the psychoanalysis crisis, stating that the main problem arises from within the analytic societies and associations themselves. He also points out some of the internal incongruences which he called "organizational and educational syncretism": problems arising from the theoretical training and supervision, as well as in the systems of accreditation and certification, among other things.

Wallerstein (2005) defends the possibility of psychoanalysis belonging to the group of sciences; but for this to happen it would be necessary for psychoanalysis to be sustained by a unified theoretical structure. Other authors, such as A. Green (2005), argue that psychoanalysis cannot be compared to other sciences, such as physics saying that pluralism was conceivable, considering that at the moment the trend was towards chaos, thus adding confusion to confusion, and giving rise to schools of thought with striking similarities to religious and sectarian methods of functioning. Green defended the need to establish, and thoroughly discuss, the differences in order to ascertain the basic theoretical principles of contemporary psychoanalysis.

More recently, Jorge Canestri (2017, p. 9), speaking about the future of EFPP, said:

> [...] psychoanalysis is not going through a particularly easy or luminous period at the moment. As we know, the economic crisis has increased difficulties that do not depend only—or perhaps even mainly—on the economy. Psychoanalysis is under attack on various fronts and its fields of action are progressively shrinking in universities, in public health systems, and in culture.
>
> We cannot exclude the responsibility of the psychoanalytical institutions themselves in contributing to this situation, although it undoubtedly varies from one country to another in the region.

We believe that the current so-called "crisis", which the psychoanalysts and group analysts are going through, is rooted in, and characterized mainly by, the insecurity that arises from:

i The rigidity of the analytic societies—The analytic societies, which were initially revolutionary in the observation of the human universe, were transformed into a kind of religion, a guardian of unique realities and gods, that demonstrates enormous difficulty in integrating contestation, thus impeding the progression of its members, as well as making the careers of the analytic societies never-ending and tedious.
ii Difficulties concerning the present economic situation.
iii The idealization of immediate and economic pragmatisms.
iv Pressure from the health systems to present low-cost and rapid results—For the last few years, we have faced the pressures of the Mental Health policy to reduce the costs of our psychotherapeutic activities in an immediate way.
v The pharmaceutical industry's pressures with the idealization of psychopharmacology and upward trends in the over-consumption of psychiatric medication.
vi Disadvantages when competing with other treatment frameworks, seemingly more effective and easier in terms of assessment.
vii International classifications based on syndromes, which have specific indications for each psychopharmacological group. The international classifications (DSM and ICD) have been corseted into syndromes, without enough consideration for the aetiology.
viii The difficulty in defining common points among the psychoanalytic and group-analytic pluralisms.

Since psychoanalytic theory is the main basis of group analysis, we can say that group analysis is doubly affected by the crisis.

We believe that it is time to define precisely what group analysis is for each one of us, and which are the main similarities and differences among group-analytic-based groups, thus defining what group analysis is not.

We will begin to focus on the controversies and ambiguities of group analysis as a theoretical and technical body.

Controversies and ambiguities within group analysis

Defining Group Analysis: we consider that there are some ambiguities and controversies about this topic.

The term "group analysis" was introduced by Trigant Burrow (1927) and later developed by Foulkes (1943) as "Group Analysis".

Foulkes conceptualized and used group analysis as a form of treatment, although he has always been concerned whether group analysis is a form of treatment equivalent to psychoanalysis in its objectives.

After the First European Symposium of Group Analysis in Estoril in 1970 (Portugal), Foulkes & Foulkes (1971) made a semantic distinction between Group Analysis and group-analytic psychotherapy.

Firstly, he said that he adopted the term Group Analysis after it had been relinquished by Trigant Burrow. Later he changed the term Group Analysis to Group Analytic Psychotherapy, after reflecting about what the best term was to express that the method was essentially based on the group; he also assumed that this method is a form of psychotherapy, yet different from psychoanalysis. Indeed, he emphasized that the fact of it being a form of psychotherapy does not mean that is a less important or less intensive treatment than psychoanalysis, whether in the individual or in the group situation. Some years later, Foulkes used the terms Group Analysis and Group Analytic Psychotherapy as synonyms, and found after some time that the use of the term "Group Analysis" was more convenient when referring to methods and theories based on and compatible with psychoanalytic and group-analytic assumptions.

Foulkes used Group Analytic Psychotherapy (Foulkes, 1975b); Group Psychotherapy (Foulkes & Anthony, 1957c); Therapeutic Group Analysis (Foulkes, 1964b) and Group Analysis in 1968.

This is a long-standing issue (Hopper, 1982) as we can see throughout the various designations used by different authors: We'll cite the following: Steinar Lorentzen—Group Analytic Psychotherapy (2014); Caroline Garland—Psychoanalytic Group Therapy (2010a); Harold Behr and Hearst (2005) called it Group-Analytic Psychotherapy, with the hyphen; Group Analysis was the designation used by: Haim Weinberg (2014), Gerhard Wilke (2018), Denis Brown (2006b), Malcom Pines (1997), Morris Nitsun (1996, 2015), Elizabeth Foulkes (1990); Claude Pigott (1990) called it Psychanalyse

Groupale; Tubert-Oklander and Tubert (2004) named it Operative Groups/ Group Analysis; the term generically used by some North American authors is Psychodynamic Group Psychotherapy.

SPGPAG applies both designations—groupanalysis and analytic group psychotherapy to refer to different frameworks regarding the group process and objectives; these last being more ambitious in the case of groupanalysis.

During World War II, some psychiatrists and psychoanalysts such as Rickman, Bion, Tom Main, Foulkes and Anthony, among others, conducted several group experiences. Meanwhile, two main trends have emerged starting from those experiences: one, headed by Foulkes, who has embedded the Freudian classical theory, the Gestalt and sociology's contributions, applied this knowledge to small groups, giving birth to the Group Analytic Society (London) (1952); and the other, the Kleinian group, developed by Bion and followers. Later, in 1971, the Group Analytic Society (London) set up the Institute of Group Analysis (IGA).

Whereas Foulkes focused primarily on therapeutic aims, Bion (1978), also a pioneer of Group Analysis, focused mainly on the group dynamics, which in our opinion might have neglected individual treatment perspective. Thus, two different points of view about group analysis have been developed: one essentially focused on the individual treatment, and another more focused on the group.

The first one—the Group Analytic perspective, has mainly therapeutic objectives, while the other is more useful to understand how to work with task-centred groups—operative groups in the narrow sense—for example, team groups, training groups, supervision groups, coaching groups, among others. These kinds of groups (the task-centred groups) have no direct therapeutic objectives, although their members may achieve indirect therapeutic benefits.

The therapeutic operative groups are mostly Bionian, predominantly in Latin America, influenced and developed by Pichon-Rivière (2000a), Zimerman (2001), Fernandes et al. (2003), Tubert-Oklander and Tubert (2004), and Osório (2007), among others.

Over the years, there has been some controversy about operative groups and the idea of the "group task". Bearing in mind that the unconscious phenomena are fostered by free association, it seems rather contradictory to base a therapeutic group on a task. However, for Pichon-Rivière every group meets around a "task" whether therapeutic or not.

Therefore, the term operative groups has been used in three main senses: in a broader sense—as therapeutic group analysis—when the objective is the cure; in a stricter sense—when the group is focused on a specific task, like working or learning, in this case without psychotherapeutic aims, though with possible indirect therapeutic benefits; and thirdly, in the broadest sense—where the operative group is seen as an "ideology" to conduct groups, be they therapeutic or working groups (Fernandes et al., 2003).

According to Tubert-Oklander and Hernández-Tubert (2014, p. 102):

> Foulkes clearly started by exploring therapeutic groups, and only later turned his attention to non-therapeutic ones, while Pichon-Rivière originally concentrated on learning, institutional, and communitarian groups, which he called operative groups, from which he developed his concepts and techniques that were also to be applied to therapeutic groups. For him, a therapeutic group was conceived as "an operative group that assumes the explicit task of attaining the healing of its members".

This concept—operative groups—is a good example of the lack of clarity coming from excessive generalization.

Moreover, the group's therapeutic perspective is conceptualized and named differently according to various associations of institutions responsible for group-analytic training.

As Hopper (1982, p. 137) refers:

> (...) the use of 'analysis' or 'psychotherapy' (...) is often (but not always) an issue in the politics and sociology of the profession rather than a problem of theoretical and technical substance (...). It is very much a matter for debate whether the term 'group analysis' is pretentious and whether it serves primarily to indicate that what we do is in essence different from what goes on in encounter groups and suchlike (p. 137).

How can, then, group analysis be defined? It is not that easy to find a clear definition of group analysis. We will quote some authors:

For Foulkes (1975b, p. 3):

> Group analysis it is not psychoanalysis of a group by a psychoanalyst. It is a form of psychotherapy by the group, of the group, including its conductor. Hence the name: group-analytic psychotherapy.

Cortesão (1991, p. 271 defines groupanalysis as:

> (...) a single and discontinuous mode of being—in the world and in life: a mode of interpreting and working through disguises and derivatives, of aggressive—destructive impulses, fantasies (generally unconscious), all of them related to death of the individual and of others. Groupanalysis is a way of dealing with Eros and Thanatos in an endless ebb and flow; with the erotic and the perverse; with the envy and conservative and destructive anality which lie beneath the unpredictability of aesthetic equilibrium.

For Morris Nitsun (1996, pp. 19–20):

> [...] Although group analysis is in most respects a distinct mode of psychotherapy, there is a sense in which it never emerged fully as separate from psychoanalysis, in spite of Foulkes's inclusion of theoretical approaches that were unrelated to psychoanalysis in any direct way. [...] Ultimately, the two approaches may not be fully separable, but the problem of separation/differentiation may be a factor in overall lack of theoretical clarity and identity in the group-analytic approach.

Jane Campbell (2005, p. 342) said that group analysis could be simple to define:

> Group analysis is based on an almost absurdly simple paradigm. You put seven people in a circle with a conductor who has established certain boundaries of time and space and confidentiality. The seven people will begin to relate to each other: they may talk, they may be silent, they may look at each other or not, they may ignore each other, but they cannot help but relate to each other since that is what human beings do. Then, this relating behaviour is potentially observed and reflected upon by all the members of the group, including the conductor. And this process of reflection, or thinking, involves not only the head, but also the heart. And that's it.

Caroline Garland (2010a, p. 11) defines psychoanalytic group therapy as:

> [...] a form of therapeutic treatment that uses the group itself as the medium for the treatment of difficulties within members of the group and within the group itself. Psychoanalytic Group Therapy takes as its basis the psychoanalytic understanding of the individual's psychic and social development and observes how this manifests itself within the social context of the small group.

Steinar Lorentzen (2014, p. 3) defines group analysis as:

> an investigative therapy which seeks to optimize interaction between group members with a view to raising awareness of group's dynamics and the individual member's intrapsychic conflicts, and eventually to contribute to correcting irrational forms of behaviour and problematic interactional patterns. The use of these insights and new corrective experiences to promote behaviour change within and outside the group can provide a starting point for more realistic self-image, for changing dysfunctional interpersonal behaviour patterns and for adoption of new, more functional ones.

Groupanalysis, as it is termed in Portugal, is used as a therapeutic way to access the unconscious, conveying introspection, insight, and development of the self. It may also be used as not primarily therapeutic, and be applied to several aims and contexts.

On the Group Analytic Society International's (GASi) website group analysis is defined as follows [Viewed 20 August 2019]. https://groupanalyticsociety.co.uk/about-gasi/group-analysis/:

> (…) a method of group psychotherapy originated by S.H. Foulkes in the 1940s. It combines psychoanalytic insights with an understanding of social and interpersonal functioning. There is an interest in group psychotherapy in the relationship between the individual group member and the rest of the group resulting in a strengthening of both, and a better integration of the individual with his or her community, family, and social network. Deriving from psychoanalysis, Group Analysis also draws on a range of other psychotherapeutic traditions and approaches: systems theory psychotherapies, developmental psychology, and social psychology. From this emerges a powerful psychotherapeutic technique. Group analysis also has applications in organizational consultancy, and in teaching and training. Group Analysts work in a wide range of contexts with a wide range of difficulties and problems. Group Analysis explores the theory, practice and experience of analytical group psychotherapy, embracing concepts derived from psychoanalytic psychology, social psychology, group dynamics, sociology, and anthropology.

Some definitions are about therapeutic Group Analysis *stricto sensu*; others may have a broader sense such as those regarding several group-analytic-based groups with different aims and different group-analytic processes that have been developed over the years. Some point out the aims while others reflect on the process, and still others convey their psychoanalytic origins, thus its therapeutic identity based on unveiling the unconscious processes. There are also those who emphasize the importance of the human relation in the group context. This diversity fully supports the necessity to clarify the concept.

Trained group-analytic conductors are easily able to conduct several kinds of groups since they tend to conceptualize applications which are somehow consequences of the adaptation to updated knowledge in general, as well as of the adaptation to current health and social policies and lifestyles.

Although we think group analysis must adapt to current changes—which is already a fact—it is appropriate to ask how far we can adapt. What are the limits? Some adjustments could even be predominantly positive, as long as we preserve our psychoanalytic/group-analytic identity.

We have the same opinion on this matter as Harold Behr (2008, p. 58) who states that "we need to be sure that in our eagerness to adapt to the new conditions, we do not mutate to such an extent that we lose our group-analytic identity".

Even if, at times, differences in facing and conceptualizing group analysis are denied, sometimes they are exaggerated. For example, there is an apparent polemic concerning the practice of group analysis in IGA and Tavistock, but in fact, some of Tavistock's groups are very similar to IGA's.

Garland, C. (2010a, p. 126) states: "In practice in the Tavistock, there exists a flexible integration of Bion's theory of group process and his psychoanalytic approach to understanding the material, with a clinical style that owes more to Foulkes."

And continues in the next page (Garland, 2010a, p. 127): "Many believe that had Bion done more group therapy, he, like Foulkes, would have found a way of using the totality of the group's interactions."

We believe she is saying that the differences between both institutions are exaggerated and that similarities must be faced as a value, disregarding past rivalries.

How to nominate the conductor is another controversial topic. We think that there is still some confusion about it. As we all know, there are also several designations, depending on groups' types and objectives and on the conductor's functions: group analyst, group-analytic psychotherapist, psychoanalytic group therapist, group therapist, conductor, leader, moderator, conveyor, and facilitator. In a recent panel of papers in which she took part (Ferro et al., 2014), Isaura Neto suggested that the avoidance of the term and concept "Group Analyst", frequently observed in several group-analytic events and settings, expressed by many members of Group Analytic Societies, is a kind of prejudice based more on the Foulkes avoidance of being rejected by the psychoanalytic "family" than a risk of confusing leadership with an autocratic and destructive way of being the main responsible for the group and each of its members. In the Portuguese Society of Groupanalysis, we all think that the groupanalyst—or should we say, his pattern (Cortesão, 1989) (a concept that will be discussed further in another chapter)—is fundamental, and has a most important role in the group-analytic process. We are all unduly influenced by psychoanalytic concepts and perspectives (Ferro, Afonso, Marques & Neto, 2014). Therefore, we call group analysts the conductors of therapeutic groups, i.e., groups in which group analysis and group-analytic psychotherapy occur.

Another ambiguous issue is the deepness of a group analysis or a group-analytic psychotherapy. Is it possible for all those who undergo a group-analytic or psychoanalytic procedure to achieve the established objectives? Our point is that someone could have undergone group analysis or analytic group psychotherapy without having truly achieved a real and deep change process. This is a real problem if applied to candidates training to be group analysts. The same issue has been raised in psychoanalysis.

Research done by Vaughan, Spitzer, Davies, and Roose (1997) revealed that only 40% of patients who underwent psychoanalysis achieve desirable changes.

We don't know of any similar research with respect to groupanalysis, although a 2008 survey (anonymous questionnaire) was conducted regarding about the Portuguese groupanalysts' identity (Carvalho, Galamba, & Neto, 2008). The aim of the study was to assess how effective Portuguese group analysts considered their groupanalysis to be. The results revealed that an average of 70% of the enquired ($n = 64$) considered that they had been sufficiently analyzed as regards their sexuality, early object relationships, narcissism, and aggressiveness.

Concerning the training criteria within the group-analytic training institutions, there are some differences having three common aspects: personal experience, theoretical programme, and supervision. They diverge in the personal experience's timing, in frequency—number of sessions per week, continuous, or in "blocks" training—, and in the ratio between the minimum theoretical course and supervision's times; the groups' constitution are also different: mixed groups or exclusively trainees' groups.

Regarding the personal experience, EFPP group section accepts that group analysis training can be achieved either in a mixed dual and group setting model or in a group setting one on its own (Constitution of the EFPP, 2017).

EGATIN (European Group Analytic Training Institutions Network) has Essential Training Standards (minimum requirements) for becoming a Qualifying Institute such as that these applying institutes have training programmes in which personal experience should be only in the group setting. However, EGATIN's members have many differences in several areas—frequency (1 or 2 sessions per week), continuity versus block training and the composition (mixed groups versus trainees' groups). The Portuguese Society of Groupanalysis, member of EGATIN, suggests that the personal experience should be predominantly in mixed groups with a minimum frequency of two sessions per week, preceded by a variable period of time in a face-to-face individual therapy setting.

As members of the Portuguese Group Analytic Society we consider it is urgent to clear up what the objectives, the group processes, matrices, technical, and theoretical assumptions, curative/therapeutic and non-therapeutic factors are in which groupanalysis and group-analytic-based groups are different or similar.

In short, what are we talking about when we talk about Group Analysis? Is this diversity a way to generate fragmentation and confusion, or by the contrary, a way of enabling connections and fostering creativity?

Ian Miller (2016) believes that every generation, by reading and re-reading other authors' concepts and theories, constructs a "vernacular psychoanalysis" that's to say, original new concepts and terms, from those personal contributions. The same may happen in Group Analysis. However, we should be careful with excessive openness, in order to preserve our group-analytic identity.

As an example, we quote the recent polemic about the Mentalization-Based Group Therapy (MBT-G) (Karterud, 2015a,b): MBT-G is rooted in Group Analysis and in analytic/dynamic group psychotherapy, the main therapeutic tenet of which is to signal and explore the significant intersubjective transactions taking place in the group. However MBT-G set aside other particular aspects of the dynamic psychotherapies; for example, one of its major deviations, is the fact that sessions are structured by therapists, who explicitly invite the patients to explore their interpersonal events, seeking to actively regulate any emotional reactions. Moreover, the patients and therapists' roles and tasks as well as the aims of the group, are very well defined and explicitly explained to the patients.

Steinar Lorentzen (2016) does not agree that this approach may be considered group-analytic, not only by the lack of correspondence between both main MBT-G and the group analysis' principles, but also because there are not yet any enlightened developments.

Others, like Peter Potthoff and U. Moini-Afchari (2014, pp. 14–15), state that,

> MBT interventions may be embedded in the repertoire of the usual analytic therapy, thus extending the analytical therapies spectrum. [...] The intersubjective field and MBT offer important concepts that utilize the perspectives held in common by the different schools of psychoanalysis and offer a bridge to connect them. Therefore, the alternative is not MBT or group analysis but MBT in group analysis.

We can allude to another example: that of multifamily groupanalysis (MFGA) (Neto & Centeno, 2014). We cannot describe it here in detail, but it is important to note that this approach is absolutely different from other so-called multifamily psycho educational approaches. It is rather an application of group-analytical concepts and technique to multifamily psychoanalysis (Badaracco, 2000). Both have the same objectives being equivalent in terms of their concepts. Multifamily psychoanalysis was introduced in the early 1960s in Buenos Aires, Argentina, by psychiatrist and psychoanalyst, Jorge Garcia Badaracco. He put together a group of patients and their families, creating a matrix where pathogenic and pathological communication and relational patterns could be easily observed, mirrored, made aware, and eventually changed.

Since then, multifamily psychoanalysis has been developed and practised by several European and American authors as a new treatment concept for mental illness, being applied to several pathologies and in several settings: institutional, outpatient, or inpatient (total or partial) as well as in the educational context. In 2001, the first Multifamily Group in Portugal was implemented by Isaura Neto and her team, at the Psychiatric Day Hospital of the Santa Maria Hospital (HSM), a public general and university hospital in Lisbon (Neto & Centeno, 2003). It has been an important therapeutic tool, having been included in the Psychiatric Day Hospital's framework since then.

In our view, the main problem seems to be the confusion that occurs when one calls something group analysis when it is *not* therapeutic group analysis. We accept that there are approaches such as MBT-G and multifamily group analysis, which, despite having some different procedures from those of therapeutic group analysis, are ruled by psychoanalytic and group-analytic concepts, and may be implemented and practised by group analysts.

The same applies to some emergent forms of applied group analysis, the most controversial forms of group-analytic-based groups—"the impossible groups" (Weinberg, 2016, pp. 330–349). Weinberg refers to some groups which do not follow the rules of the therapy textbook, but nevertheless their members "are still able to work at deep levels, create intimate relationships, and benefit from the group". Weinberg lists a few:

a   Demonstration groups (demo groups);
b   Institute groups at the American Group Psychotherapy Association (AGPA);
c   Resident groups where members do not attend meetings regularly;
d   Non-western groups where the culture does not allow a stormy stage;
e   Groups that function well in times of war and terror;
f   Inpatient groups in a psychiatric ward in which the membership changes from one session to another (and indeed Yalom (1995) developed a specific model based on a one session intervention); and
g   Internet groups where the boundaries are incredibly loose.

The Internet groups mentioned above should not be mistaken with the more recent online therapy groups. These last differ from the former in that they are synchronic by video conference. As Weinberg writes, in this modality, the group dynamic seems to be very similar to group analysis and psychoanalytic group psychotherapy (Martins, Perestrelo & Neto, 2018; Weinberg, 2020).

In summary, we would say that there are several types of groups, with different characteristics and objectives which are based in the group-analytic framework as well as conceptualized and conducted by group analysts; therefore, it is important to characterize them.

The group-analytic cluster—a kind of brand

Besides the groups of Therapeutic Group Analysis, we will distinguish seven other forms of group-analytic-based groups. These eight items constitute, in our opinion, a "group analytic cluster":

1 Therapeutic Group Analysis (for some authors this setting is called Group Analytic Psychotherapy, for other authors it is called Operative Groups (in the broader sense)
2 Group Analytic Psychotherapy (Short- and Long- term Groups) Institutional Group Analytic Psychotherapy (Outpatient, Day Hospital and Ward Groups)/Operative Groups (in the broader sense)
3 Multifamily Group Analysis (Neto, 2017)/Parents' Groups
4 Mentalization-Based Treatment—Group
5 Internet Groups
6 Group Analytic Coaching
7 Experiential Groups/T-Groups/Demo Groups
8 Task-Centred Groups/Operative Groups (strict sense)/Supervision/Balint Groups/Team Work Groups.

We have based our choice in what we know directly from our own practice of these groups. We considered that in all of them there was at least one common feature: the importance of unconscious forces and phenomena within every individual and every group. Moreover, we took account of the opinion of the group analysts who wrote about them, stating that they were group-analytic-based groups. This way we considered the existence of a common ground which we call a cluster. We also think that this identity may perform as a kind of brand. Why a Brand? In a certain way, we want to advertise groupanalysis and convince other professionals that is a very useful model to understand individuals and groups; thus we want to sell groupanalysis. A brand highlights the idea of something more cohesive, more institutional.

The present GASi has many members who are not truly trained group analysts. Nevertheless, they are definitely interested in group analysis and conduct several kinds of groups.

The group-analytic cluster/brand—the tables

To further clarify what we have said before, we created eight tables in order to emphasize the main differences and similarities of the Group Analytic Cluster. The first one concern therapeutic Group Analysis followed by the others group-analytic-based groups.

We divided each table in two main topics: The Objectives of each group framework, and their respective Group Analytic Processes.

The objectives are changes to be achieved, previously established between the conductor, each one of the group members, and the group itself

Regarding the group-analytic process, Cortesão (1989, p. 31, translated from the Portuguese), defines it as

> The groupanalytic process is the mode through which the various theoretical and technical dimensions that contribute to giving a framework and form to groupanalytic therapy are structured, organized, and perform a function.

We believe that the function mentioned by Cortesão corresponds in fact to the objectives.

We have included in the group-analytic process the following items: (a) the focus of the group-analytic process, which may be the individual and/or the group; (b) the conductor's pattern/leadership activity/dynamic administration; and (c) the matrix's characteristics, including the setting.

The features displayed on the tables were chosen according to our own experience/knowledge about the several frameworks, as well as to other authors' oral and written contributions. We took into account the most paradigmatic as well as the most controversial features. We did not mention every phenomenological factor—such as, for instance, mirroring, resonance, etc., because we consider that they are somehow implicit in the free-floating discussion and in the ego training in action, which are paradigmatic features in group-analytic theory and practice.

The tables were built in order to make the comparison between both similarities and differences of the eight forms of group-analytic-based groups possible.

Therefore the last four columns present four parameters: "Yes"; "No"; "PSB" (possible); and "NA" (not applicable). We consider a "Yes" when the issue is a typical characteristic of the group's application, and by that reason it must occur; we consider a "No", when the item does not occur, and does not characterize the application; it is a "PSB" when it may occur, although this occurrence may not be essential to characterize that specific group; finally it is a "NA" when it does not apply.

Regarding the item "conductor's designation", we considered the designations commonly used in the literature for each type of group, independently of the conductor's group-analytic training. For instance, we know that some of the group-analytic-based groups, like the Mentalization-Based Treatment Group or the Group Analytic Coaching, might be conducted by group analysts; nevertheless, in the tables, we choose to designate them as group therapists/conductors/moderators/facilitators rather than group analysts.

Table 2.1

		GROUP DESIGNATION			YES	NO	PSB	NA
		ANALYTIC CURE/LONG LASTING RESULTS						
		SYMPTOMATIC RELEASE / EGO-DYSTONIC CHANGES						
		EGO-SYNTONIC CHANGES						
		INDIRECT THERAPEUTIC BENEFITS						
OBJECTIVES / DESIRABLE RESULTS		MENTALIZATION CAPACITIES						
		SELF KNOWLEDGE/INSIGHT						
		LEARNING						
		EMPATHY						
		AUTONOMY						
GROUP PROCESS	PROCESS FOCUSED	ON THE INDIVIDUAL						
		ON THE GROUP						
	PATTERN/ LEADERSHIP ACTIVITY/DYNAMIC ADMINISTRATION	PREVIOUS THERAPEUTIC ALLIANCE						
		NON-INVASIVE CONDUCTION,EMPATHY,CONTINUITY,PUNCTUALITY						
		CT AWARENESS						
		COUNTER-TRANSFERENCE DISCLOSURE						
		INDIVIDUAL INTERPRETATION						
		GROUP-AS-A-WHOLE INTERPRETATION						
		TRANSFERENCE INTERPRETATION						
		GENETIC RECONSTRUCTION						
		HERE AND NOW						
		THERE AND THEN						
		CO-THERAPY						
		CONDUCTOR'S DESIGNATION	GROUP ANALYST					
			GROUP THERAPIST					
			CONDUCTOR /CONVEYOR					
			MODERATOR / FACILITATOR					
		CONDUCTOR MEMBERS' SELECTION						
	MATRIX	REGRESSION						
		FREE-FLOATING-DISCUSSION						
		EGO-TRAINING-IN-ACTION						
		EMOTIONAL TRANSFORMATIVE EXPERIENCES						
		SETTING	GROUP'S FORM AND COMPOSITION	SMALL				
				MEDIUM				
				LARGE				
				CLOSED				
				OPEN				
				SLOW-OPENED				
			PLACEMENT	CIRCLE(S)				
			ASEPSIS	CLOSE RELATIONSHIPS				
				CONTACT OUT OF SESSIONS				
			CONFIDENTIALITY	MEMBERS IDENTITY				
				GROUP CONTENTS				
			FREQUENCY	MORE THAN 1 SESSION WEEK				
				OTHER FREQUENCIES				
			DURATION	SESSION	60 TO 120 MIN			
				PROCESS	LIMITED TIME			

Table 2.2

Group analysis: therapeutic group analysis, groupanalysis, operative groups (in the broader sense)					YES	NO	PSB	NA
OBJECTIVES / DESIRABLE RESULTS	ANALYTIC CURE/LONG LASTING RESULTS				x			
	SYMPTOMATIC RELEASE / EGO-DYSTONIC CHANGES				x			
	EGO-SYNTONIC CHANGES				x			
	INDIRECT THERAPEUTIC BENEFITS							x
	MENTALIZATION CAPACITIES				x			
	SELF KNOWLEDGE/INSIGHT				x			
	LEARNING				x			
	EMPATHY				x			
	AUTONOMY				x			
GROUP PROCESS	PROCESS FOCUSED	ON THE INDIVIDUAL			x			
		ON THE GROUP			x			
	PATTERN/ LEADERSHIP ACTIVITY/DYNAMIC ADMINISTRATION	PREVIOUS THERAPEUTIC ALLIANCE			x			
		NON-INVASIVE CONDUCTION,EMPATHY,CONTINUITY,PUNCTUALITY			x			
		CT AWARENESS			x			
		COUNTER-TRANSFERENCE DISCLOSURE			x			
		INDIVIDUAL INTERPRETATION			x			
		GROUP-AS-A-WHOLE INTERPRETATION			x			
		TRANSFERENCE INTERPRETATION			x			
		GENETIC RECONSTRUCTION			x			
		HERE AND NOW			x			
		THERE AND THEN			x			
		CO-THERAPY				x		
		CONDUCTOR'S DESIGNATION	GROUP ANALYST		x			
			GROUP THERAPIST				x	
			CONDUCTOR / CONVEYOR				x	
			MODERATOR / FACILITATOR			x		
		CONDUCTOR MEMBERS' SELECTION			x			
		REGRESSION			x			
		FREE-FLOATING-DISCUSSION			x			
		EGO-TRAINING-IN-ACTION			x			
		EMOTIONAL TRANSFORMATIVE EXPERIENCES			x			
	MATRIX	SETTING	GROUP'S FORM AND COMPOSITION	SMALL	x			
				MEDIUM		x		
				LARGE		x		
				CLOSED		x		
				OPEN		x		
				SLOW-OPENED	x			
			PLACEMENT	CIRCLE(S)	x			
			ASEPSIS	CLOSE RELATIONSHIPS		x		
				CONTACT OUT OF SESSIONS		x		
			CONFIDENTIALITY	MEMBERS IDENTITY	x			
				GROUP CONTENTS	x			
			FREQUENCY	MORE THAN 1 SESSION WEEK	x			
				OTHER FREQUENCIES		x		
			DURATION	SESSION 60 TO 120 MIN	x			
				PROCESS LIMITED TIME		x		

Table 2.3

		GROUP ANALYTIC PSYCHOTHERAPY (SHORT AND LONG TERM GROUPS) /INSTITUTIONAL GROUPS/OPERATIVE GROUPS (IN THE BROADER SENSE)			YES	NO	PSB	NA
	OBJECTIVES / DESIRABLE RESULTS	ANALYTIC CURE/LONG LASTING RESULTS					x	
		SYMPTOMATIC RELEASE / EGO-DYSTONIC CHANGES			x			
		EGO-SYNTONIC CHANGES					x	
		INDIRECT THERAPEUTIC BENEFITS						x
		MENTALIZATION CAPACITIES			x			
		SELF KNOWLEDGE/INSIGHT			x			
		LEARNING			x			
		EMPHATY			x			
		AUTONOMY			x			
GROUP PROCESS	PROCESS FOCUSED	ON THE INDIVIDUAL			x			
		ON THE GROUP			x			
	PATTERN/ LEADERSHIP ACTIVITY/DYNAMIC ADMINISTRATION	PREVIOUS THERAPEUTIC ALLIANCE					x	
		NON-INVASIVE CONDUCTION,EMPATHY,CONTINUITY,PUNCTUALITY			x			
		CT AWARENESS			x			
		COUNTER-TRANSFERENCE DISCLOSURE					x	
		INDIVIDUAL INTERPRETATION			x			
		GROUP-AS-A-WHOLE INTERPRETATION			x			
		TRANSFERENCE INTERPRETATION			x			
		GENETIC RECONSTRUCTION			x			
		HERE AND NOW			x			
		THERE AND THEN			x			
		CO-THERAPY					x	
		CONDUCTOR'S DESIGNATION	GROUP ANALYST				x	
			GROUP THERAPIST		x			
			CONDUCTOR /CONVEYOR				x	
			MODERATOR / FACILITATOR			x		
		CONDUCTOR MEMBERS' SELECTION					x	
	MATRIX	REGRESSION					x	
		FREE-FLOATING-DISCUSSION			x			
		EGO-TRAINING-IN-ACTION			x			
		EMOTIONAL TRANSFORMATIVE EXPERIENCES			x			
		SETTING	GROUP'S FORM AND COMPOSITION	SMALL	x			
				MEDIUM	x			
				LARGE		x		
				CLOSED			x	
				OPEN			x	
				SLOW-OPENED			x	
			PLACEMENT	CIRCLE(S)	x			
			ASEPSIS	CLOSE RELATIONSHIPS		x		
				CONTACT OUT OF SESSIONS			x	
			CONFIDENTIALITY	MEMBERS IDENTITY			x	
				GROUP CONTENTS	x			
			FREQUENCY	MORE THAN 1 SESSION WEEK			x	
				OTHER FREQUENCIES	x			
			DURATION	SESSION 60 TO 120 MIN	x			
				PROCESS LIMITED TIME			x	

Table 2.4

			MULTIFAMILY GROUP ANALYSIS / PARENTS GROUPS			YES	NO	PSB	NA
	OBJECTIVES / DESIRABLE RESULTS		ANALYTIC CURE/LONG LASTING RESULTS				x		
			SYMPTOMATIC RELEASE / EGO-DYSTONIC CHANGES			x			
			EGO-SYNTONIC CHANGES					x	
			INDIRECT THERAPEUTIC BENEFITS						x
			MENTALIZATION CAPACITIES			x			
			SELF KNOWLEDGE/INSIGHT			x			
			LEARNING			x			
			EMPATHY			x			
			AUTONOMY			x			
GROUP PROCESS		PROCESS FOCUSED	ON THE INDIVIDUAL			x			
			ON THE GROUP			x			
		PATTERN/ LEADERSHIP ACTIVITY/DYNAMIC ADMINISTRATION	PREVIOUS THERAPEUTIC ALLIANCE					x	
			NON-INVASIVE CONDUCTION,EMPATHY,CONTINUITY,PUNCTUALITY			x			
			CT AWARENESS			x			
			COUNTER-TRANSFERENCE DISCLOSURE					x	
			INDIVIDUAL INTERPRETATION					x	
			GROUP-AS-A-WHOLE INTERPRETATION					x	
			TRANSFERENCE INTERPRETATION					x	
			GENETIC RECONSTRUCTION					x	
			HERE AND NOW					x	
			THERE AND THEN					x	
			CO-THERAPY			x			
			CONDUCTOR'S DESIGNATION	GROUP ANALYST			x		
				GROUP THERAPIST		x			
				CONDUCTOR / CONVEYOR				x	
				MODERATOR / FACILITATOR			x		
			CONDUCTOR MEMBERS' SELECTION					x	
		MATRIX	REGRESSION					x	
			FREE-FLOATING-DISCUSSION			x			
			EGO-TRAINING-IN-ACTION			x			
			EMOTIONAL TRANSFORMATIVE EXPERIENCES					x	
			SETTING	GROUP'S FORM AND COMPOSITION	SMALL			x	
					MEDIUM			x	
					LARGE			x	
					CLOSED			x	
					OPEN			x	
					SLOW-OPENED			x	
				PLACEMENT	CIRCLE(S)	x			
				ASEPSIS	CLOSE RELATIONSHIPS	x			
					CONTACT OUT OF SESSIONS			x	
				CONFIDENTIALITY	MEMBERS IDENTITY			x	
					GROUP CONTENTS	x			
				FREQUENCY	MORE THAN 1 SESSION WEEK			x	
					OTHER FREQUENCIES	x			
				DURATION	SESSION 60 TO 120 MIN	x			
					PROCESS LIMITED TIME			x	

The group-analytic cluster 47

Table 2.5

MENTALIZATION-BASED GROUP THERAPY (MBT-G)					YES	NO	PSB	NA
OBJECTIVES / DESIRABLE RESULTS			ANALYTIC CURE/LONG LASTING RESULTS				x		
			SYMPTOMATIC RELEASE / EGO-DYSTONIC CHANGES			x			
			EGO-SYNTONIC CHANGES					x	
			INDIRECT THERAPEUTIC BENEFITS						x
			MENTALIZATION CAPACITIES			x			
			SELF KNOWLEDGE/INSIGHT			x			
			LEARNING			x			
			EMPATHY			x			
			AUTONOMY			x			
GROUP PROCESS	PROCESS FOCUSED		ON THE INDIVIDUAL			x			
			ON THE GROUP					x	
	PATTERN/ LEADERSHIP ACTIVITY/DYNAMIC ADMINISTRATION		PREVIOUS THERAPEUTIC ALLIANCE					x	
			NON-INVASIVE CONDUCTION,EMPATHY,CONTINUITY,PUNCTUALITY			x			
			CT AWARENESS			x			
			COUNTER-TRANSFERENCE DISCLOSURE					x	
			INDIVIDUAL INTERPRETATION				x		
			GROUP-AS-A-WHOLE INTERPRETATION				x		
			TRANSFERENCE INTERPRETATION					x	
			GENETIC RECONSTRUCTION				x		
			HERE AND NOW			x			
			THERE AND THEN					x	
			CO-THERAPY					x	
			CONDUCTOR'S DESIGNATION	GROUP ANALYST				x	
				GROUP THERAPIST		x			
				CONDUCTOR / CONVEYOR				x	
				MODERATOR / FACILITATOR				x	
			CONDUCTOR MEMBERS' SELECTION					x	
	MATRIX		REGRESSION					x	
			FREE-FLOATING-DISCUSSION					x	
			EGO-TRAINING-IN-ACTION			x			
			EMOTIONAL TRANSFORMATIVE EXPERIENCES					x	
			GROUP'S FORM AND COMPOSITION	SMALL		x			
				MEDIUM		x			
				LARGE				x	
				CLOSED				x	
				OPEN				x	
				SLOW-OPENED				x	
		SETTING	PLACEMENT	CIRCLE(S)		x			
			ASEPSIS	CLOSE RELATIONSHIPS				x	
				CONTACT OUT OF SESSIONS				x	
			CONFIDENTIALITY	MEMBERS IDENTITY				x	
				GROUP CONTENTS		x			
			FREQUENCY	MORE THAN 1 SESSION WEEK			x		
				OTHER FREQUENCIES		x			
			DURATION	SESSION	60 TO 120 MIN	x			
				PROCESS	LIMITED TIME			x	

Table 2.6

		INTERNET GROUPS			YES	NO	PSB	NA
	OBJECTIVES / DESIRABLE RESULTS	ANALYTIC CURE/LONG LASTING RESULTS				x		
		SYMPTOMATIC RELEASE / EGO-DYSTONIC CHANGES					x	
		EGO-SYNTONIC CHANGES					x	
		INDIRECT THERAPEUTIC BENEFITS						x
		MENTALIZATION CAPACITIES					x	
		SELF KNOWLEDGE/INSIGHT					x	
		LEARNING			x			
		EMPATHY					x	
		AUTONOMY					x	
GROUP PROCESS	**PROCESS FOCUSED**	ON THE INDIVIDUAL			x			
		ON THE GROUP					x	
	PATTERN/ LEADERSHIP ACTIVITY/DYNAMIC ADMINISTRATION	PREVIOUS THERAPEUTIC ALLIANCE						x
		NON-INVASIVE CONDUCTION,EMPATHY,CONTINUITY,PUNCTUALITY			x			
		CT AWARENESS			x			
		COUNTER-TRANSFERENCE DISCLOSURE					x	
		INDIVIDUAL INTERPRETATION					x	
		GROUP-AS-A-WHOLE INTERPRETATION					x	
		TRANSFERENCE INTERPRETATION					x	
		GENETIC RECONSTRUCTION					x	
		HERE AND NOW					x	
		THERE AND THEN					x	
		CO-THERAPY				x		
		CONDUCTOR'S DESIGNATION	GROUP ANALYST				x	
			GROUP THERAPIST		x			
			CONDUCTOR / CONVEYOR		x			
			MODERATOR / FACILITATOR			x		
		CONDUCTOR MEMBERS' SELECTION					x	
	MATRIX	REGRESSION					x	
		FREE-FLOATING-DISCUSSION			x			
		EGO-TRAINING-IN-ACTION			x			
		EMOTIONAL TRANSFORMATIVE EXPERIENCES					x	
		GROUP'S FORM AND COMPOSITION	SMALL				x	
			MEDIUM				x	
			LARGE				x	
			CLOSED				x	
			OPEN				x	
			SLOW-OPENED				x	
		SETTING	PLACEMENT	CIRCLE(S) (VIRTUAL CIRCLE)	x			
			ASEPSIS	CLOSE RELATIONSHIPS		x		
				CONTACT OUT OF SESSIONS			x	
			CONFIDENTIALITY	MEMBERS IDENTITY	x			
				GROUP CONTENTS	x			
			FREQUENCY	MORE THAN 1 SESSION WEEK			x	
				OTHER FREQUENCIES			x	
			DURATION	SESSION 60 TO 120 MIN	x			
				PROCESS LIMITED TIME			x	

Table 2.7

		GROUP ANALYTIC COACHING			YES	NO	PSB	NA
OBJECTIVES / DESIRABLE RESULTS		ANALYTIC CURE/LONG LASTING RESULTS				x		
		SYMPTOMATIC RELEASE / EGO-DYSTONIC CHANGES				x		
		EGO-SYNTONIC CHANGES					x	
		INDIRECT THERAPEUTIC BENEFITS					x	
		MENTALIZATION CAPACITIES			x			
		SELF KNOWLEDGE/INSIGHT			x			
		LEARNING			x			
		EMPATHY			x			
		AUTONOMY			x			
GROUP PROCESS	PROCESS FOCUSED	ON THE INDIVIDUAL			x			
		ON THE GROUP			x			
	PATTERN/ LEADERSHIP ACTIVITY/DYNAMIC ADMINISTRATION	PREVIOUS THERAPEUTIC ALLIANCE						x
		NON-INVASIVE CONDUCTION,EMPATHY,CONTINUITY,PUNCTUALITY			x			
		CT AWARENESS			x			
		COUNTER-TRANSFERENCE DISCLOSURE					x	
		INDIVIDUAL INTERPRETATION					x	
		GROUP-AS-A-WHOLE INTERPRETATION					x	
		TRANSFERENCE INTERPRETATION				x		
		GENETIC RECONSTRUCTION					x	
		HERE AND NOW					x	
		THERE AND THEN					x	
		CO-THERAPY					x	
		CONDUCTOR'S DESIGNATION	GROUP ANALYST				x	
			GROUP THERAPIST				x	
			CONDUCTOR / CONVEYOR		x			
			MODERATOR / FACILITATOR		x			
		CONDUCTOR MEMBERS' SELECTION					x	
	MATRIX	REGRESSION					x	
		FREE-FLOATING-DISCUSSION					x	
		EGO-TRAINING-IN-ACTION			x			
		EMOTIONAL TRANSFORMATIVE EXPERIENCES			x			
		SETTING	GROUP'S FORM AND COMPOSITION	SMALL	x			
				MEDIUM	x			
				LARGE		x		
				CLOSED			x	
				OPEN		x		
				SLOW-OPENED			x	
			PLACEMENT	CIRCLE(S)	x			
			ASEPSIS	CLOSE RELATIONSHIPS		x		
				CONTACT OUT OF SESSIONS			x	
			CONFIDENTIALITY	MEMBERS IDENTITY			x	
				GROUP CONTENTS	x			
			FREQUENCY	MORE THAN 1 SESSION WEEK		x		
				OTHER FREQUENCIES	x			
			DURATION	SESSION 60 TO 120 MIN	x			
				PROCESS LIMITED TIME	x			

Table 2.8

		EXPERIENTIAL GROUPS / T-GROUPS /DEMO GROUPS			YES	NO	PSB	NA
		ANALYTIC CURE/LONG LASTING RESULTS				x		
		SYMPTOMATIC RELEASE / EGO-DYSTONIC CHANGES				x		
		EGO-SYNTONIC CHANGES				x		
		INDIRECT THERAPEUTIC BENEFITS				x		
OBJECTIVES / DESIRABLE RESULTS		MENTALIZATION CAPACITIES				x		
		SELF KNOWLEDGE/INSIGHT				x		
		LEARNING			x			
		EMPATHY					x	
		AUTONOMY					x	
	PROCESS FOCUSED	ON THE INDIVIDUAL			x			
		ON THE GROUP			x			
		PREVIOUS THERAPEUTIC ALLIANCE						x
		NON-INVASIVE CONDUCTION, EMPATHY, CONTINUITY, PUNCTUALITY			x			
		CT AWARENESS			x			
		COUNTER-TRANSFERENCE DISCLOSURE					x	
		INDIVIDUAL INTERPRETATION					x	
		GROUP-AS-A-WHOLE INTERPRETATION					x	
	PATTERN/ LEADERSHIP ACTIVITY/DYNAMIC ADMINISTRATION	TRANSFERENCE INTERPRETATION					x	
		GENETIC RECONSTRUCTION					x	
		HERE AND NOW			x			
		THERE AND THEN					x	
		CO-THERAPY					X	
		CONDUCTOR'S DESIGNATION	GROUP ANALYST				x	
			GROUP THERAPIST				x	
GROUP PROCESS			CONDUCTOR / CONVEYOR			x		
			MODERATOR / FACILITATOR			x		
		CONDUCTOR MEMBERS' SELECTION					x	
		REGRESSION					x	
		FREE-FLOATING-DISCUSSION			x			
		EGO-TRAINING-IN-ACTION			x			
		EMOTIONAL TRANSFORMATIVE EXPERIENCES					x	
				SMALL	x			
				MEDIUM	x			
			GROUP'S FORM AND COMPOSITION	LARGE	x			
				CLOSED	x			
	MATRIX			OPEN		x		
				SLOW-OPENED		x		
			PLACEMENT	CIRCLE(S)	x			
		SETTING	ASEPSIS	CLOSE RELATIONSHIPS			x	
				CONTACT OUT OF SESSIONS			x	
			CONFIDENTIALITY	MEMBERS IDENTITY				x
				GROUP CONTENTS	x			
			FREQUENCY	MORE THAN 1 SESSION WEEK		x		
				OTHER FREQUENCIES	x			
			DURATION	SESSION	60 TO 120 MIN	x		
				PROCESS	LIMITED TIME	x		

The group-analytic cluster 51

Table 2.9

TASK-CENTRED GROUPS: OPERATIVE GROUPS (STRICT SENSE)/ SUPERVISION GROUPS / BALINT GROUPS / TEAM WORK GROUPS					YES	NO	PSB	NA
OBJECTIVES / DESIRABLE RESULTS				ANALYTIC CURE/LONG LASTING RESULTS				x
				SYMPTOMATIC RELEASE / EGO-DYSTONIC CHANGES				x
				EGO-SYNTONIC CHANGES				x
				INDIRECT THERAPEUTIC BENEFITS			x	
				MENTALIZATION CAPACITIES			x	
				SELF KNOWLEDGE/INSIGHT			x	
				LEARNING	x			
				EMPATHY			x	
				AUTONOMY			x	
GROUP PROCESS	**PROCESS FOCUSED**			ON THE INDIVIDUAL			x	
				ON THE GROUP	x			
	PATTERN/ LEADERSHIP ACTIVITY/DYNAMIC ADMINISTRATION			PREVIOUS THERAPEUTIC ALLIANCE				x
				NON-INVASIVE CONDUCTION,EMPATHY,CONTINUITY,PUNCTUALITY	x			
				CT AWARENESS	x			
				COUNTER-TRANSFERENCE DISCLOSURE			x	
				INDIVIDUAL INTERPRETATION			x	
				GROUP-AS-A-WHOLE INTERPRETATION	x			
				TRANSFERENCE INTERPRETATION			x	
				GENETIC RECONSTRUCTION		x		
				HERE AND NOW	x			
				THERE AND THEN		x		
				CO-THERAPY				x
		CONDUCTOR'S DESIGNATION	GROUP ANALYST			x	
			GROUP THERAPIST			x	
			CONDUCTOR /CONVEYOR	x			
			MODERATOR / FACILITATOR	x			
				CONDUCTOR MEMBERS' SELECTION				x
	MATRIX			REGRESSION			x	
				FREE-FLOATING-DISCUSSION			x	
				EGO-TRAINING-IN-ACTION	x			
				EMOTIONAL TRANSFORMATIVE EXPERIENCES			x	
		SETTING	GROUP'S FORM AND COMPOSITION	SMALL			x	
				MEDIUM			x	
				LARGE		x		
				CLOSED			x	
				OPEN			x	
				SLOW-OPENED			x	
			PLACEMENT	CIRCLE(S)	x			
			ASEPSIS	CLOSE RELATIONSHIPS			x	
				CONTACT OUT OF SESSIONS			x	
			CONFIDENTIALITY	MEMBERS IDENTITY			x	
				GROUP CONTENTS	x			
			FREQUENCY	MORE THAN 1 SESSION WEEK			x	
				OTHER FREQUENCIES			x	
			DURATION	SESSION 60 TO 120 MIN	x			
				PROCESS LIMITED TIME				x

Concluding remarks

After analyzing the tables, we noticed that they all share some common features. Therefore, we may define group analysis in a broader sense as a cluster set of psychological group interventions based on the therapeutic group-analytic framework. These interventions share six common characteristics:

- The importance of unconscious mental processes, both in individuals and in groups.
- They are handled in groups taking advantage of the group's relational dynamics.
- Group members are in circles including the conductor; we consider that even the online groups are handled in "virtual circles".
- A non-intrusive conduction. The conductor must understand and maintain the group-analytic matrix, being the conveyer of a non-invasive, supportive, and empathic pattern.
- A holding environment based on a non-intrusive conduction, authenticity, coherence, empathy, confidentiality, punctuality and constancy, bearing in mind the countertransference awareness.
- The opportunity to develop learning and self-knowledge's skills.

Therefore, we consider that there is a group-analytic identity in this cluster, performing as a kind of brand.

We do believe that this way of analyzing and comparing the main objectives, and group-analytic processes of these several group-analytic frameworks, can contribute to the definition and operationalization of the so-called group analysis, which will facilitate research. Moreover, it will raise the credibility of group analysis pushing group-analytic conceptualization to the front row of open systems conceptualizations, allowing group analysis to integrate critically new concepts, thus new applications.

Finally, we will answer the central question which we asked at the beginning of this chapter: Is there one group analysis or several?

We believe that there are two ways of looking at groupanalysis; and therefore, two ways to practise it:

1 In the strict sense, which includes Therapeutic Group Analysis and Group Analytic Psychotherapy/Psychoanalytic Group Psychotherapy/Operative Groups in the broader sense;
2 In the broader sense: the Group Analytic Cluster.

Chapter 3

The Portuguese school of groupanalysis

The integration of psychoanalytic concepts in groupanalysis

Sara Ferro and Margarida França

Preliminary considerations

Since 1956—when Eduardo Cortesão introduced groupanalysis in Portugal—Portuguese groupanalysts have been concerned with the integration and use of psychoanalytic conceptualizations in groupanalytic practice. In his book published in 1989, Cortesão states "psychoanalysis and groupanalysis are conceptualized and described as research and therapeutic methods with common theoretical grounds but different operative procedures" (Cortesão 1989, p. 36, translated from the Portuguese). Until his death in 1991, he sought to review and reformulate the groupanalytic theory as proposed by Foulkes, adding concepts and revising aspects which allowed him to state that, regarding psychoanalysis, groupanalysis should be understood as a different yet not contradictory situation (Cortesão, 1989).

The apparent constraints on approaching groupanalysis and psychoanalysis seem to have very little to do with the difficulty in understanding their conceptual interdisciplinary relationship. Cortesão (1989, p. 49, translated from the Portuguese), about the use of the expression group analysis coined by Foulkes, wrote:

> Nevertheless, the inclusion of the word analysis on the binomial term group analysis was perceived as an intrusion among the psychoanalytical establishment of the British Psychoanalytic Society. Such reaction led some psychoanalysts—not all—at that time, to consider Foulkes as somehow a heretic psychoanalyst.

Eduardo Cortesão trained with Foulkes, towards whom he nourished admiration and friendship. However, these facts did not prevent him from revealing a certain apprehension regarding a vision of group analysis that was, in his opinion, too practical and which leads to conceptual confusion between psychoanalysis, group analysis, and psychoanalytic group psychotherapy.

Perhaps the fact that psychoanalysis and groupanalysis were introduced in Portugal at about the same time influenced Cortesão's spontaneity, since the beginning, to suggest the agglutination of the binomial term "group analysis" to create the new term "groupanalysis", with the intention of simplifying the natural evolution of concepts and writing, as long it did not alter its essence (Cortesão, 1989). In this chapter, we will employ the word groupanalysis, instead of the expression group analysis, as Cortesão proposed and as used by the Portuguese Groupanalytic Society.

This chapter intends to be an overview of this interdependence between the theoretical psychoanalytic field and the construction of a groupanalytic metatheory. We will focus on the way concepts have developed in order to maintain its psychoanalytic identity and how these concepts apply to the group setting: which are the most important psychoanalytic tools and concepts used in groupanalysis; how they are integrated by groupanalysts and what they are called.

Cortesão's legacy

Perhaps the relevance of the psychoanalytic theory in Cortesão's mind was one of the main reasons that led him to build concepts like "pattern"; to conceptualize groupanalysis as a process; to emphasize the analysis of the regression, the importance of resistance, or the dynamic transference-countertransference. He spoke about "group transference neurosis"—meaning the transference neurosis of each patient in the broad context of the group—and about working through. He looked at interpretation as the engine that promotes groupanalytic insight, electing transferential interpretation, mostly commutative (closely related with Strachey's mutative interpretation (Cortesão, 1989)) as a privileged way to attain deepest transformation.

Pattern

In 1967, when Cortesão discussed with Foulkes and other colleagues his idea about the importance of the groupanalyst's function and the need for further conceptualization on this issue, it was not welcome (Cortesão, 1967a). Considering that psychoanalytic and group-analytic theories and conceptualizations, as are all other theories, are born in and from a specific context, we believe that Foulkes' and Cortesão's surrounding contexts bore little resemblance to each other, which is what prevented Foulkes from accepting the assignment of too much power/responsibility to the groupanalyst.

In this chapter we will restrict ourselves to addressing why Cortesão's concept of pattern bears the unequivocal brand of psychoanalysis. Other chapters of this book will discuss in detail several other features of the concept.

The pattern's integration in the group matrix induces the working-through that allows the group matrix to become a place of psychological birth and development for each of the participants (Cortesão, 1989). It is because of the pattern that the matrix may constitute an operative base for intra and inter psychic relations, capable of containing, integrating, and eventually bringing each patient's individual contribution into a higher operational level. It becomes an internal space with its own temporality that comprehends its past and a future in which its goals and accomplishments are projected (Cortesão, 1989).

The groupanalyst conveys the pattern. His personality, features like tolerance, honesty, and empathic attitude, are part of the pattern's nature. These are connected to the use of the groupanalyst's countertransference: his awareness of his own blind spots and of his own personal internal matrix (this concept is developed in Chapter 4 of this book). This aim can only be attained properly if the groupanalyst himself has been in a groupanalytic process, being a patient in a heterogeneous group (with patients seeking treatment aside from training) for a certain amount of times (usually no less than four years) on a twice a week basis. Similarly to psychoanalytic training, a groupanalyst trained by the Portuguese Society of Groupanalysis and Analytic Group Psychotherapy must have the need to understand deeply his or her unconscious processes in order to deal with group members and the group's transferential processes.

We think that, aside from the powerful connotation of the word 'leader' in German which could set up Foulkes's resistance to the idea of the importance of a leader in the group, perhaps Cortesão never really knew how to convey the message. César Dinis (2000a) writes about the responsibility groupanalysts bear, mostly like parental figures towards their children: the responsibility is never symmetrical. In classical psychoanalysis, the psychoanalyst appears as an intangible figure, while transference is considered a resistance and countertransference means that powerful projective identification mechanisms are at work.

Nowadays, psychoanalysis looks at countertransference as much more complex phenomenon, and at the relationship between patient and analyst as a two-way stream. Needless to state that in groupanalysis, because transference and counter transference phenomena are multiple and happening all the time between so many individuals and the group as a whole, we sense that the "leader's" role is being reviewed every second. Obviously, a groupanalyst cannot hide behind silence or remain unseen by the patient. His character, personality, and authenticity have to be proven because that is what the group demands. We believe Cortesão and his followers sensed the potential a good enough groupanalyst could have by intervening more sensibly than a passive one who would trust the group to fulfil its task, that is, to have the holding and handling functions for the primitive anxieties that could emerge. That is why Cortesão conceptualized the pattern which will be thoroughly explored in another chapter. We approach this issue to explain how our psychoanalytic point of view,—with the importance given to regression, transference, and countertransference and working through,—relies on a groupanalyst with a sense of his importance in the group's outcome.

The pattern's function, particularly as regards the attitudes the groupanalyst has to convey in the matrix, relates specifically with the analyst's psychoanalytic function of the personality. In order to provide the access to a groupanalytic function of the personality for his or her analysands, the groupanalyst will have an overall interpretative activity through clarifications, analogies, metaphors, confrontations, reformulations, and transference interpretations about the contents being communicated.

The pattern's objective is linked to the groupanalytical goals which are to promote intellectual and emotional insight and significant change in each patient's self in terms of "structure, differentiation and operation, with relative autonomy and a coherent and natural dependence" (Cortesão, 1989, p. 123, translated from the Portuguese). In its aims, groupanalysis is compatible with psychoanalysis, although the outputs of both analytical processes may not achieve the same objectives.

The final goal of a groupanalysis matches the patient's internalization of the pattern which will provide the internalization of an analytic attitude (Neto & Babo, 2000). According to Neto, it is a process that "operate[s] intra-psychic modifications that have relational consequences" (Neto & Centeno, 2005).

Process

We emphasize that Cortesão insisted on the need to conceptualize groupanalysis as a process to clarify in what way the theoretical and technical dimensions are structured, organized, and perform their role. As Guilherme Ferreira (2015b, p. 469) states,

> his point of view was based on a purely therapeutic process [...] (and) perceived the groupanalytic process as included in the psychoanalytic theory as a whole, and thus, integrating the technical and clinical management of the metapsychological formulation and the minutiae of object relations: in a specific group situation, which is different, but not inconsistent with the dual situation of psychoanalysis.

In this sense, Cortesão agreed with authors who think the setting is not part of what might define psychoanalysis as much as the technical procedures the analyst must attempt to attain psychoanalytic cure (Etchegoyen, 2002). Therefore, the process is the path through which the dimensions of groupanalysis engage to fulfil its goals. We believe Cortesão created new concepts in groupanalysis or adapted pre-existent psychoanalytic ones in order to clearly establish what prerequisites groupanalysis must have.

Similar to free association in psychoanalysis, the intense emotional interchange that develops within the group allows the groupanalytic process to occur: the transferential processes are revealed through regression, fixation points, and repetition-compulsion phenomena. In the group, the regressive phenomena always have a brand of individuality in spite of the existence of real others.

The therapeutic action targets the individual and not the group. A therapeutic group never offers itself as a patient formulating a request for help; the group in itself does not constitute a mental apparatus and, finally, insight arises differently and punctually for each member of the group. This kind of approach of the individual in the group is very different from a psychotherapeutic/psychoanalytic process of the group. It is the individual, better said, the person, that is the goal of the therapeutic action although what is communicated is understood within the broad dynamic communication network that constitutes the group matrix (Dinis, 2002).

Aside from the topographic and dynamic dimensions, looking at the relational aspect of group phenomena is of most importance: what is occurring within the matrix is producing its effects on the individual's intrasubjectivity.

The way the individual is the core of the analytic process in groupanalysis also becomes obvious when looking at the way transference and interpretation are managed from a psychoanalytic point of view: the levels of interpretation identified by Cortesão start from a here-and-now perspective, achieving a genetic-evolutionary and meaning perspective that will allow authentic and durable change in the individual. Transference and interpretation are fundamental criteria to describe the analytic/groupanalytic process.

Nevertheless, Cortesão highlighted that the "technical dimensions in groupanalysis although related to the theoretical constructions and clinical significance relevant in psychoanalytic theory and technique also depend on specific aspects of a groupanalytic technical theory" (Cortesão, 1989, p. 37, translated from the Portuguese). We think that in order to try to integrate both perspectives, he elaborated on the analyst's role, created the concept of pattern and approached the way working-through is possible in a group setting.

Group transference neurosis, interpretation, and working-through

Transference is necessary for the analytic process to occur and is the natural outcome of the contract and the rules of the setting and of the very initial request of the patient which implies right from the start an infantile emotional attitude in the face of a caregiver (Dinis, 1994). It is this specific and original relation that will lead to the re-enactment of the relational infantile movements, to the enlightenment of the original objects' significance and to the revelation of the defence mechanisms gathered by the individual to deal with a more or less unfavourable environment: that is, it will lead to the transference neurosis and its interpretation.

While in our view transference neurosis would be better termed transference structure as suggested by Ferreira (2015b), we will apply the original Freudian terminology in order to avoid conceptual confusion. Transference neurosis is established by each member individually in the group matrix within the here-and-now situation and becomes identifiable by the appearance of repetitive and inadequate behaviour in view of whatever is happening between the participants. The internal objectal structure of each participant becomes evident and may be perceived according to one's primitive objectal relations and the repetition of unsolved conflicts from the past in the here-and-now of the sessions; the traumatic events and relational patterns are experienced with the same emotional intensity as they originally were.

Although these phenomena take place in a group setting they should not be confused with group as a whole transference. As Dinis (1994, p. 11, translated from the Portuguese) synthesizes:

> I intend to mean the complexity of the transferential movements, positions and attitudes of each group member as an individual process, unique in its singularity, and unrepeatable by another patient, within the specificity of its nuances and of its path, notwithstanding the common denominator regression in a group context. The expressions group neurotic transference or transference neurosis in groupanalysis are justified as a reference to its emerging and evolving context.

Obviously, no analysand's transferential neurosis is independent of its context. In this sense, the group is the means, and the analysis of each member is the goal.

Ferreira (2005) adds that according to Cortesão, transferential evolvement always implies a connection with the groupanalyst producing a triangular transferential structure within the matrix and variable cathexes that match the therapeutic working-through of the Oedipus complex or of the dyadic situation. Similarly to psychoanalysis, the group transference neurosis/transference structure develops with the analyst's participation through transference-countertransference as a dynamic and dialectical unity.

The pattern conveyed by the groupanalyst reinforces individuality. Interpretation is the main tool and is mostly addressed to the individual patient and not to the group. If that is not so, the group will tend to operate on a psychotherapeutic level and not on an analytic one (Dinis, 1994). Even when transference interpretations are addressed to the group, their meaning is particularized to each member according to his or her transference neurosis (Dinis, 2001, 2005).

Cortesão (1971) defended an interpretation theory with different levels of interpretation, which is the object of Chapter 6. We highlight that for him, commutative interpretation—inspired by Strachey's mutative interpretation—is the settlement of an interpretation of the transference with the particularity of promoting the transition to a more complex communication level, thereby deepening its meaning and also promoting the mutative effects in Strachey's sense. This kind of interpretation is related to the process of working-through. Working-through aims to change the initial intellectual or cognitive insight into an emotional insight and progress from there to the analytic insight, which is capable of promoting durable and significant change (Abreu-Afonso et al., 2015).

Cortesão writes about the concept of working-through in its diverse meanings, emphasizing that the use of the concept is still unclear, although most authors seem to agree in considering it a part of the psychoanalytic process: an important technical instrument as well as a theoretical construct (Cortesão, 1989). For him, working-through is a clinical and descriptive concept that requires skills from the analyst in handling transferential movements, interpretation, and reconstruction. It is invested in constancy and time features, and presents itself with a silent evolution.

To Cortesão (1989), analytic labour and working-through are two different concepts. Analytic labour is related to insight. It focuses on the resistances that prevent insight and promotes the passageway of unconscious material to consciousness. The process of working-through would result from the insight of different insights (Cortesão, 1989). It is a process with which the analysis integrates interpretations overcoming resistances, acceptance of repressed material, and release of repetitive mechanisms.

In groupanalysis, working-through operates through the pattern's action with the collaboration of the group matrix (Ferreira, 2004). From the interaction of these three entities arises the possible solution of the group's transference neurosis/structure of each one of the patients in the group.

In analytic group psychotherapy, symptoms and ego-dystonic traits may be changed. This relies mostly on the phenomenon Foulkes describes as ego training in action.

For the Portuguese school of groupanalysis, what mostly distinguishes analytic group psychotherapy and groupanalysis is that in the latter, the group transference neurosis/structure can be analyzed and worked through, while in the former, the group transference neurosis/structure is recognizable but will not be analyzed.

In short, what seems to clearly separate the two processes "is (that) the transforming capacity in groupanalysis occurs essentially due to the analysis of the transference and resistances of each member of the group. Whereas, in analytic group psychotherapy, the psychotherapeutic process is mainly focused on the mirror phenomena, on the interaction and relation between the group members, and the interaction and relation of each of them with the objects in their actual lives" (Neto & Centeno, 2005). This has been discussed in more detail in Chapter 2.

Another concept that relates to Cortesão's (1991) perspective on working-through is the concept of aesthetic equilibrium, obviously inspired by psychoanalytic theory. It is the real aim of groupanalysis and it requires a previous dynamic process of internalizations of new object representations and an ability to think with new representations. This would result from a work of elaboration of the negative: the connections with primitive objects, ancient needs, thoughts where grandiose images of the self are predominant, must be abandoned so that a mourning process becomes viable; this triggers the transition from a narcissistic world obeying the primary process towards an objectal real world ruled by the wish for laws with the necessary acceptance of human limitation (Filipe, 2000a).

In these conditions, a change and maturation of psychic structure is achieved as well as behavioural modification and the establishment of an aesthetic equilibrium (Cortesão, 1991), which translates into a state where object representations are less persecutory, less split, less distorted, and more identifiable with a relative autonomy (object representations that the early relations never allowed to develop). At the end of the process, the groupanalytic function of personality of the groupanalyst conveyed by the pattern will be introjected by the patients allowing them to access a self-analytic attitude which will endure after leaving groupanalysis.

Further on, we will refer to Rita Leal's concept of the personal group matrix (Leal, 1968) and her perspective regarding the objective of groupanalysis. She defined this concept as the experience accumulated during the human life cycle, from childhood to old age, located inside a complex network of relationships. She also called it 'internal interpersonal network' and 'individual relationship matrix' (Leal, 1968) as well as internal relational matrix (Dinis, 1994). In Portugal, we use mostly this last nomination, although according to Guilherme Ferreira, Foulkes preferred 'personal group matrix' (Ferreira, 2015b). Nevertheless it seems important to state here that, in our opinion, aesthetic equilibrium as Cortesão conceptualized only happens because of the transformation of one's personal group matrix (or internal relational matrix) through the action of the dynamic matrix and the pattern.

Other concepts in groupanalysis

Personal group matrix and metadramatic communication

Rita Leal (1968) introduced the concept of the personal group matrix (intimately connected with object relations theory and with Pichon-Rivière's concept of the matrix which postulates the internalization of relational objects). Personal group matrix is an internal individual structure originated through mirroring in the dyadic mother-infant interaction and influenced afterwards by the others in the family and after that by other groups. Rita Leal (1968, 1981, 1994b) assumes that this structure will determine the behaviour and communication features of each individual and can change through re-experiencing early pre-verbal emotional situations in the groupanalytic matrix. This would represent a precondition to the individual's evolution.

Regarding Rita Leal's perspective, it is possible to approach primitive relational features of patients through the transferential phenomena they project in the groupanalytic matrix and through the analyst's answers emerging as a proto-conversational dialogue as happens in early childhood. This is what may lead the arrested development to resume. Her conceptualization shows the importance of drawing knowledge from different disciplines and the crucial contribution of developmental psychology.

Language emerges from a context of trading responses in a nondenotative register between a baby and his caregiver, in a dialogue going back and forth, mediated by voice and gaze, in a mutually satisfactory mirroring. This situation will be re-enacted in the groupanalytic setting and this way the basic paradigm of groupanalysis embraces the importance of seeing and being seen (Neto, 2012) to attain differentiation: the establishment of empathy which is firstly suggested by the visual perception of the physical manifestation of emotions with a consequent enhancement of biological communication skills. Language arises from prelinguistic forms based on response search reactions in which the biological rhythms stand as major in early psychological development.

Azevedo e Silva (1971, 1994) alludes to the effectiveness of the groupanalyst's communication and suggests what he calls metadramatic communication. The groupanalyst intentionally resorts to a kind of communication identical to the primary process of the mental apparatus thus becoming accessible to much regressed patients.

One important aspect that we have been discussing over the years amongst Portuguese groupanalysts is how a deep transformation or 'cure' can be achieved through groupanalysis. Rita Leal and Cortesão seem to have different points of view.

In Rita Leal's perspective, cure in groupanalysis does not need the analysis of group transference neurosis/structure. Therefore, we could consider that she gives a more psychoanalytic and developmental perspective to Foulkes' perspectives, building bridges between Cortesão's deeply psychoanalytic view and Foulkes more social one.

Her research method, centred in developmental psychology, diverges from Cortesão's, which is centred in psychoanalytic research. In this sense, Ferreira highlights that Rita Leal's point of view could be understood as an epistemological criticism of Cortesão's thinking.

Nowadays, the SPG tends to integrate both perspectives. Regarding the personal group matrix conceptualization, Ferreira (2004, 2005) suggests that it is through the integration of this construct in a triangle with the concepts of pattern and matrix that we are able to achieve a groupanalytic metatheory.

We believe that the transference-countertransference dynamic is what introduces each one's personal internal matrix into the dynamic matrix and the processes of mirroring, resonance, and ego training in action are responsible for new introjections which will alter the original personal group matrix of each member. The dynamic interactions are mediated by a holding environment and the authenticity of the analyst.

Inner space of optional doubt

Since the 1970s, Portuguese groupanalysts have been influenced by Winnicott's (1958) concept of good enough mother and Bion's (1962, 1965) concept of maternal reverie, mainly because of their connection with the attitude a groupanalyst should be able to provide to the group. Azevedo e Silva (1971, 1994), suggested that groupanalysis could create a psychological space which he called inner space of optional doubt. People use defence mechanisms to hide mental suffering from themselves, and that becomes obvious in a groupanalytic setting. Azevedo e Silva highlights that in order for the patients to free themselves from the compulsory need to find immediate solutions for their anxieties through these defence mechanisms, the groupanalyst—through the use of metadramatic communication already mentioned above—must create the possibility of a space of freedom in which the analytical labour becomes fertile because of the vast optional field it enables.

It is our view that this idea is in line with Cortesão's conceptualization of pattern. The analyst's attitude will create this psychological space, favouring the multiplicity of perspectives in the group, and in each member's mind, allowing the enhancement of mental creativity and discovery. It is not the group by itself that will produce this development. The SPG has been stressing over the years the importance of regarding the role of the conductor in the process; i.e., the pattern. As Lorentzen (2010) so clearly stated revealing Pine's informal words, even Foulkes "could be quite active and assertive as a conductor".

The individual in/and the group: the empathic resonance box

Among Cortesão's followers, César Vieira Dinis has been the most diligent in shedding light on the concepts of group transference neurosis and countertransference, relating them to how groupanalysis might provide cures and how it can be compared to psychoanalysis in terms of the similarity of their goals. He approaches the way each individual must be taken care of in the group in his own individuality so that the transference neurosis may occur and be solved.

According to several Portuguese groupanalysts—mostly influenced by object relations theory—psychopathology has many roots in early childhood and in the way people interact with the environment particularly with their first caregivers. Depressive and narcissistic disorders, for example, are considered to emerge from empathic failures of the environment in the early developmental stages. In modern psychoanalysis (ORT, self psychology, intersubjectivism, and relational paradigms), treating these conditions implies returning to those (mostly nonverbal) infantile experiences, bringing the patient to enact them through transference and understand them after translating them in a verbal and symbolic manner, but also changing the affective way the caregiver (currently the analyst) responds to those childhood unsatisfied needs of recognition and validation. Nowadays, analyst's features such as neutrality are called into question and many have tried in recent works to integrate the analyst's authenticity with the classical Freudian positions (Greenberg, 1986; Neto, 2001).

When we look at groupanalysis the way it is taught and practised in Portugal we have to ask the question: how can this psychoanalytical conceptualization of the treatment process apply in a group where several patients have different and conflicting needs?

Selection, empathic symmetry, and the analyst's personhood
Reminding us of the importance of selection, César Dinis talks about the need of a desirable empathic equity from the groupanalyst. He questions the reach of the neutral attitude Bion (1967b) defends by suggesting that the analyst should have "memory" and "desire" when facing "transferential tempests" (Dinis, 2004). The groupanalyst should contain them and return with a significance hypothesis. He defends that regarding the analyst' protagonism "it is mixed with his task as a conveyor and guardian of the Pattern and with his responsibility as a therapist/caregiver. To cast it out, differing it to the group would be [...] a technical flaw and deontological laxness" (Dinis, 2004, p. 15, translated from the Portuguese).

The analyst's narcissism and responsibility
As Dinis states, it is necessary that "the groupanalyst manages to make the honest resignation of his own narcissistic needs and prejudices compatible with the thorough conscious of his analytic power. It is expected that, like from parents to children, he will know how to use that immense power to his analysands' benefit" (Dinis, 2005, p. 15, translated from the Portuguese).

The huge responsibility of the groupanalyst starts even before a patient enters a group. It is never too much to reinforce the importance of patient's selection and the tremendous consequences of a sloppy examination of the groupanalyst's countertransference, not just for a single patient but also for the whole group. As Dinis states (2004, 2005), groupanalysts must listen either to their own countertransference, or the group's and patient's tolerance of frustration. It will always be the measure of empathy that dictates the fate of the needs and vulnerabilities that emerge in a group (Dinis, 2004, 2005).

Empathic resonance box

As empathy is considered the crucial ability of a good enough groupanalyst, how may the rest of the group take part in the meeting that should take place between the analyst and each individual, if we bear in mind Stern's moments of meeting (Stern, 2004a; Stern et al., 1998)? Dinis maintains that the group who has integrated the pattern will use interpretations to individual members as the nurturing of rational insight and commitment to the process for all the others. Nevertheless, only an interpretation directed towards a specific analysand with the right timing will produce the desired change (Dinis, 1994). That is when the group might behave as an empathic resonance box, reverberating what is interpreted, becoming an agent of change as it accepts and participates in the creation of new meanings. This articulates the groupanalyst's attention to the individual level where change operates, the deepening of the matrix, the co-construction that the group represents of a truly relational/intersubjective space (similar to Baranger's analytic field conceptualization; Baranger et al., 1980). In summary, we believe the consequence for the other members of a group of a meeting moment is amplified by the idea translated in the concept of the empathic resonance box.

Dinis states that groupanalysis operates as follows: the group is the means, each member's analysis is the goal; likewise, the nuclear family and all the interpersonal and transpersonal sets to which the individual belong throughout his life are the environment, while structuring identity and attaining autonomy is the desired conquest (Dinis, 1994). While defending a psychoanalytical way of treating the individual in the group, César Dinis and other followers of Cortesão fostered groupanalytic concepts that nowadays we can easily relate to the intersubjective/relational paradigm as well as to the perspectives of the Boston Study Group.

Specificities in groupanalysis

To see and to be seen

In the groupanalytic setting, eye contact allows that phenomena that are specific in groups, such as mirroring and resonance, enhance empathic responses. The groupanalyst also affords a deeper perception and understanding of aggressiveness and of the narcissistic disturbances usually connected to it. Aggressiveness becomes clearer in this setting. Therefore in the groupanalytic matrix, two pathways with opposite potential coexist: the constructive and the destructive. These paths must be integrated in order to achieve a therapeutic evolution and positive transformation.

By seeing the patient, the groupanalyst observes unconscious phenomena translated in facial expressions, gestures, body movement, etc., that might witness the affective charge of prelinguistic experiences from early stages in the development of the mental apparatus. This way it becomes possible to overcome the symbolic barrier, establishing an intensely empathic communication in a sustaining environment (holding), without which analytic labour would be compromised or become hostage to non-transforming intellectualizations and rationalizations. To see and be seen (Neto, 2012) in the groupanalytic setting favours therapeutic handling in the basic fault area (Balint, 1968) where, for the patient, symbolic communication may be inaccessible. Mutual observation allows the validation of nonverbal communicational exchange that operates at an unconscious level, triggering introjections and internalizations at a primitive level, providing reparation.

From our point of view, this hypothesis sustains the therapeutic/analytic approach of the underlying phenomena of communicational processes at a preverbal level (Ferro, 2012); it points out the need to investigate the conditions for the introjective processes to occur and to discover techniques that promote the transformation of body and action experiences into mentalization.

What we have been writing is easy to relate to the meeting moments conceptualization (Stern et al., 1998). It is about choosing not to reduce transference to the discourse and not to remember childhood events and elaborate those repressed memories; instead we must pay attention to the possibility of investigating and registering nonverbal and unconscious communication features. We assume that this point of view also bridges with relational psychoanalysis.

Treating difficult patients—basic fault, narcissism, and aggressiveness

Cortesão (1989) and some of his followers, such as Ferro (1997), Neto (2010b, 2014) and Neto and Dinis (1994) approached the possibility of treating psychotic, borderline, narcissistic pathologies, and the implicit narcissistic aspects in personality and character development which mould psychopathology, as well as working through aggressiveness. They highlighted the contributions of Balint (1968), Kohut (1984), and Kernberg (1976), among others, applying their ideas to groupanalysis.

Groupanalytic labour with the pathologies mentioned above develops on two levels: the oedipal level and the pre-oedipal level that Balint conceptualized as the basic fault area. For Cortesão, Balint's conceptualizations—the basic fault and new beginning—are manifest in a groupanalytic setting. One of the features of the function of the groupanalytic setting is to facilitate the emergence of regressive phenomena that always have a brand of individuality, in spite of the whole groupanalytic process (Cortesão, 1989).

Self psychology introduces an additional perspective on understanding and dealing with patients with narcissistic pathology in groupanalysis. When someone has experienced empathic failure in early life, their basic narcissistic self-structures are activated in the group and the individual repeats in the here-and-now the trauma he or she suffered in childhood due to the failure of non-responsive self-objects. Annihilation and fragmentation anxieties emerge as well as loss of self-cohesion experience and aggressive verbal manifestations. The repairing potential of these flaws exist in the groupanalytic setting; it may be used by the groupanalyst when he or she provides a sustaining/holding environment and allows the patient to use him/her as self-object. Another member of the group, or even the group as a whole, is allowed and able to perform that role. Kohut's empathy conceptualization is important: the groupanalyst's attitude resembles the mother/baby relationship described in Winnicott's good enough mother conceptualization or Bion's reverie and alpha function constructs.

In our view, in deficit pathologies and in the absence of a patient's insight, the groupanalyst's initial objective may be to stimulate the patient with interventions that draw on structuring visual features and words being considered as sonorous bodies in their material and affective outlook, the value of which comes from their tone, rhythm and manner of articulation (Anzieu, 1976). Interpretative activity may not be used on drive and defence behaviour when in the presence of fragmentation anxieties that threaten the self's cohesion, usually accompanied by aggressive manifestations. In these situations interpretation should aim to understand the threat of self-disorganization and try to clarify the genetic-evolutionary comprehension of the phenomena presented in the group (the enactment of mirroring and idealizing transferences and the aggressive verbal attitudes). This way self-disintegration may be avoided. In this context, defence and resistance are understood more as a way to protect the self of the eventual failure of self-objects that would expose the individual to a re-traumatization than as an attempt to repress unacceptable desires. It is not the conflict resolution that is at stake. We stand before a pathology of the deficit (Bleichmar, 1997, 2004).

In approaching the treatment of "difficult patients", Kohut's empathy concept has a special relevance: it suggests a similar attitude to the mother-baby relation of Winnicott's conceptualization of 'good enough mother' and to Bion's alpha function and reverie. Besides understanding the group's interaction within a Kohutian perspective, Cortesão emphasized the importance of addressing aggressiveness (Cortesão, 1989) using other contributions such as ego psychology and the theories of Kernberg. Kernberg (1979) insisted on the importance of envy, attacks on the object and on the intrapsychic and interpersonal conflicts; he insisted on handling hostile transference and grandiose expectations through the systematic interpretation of these phenomena.

We consider that interpretative activity must be flexible, resorting to both Kernberg's and Kohut's perspectives, depending on different narcissistic pathologies.

Nevertheless, we highlight that interpreting aggressiveness in the group is fundamental for the group's survival (Neto, 1993). Failing to elaborate aggressiveness in the group reflects on the construction of (latent and manifest) destructive phenomena that Nitsun (1996) calls the anti-group.

We believe that what is intended is the simultaneous elaboration of both aggressiveness and positive attachment phenomena that lead to a balance between relational movements that will generate creativity, and aggressive phenomena handled in a psychoanalytic perspective in a process of realization through negative that will allow more adequate experiences.

Dreams

As Freud inferred in the beginning of the 20th century, studying dreams gives access to unconscious processes. Freud concentrated on discovering the latent meaning and hidden impulses or wishes underlying the dream (Neto, 2006). Modern psychoanalytic perspectives seek to understand dreams through manifest imagery and the metaphorical meanings contained within it, which may reflect impulses and wishes, as Freud observed, but also a spectrum of emotions, past experience, recent events, defensive operations, perceptions of self and others, conflicts, problems, and attempts at their resolution (Neto, 2006). Therefore, groupanalysis—as is the case with psychoanalysis, uses dreams as important clinical tools.

Any dream may be observed from multiple perspectives: life context, intra-psychic conflict, present and past relational conflicts, and therapeutic relation (Neto, 2006). All these aspects concur with the emergence of a dream. Some functions of dreaming are well studied, and psychoanalysis has been successfully confirmed by neuropsychoanalysis (Nava, 2003). What interests us the most is the elaborative function of dreaming "in the sense that it searches for a solution for problems that occupy one's mind as Ferenczi has pointed out first-hand (1934) and then was emphasized by Meltzer (1984)" (Nava, 2003, p. 229, translated from the Portuguese).

This leads us to another aspect of dreaming that probably is what enhances the importance of dreams in a groupanalytic setting: the fact that in group analysis resonance as described by Foulkes is also extended to dreams. As Nava (2003) stresses, telling a dream in a group easily awakes, in association, the lost memory of another member's dream. Obviously, this happens with everything that is communicated within the group. Nevertheless, dreams seem to benefit from a special status—perhaps because of its transitional character in Winnicott's sense: conscious processes are set aside more easily when the subject is a dream. Neto (2010b) refers to her vast experience treating schizophrenic patients in a Day Care Hospital when she states that for these patients hearing other people's dreams in the group context enables them to expand their interest in their own mental life.

We do consider that taking dreams seriously in groupanalysis is very important. For Neto (2006), dreams may serve as the initial indicators of transference, resistance, impending crisis, acting-out, conflict resolution, and decision-making.

Besides their potential in helping the analyst's task, there is one specific and major aspect we would like to consider. If we approach dreams as interpersonal phenomena emerging from the group, then we can consider the dream as being related to working-through (Abreu-Afonso, 2004; Nava, 2003). Moreover, when we acknowledge that dreams may also be charged with implicit relational memories from a preverbal stage of development, they give analysts another pathway other than transference to deeply understand and relate to their patients.

Saying that a dream of someone that is in groupanalysis may be mostly determined by the group is not the same as saying that it is the group's dream. As Neto emphasizes, "Before everything else the dream belongs to the person who dreamt it! And it is that person who should start the process of unveiling its secrets and mysteries" (Neto, 2006, p. 7). The group and the groupanalyst must not arrive immediately with one or multiple interpretations that would probably lead to a rationalized discussion (Afonso, 2004). The therapist should nurture the free-floating discussion environment and tolerate the uncertainties the process implies. Attention should be not only on the content of the dream but also on the way it is communicated, its timing and tone, as well as all the rhythm of the groupanalytic process in that moment.

And what about the groupanalyst? There are two important aspects: one is that groupanalysts must be comfortable with their own dreams and with dreaming (Afonso, 2004); and the other is that "dreams may be also a way for the therapist to think about the patient. Therefore, one should pay attention to the therapist's dreams with the patients at their care" (Neto, 2006, p. 6).

Other contributions

The positive contribution that the neurosciences have made to psychoanalysis and to groupanalysis is undeniable. This contributes to deepening and validating its concepts and results in opening new perspectives on therapeutic action.

It is important to have an integrated perspective coming from different fields of knowledge such as cellular biology, brain imaging and behavioural neurology, and computing sciences which gave birth to cognitive neuroscience.

Neurosciences contribute to the understanding of the human brain as the organ through which the relationship between individuals becomes possible.

Genetic determinism is not enough to induce the brain's maturation; internal and external stimuli complement the genetic configuration through the establishment of neuronal circuits. This process begins in the first years of life and goes on throughout life. Neurosciences highlight the fundamental role of relationality and demonstrate that the brain needs the establishment of adequate relations to achieve full maturation.

Research on memory also represents an important contribution. Different memory systems with different locations in the brain were established and this could be related to two types of unconscious: repressed (the Freudian unconscious) and non-repressed (procedural memory). These discoveries influence the theory and practice of psychoanalysis, clearly supporting relational perspectives on psychological and psychopathological development. Transferential processes are, in our perspective, the only way some early implicit memories may be acknowledged thus worked through.

Several authors from psychoanalysis have been working on these conclusions: Christopher Bollas's (1987) "what is known but is not thought"; Daniel Stern's (Stern et al., 1998) "implicit relational knowledge"; James Fosshage's (1994, 2005) and the concept of implicit mental model. Neuronal plasticity confirms what psychoanalysis and groupanalysis have defended: that it is possible to transform early behavioural and relational patterns due to experiences held in a psychotherapeutic context that may become registered in a long-lasting way.

Neurosciences confirm the importance of the intersubjective early relationship (Nava, 2007). They validate Stern's conceptualizations that we will approach below (Stern, 1977, 1998).

The concept of internal object and events described as transference, resistance, hostile transference, empathy, or projective identification, can be deeply understood as they continue to be supported by neurosciences discoveries.

Psychoanalysis and the neurosciences have been studying the self and self-representation, yet their knowledge has not been fully integrated. Yet there are some areas that are confluent and ideas that overlap. Works on the ego, a common interest of both neuroscience and psychoanalysis, approach Freud's ego characteristics as functions assigned to the prefrontal lobes (Damásio, 1994).

We recall how research on neuron mirrors and its obvious connection with empathy confirm that to see the other allows a deeper communication (Nava, 2007). Considering empathy's neurophysiologic basis, we can suppose that the possibility of seeing and being seen (Neto, 2012), as is the case in the groupanalytic setting, enhances the transforming potential of the therapeutic relationship.

Training

Since its foundation, the Portuguese Society of Groupanalysis has highly valued improvement in, and discussion about, training, with the purpose of better serving groupanalysis and those who benefit from it. As in psychoanalysis, training has three pillars: the personal groupanalysis, the theoretical course, and supervision.

Applying for membership as a candidate and beginning the theoretical course demands that one has been in a group of groupanalysis for at least one year two times per week. The theoretical course lasts for four academic years, with once a week sessions, and with several trainers. These sessions may be exclusively theoretical or, later in the course, be divided between theory of technique and clinical seminars. The first two years are mostly about psychoanalytic theory and psychopathology and the last two years focus essentially on groupanalysis and its technical aspects. Supervision should be undertaken, individually or in group, with the same supervisor or several, for as long as the training lasts, i.e., until the candidates present a final work as a conductor of a group of groupanalysis running for two years. Personal groupanalysis goes on until the candidate feels ready to leave, a fact that should be supported by the groupanalyst and, ideally, by the group. Nevertheless, the minimum period of time usually accepted is from four to six years, although the majority of candidates in the Portuguese Society of Groupanalysis have had much longer personal groupanalysis (Carvalho, Galamba & Neto, 2008).

One aspect we would like to highlight in this chapter is the importance of personal groupanalysis because of its direct relation with the way groupanalysis is conceived by the Portuguese school of groupanalysis. The personal groupanalysis takes place in a mixed group, i.e., a group with patients who are 'candidates', and other 'regular' patients. There are several reasons for this requirement that will be discussed in a later chapter. Nevertheless we highlight that, as with psychoanalysis, groupanalysts in Portugal must "have a clear consciousness of their own emotions and needs, without which there cannot be a healthy narcissism neither the possibility to move forward towards autonomy" (Neto, 1993). Only after facing and working through one's painful feelings in a groupanalytic setting will the future groupanalyst be able to tolerate being a receptacle of similar emotional states delivered by his or her patients, avoiding the traumatic repetition of their own relations with their parental self-objects in the here-and-now of the transferential-countertransferential process (Neto, 1993).

Why must one's own analytic treatment take place in a group and not in a dyadic setting? We believe there are two main reasons. The first is that since we understand that groupanalysis is the most effective setting for observing and treating pathological character traits, not undergoing groupanalysis would surely be an impediment to one becoming a well prepared groupanalyst (Neto & Centeno, 2005; Neto, 2014; Zimerman, Osório et al., 1997). The second is the obvious fact that seeing the treatment of patients in a group being done in an authentic manner provides tools for the future groupanalyst that otherwise would only be read and intellectually assimilated. This perspective will be discussed in another chapter.

Supervision, as practised by senior members of the SPG, is considered both as a way of refining theoretical knowledge and as a process of opening new perspectives on the patients and oneself, mostly regarding the candidates' blind spots not yet touched by their own groupanalytic processes. It is not a purely academic training, like in a teaching model, where the supervisor would present as the one who knows; but neither is it an analysis for there is no place for interpretations and regression is not stimulated. It is probably something in between and we believe that this is better achieved when supervision in undertaken in a group setting.

We would like to add that we recognize we have an intense and highly demanding training programme in Portugal and not everyone who finishes the theoretical course manages to become a groupanalyst. Nevertheless, we believe that because we conceive groupanalysis as a psychotherapeutic process capable of deep transformation of the individual, the standards a candidate must achieve must remain high.

Concluding remarks

Throughout this chapter it has been our intention to summarize the main features of groupanalysis as it is understood and practised by the members of the Portuguese Groupanalytic Society. We have emphasized that psychoanalysis is at the core of its conceptualization. Its inherent specificities are the basis of its own identity, in spite of Foulkes' conceptualization of the group situation as integrated.

Over the years, groupanalysts have paid attention to updated knowledge in different related fields such as the developmental and behavioural sciences, social psychology, ecology, communication, linguistics and, more recently, the neurosciences, not putting aside the links to art, history and philosophy.

This scientific interchange is based on the recognition of a thought characterized by hyper complexity (Morin, 2008), highlighting openness to dialogue as a way of contributing to groupanalysis attaining epistemological citizenship.

It has also been our intention to introduce the discussion of core themes, such as:

- The relevance of integrating psychoanalytic concepts such as metapsychology, object relations theory, ego and self psychology, and the intersubjective and relational paradigms.
- The importance of the pattern in relation with the groupanalyst's authority and responsibility in different group-analytic frameworks.
- Transference neurosis and its resolution also happens in the multiple relational context of the group being approached individually in the group.

- Accepting that the target of therapeutic action in groupanalysis is each member of a group separately and not the group as a whole. Therefore, groupanalysis is a form of treatment of the individual in the group and through the group.
- The imperative that trainees have their own experience as patients in a group with other patients, whose aim does not include training in groupanalysis.

Finally, we would also like to add that we are obviously still on the quest to improve our model. Communicating our points of view and bringing them to a broader forum seems to be a good way to become better groupanalysts.

Chapter 4

The concepts of groupanalytic matrix and personal group matrix

Paulo Motta Marques and João Carlos Melo

Theoretical framework: historic and evolutive perspectives

The concept of matrix emerges in groupanalysis as a concept that enables the comprehension of interpersonal, transpersonal, and intrapersonal functioning in a systemic and integrated manner. In this chapter, we broach the concepts of the group-analytic matrix and the personal group matrix, their definition and importance for groupanalysis, as well as other similar concepts, which will allow a further understanding of the evolution and the potentialities of this idea of matrix in the group context, both in a theoretical-conceptual framework, as well as in a clinical one.

Therefore, initially, the theoretical, historical, and evolutive background of the matrix concept will be presented, which was accomplished with the contribution of various authors over time. These authors concentrated primarily on this approach in respect of the concepts of group matrix, group-analytic matrix, and personal group matrix. Emphasis will be placed on the contribution of Portuguese authors and the comprehension of these concepts in the Portuguese school of groupanalysis.

Consequently, the clinical part will be presented giving two illustrative examples of the manner in which the group-analytic matrix functions as well as how it interacts with the personal group matrix. Thereafter, conclusions will be summarized.

The concept of groupanalytic matrix and the concept of personal group matrix are well organized concepts—the former developed by Eduardo Luís Cortesão and the latter, by Maria Rita Mendes Leal. Both concepts reflect, each one in its own specific manner, the importance of the concept of matrix in the group-analytic context. The definitions of personal group matrix and internal relational matrix seem to be equivalents with regard to the conceptualization of internal matrix preconized by Maria Rita Mendes Leal.

The concepts of the groupanalytic matrix and the personal group matrix are inherent to groupanalysis, where they define important aspects and may be understood in a related manner in the group-analytic process. They are concepts with a pronounced psychoanalytic dimension. Sara Ferro (2010) referring to the concepts and development of groupanalysis, highlights the importance of psychoanalytic theory, and points out that the psychoanalytic concepts are conjointly introduced with communication theory and Gestalt and may be considered to be of greater or lesser importance.

In order to contextualize the concepts of groupanalytic matrix and personal group matrix in broader terms one cannot forget that we all live embedded in groups from birth to adulthood. The individuals' diverse learning experiences are inherent to the different groups and their respective matrices, which influence their development. The family group emerges as the most important and fundamental matrix. Groups at school, groups of friends, and groups at work are also an integral and structuring part of psychological organization. When of a therapeutic nature, however, the analytic group emerges, where a matrix of interactions between its members is organized and developed, leading to the possibility of personal transformation.

Various authors have elaborated on the concept of the matrix, with similar perspectives but also with some differences, thus introducing new aspects to their conceptualizations.

The concept of matrix was initially introduced into psychology by various researchers and clinicians who were dedicated to the study of small groups, in the late 1940s and early 1950s, simultaneously with Kurt Lewin's notion of the dynamics involving the group as a whole (Torres, 2010).

Although centred on the individual mind seemingly implying something systemic, this idea of the matrix had, however, already been suggested to a certain extent by Freud in 1895, when he conceived of the ego as a network of neurons which undergo cathexis in relation to each other (Freud, 1950).

In addition, while elaborating on group psychology and referring to the fact that each individual is a component of many groups with various aspects of identification to those groups, Freud (1921) introduced his concept of the ideal of the self, according to various models. Perhaps here one might potentially discern the conceptualization of a certain internal matrix, although not specifically referred to as such by Freud.

In 1913, Trigant Burrow, stated that the preconscious subjective phase alludes to "a phase of development in which the psychic organism is at one with its surrounding medium" (Burrow, 2013a), thus organizing the conscience's primary matrix. Pertegato (2014) highlights the fact that it was Burrow who introduced the concept of matrix at the time; a concept which would later become so central in group analysis.

In 1926, Burrow (2013b) mentioned the existence of an ontogenetic matrix of development but simultaneously the existence of a phylogenetic matrix in which the individual develops from the social point of view.

From a different perspective, nonetheless with repercussions in group psychotherapy, a perception worthy of mention is that of Jacob Moreno who approaches the idea of the matrix in the context of his conception of child development. In 1944, Moreno and his wife, Florence Moreno, published a paper entitled "Spontaneity Theory of Child Development", in which they address the concept of the identity matrix, and which was later included in the book *Psychodrama—volume I*, published in 1944 (Moreno & Moreno, 1944).

For Moreno, the individual develops from a primary relational network which commences very early on, even before birth and includes biological, socio-cultural, and psychological aspects. He designated this matrix as the identity matrix, and it comprises the child's relational learning process. Whatever eventual repercussions the term identity matrix may have found in the Foulkesian concept of the group matrix, these are not explicit in the literature encountered. There might be a possible connection in Foulkes as early as 1948; however, when, for example, upon reflecting on the matters of the individual and the social, and the close interaction between both, he refers to the concept of the social network, and to Moreno's concept of the social atom, in an attempt to illustrate the place and the role of the individual in the group and in the social (Foulkes, 2005).

Bion (1961b, c) proposed the existence of a thought matrix that embraces the group as a whole and isn't limited to the individual, which apparently is not related to the mathematics of a sociometric matrix but places emphasis on the notion of emotional forces in the group as a whole. Bion's notion of the matrix later (1951/52) evolved into the concept of the proto-mental matrix (Bion, 1961d, 1961e) comprising the dynamic combination of three basic emotional states in the human species (dependency, the fight-flight response, and mating). Rickman (1950), who worked with Bion, also used the term matrix as a metaphor to describe a psychology of multiple individuals that could incorporate psychoanalytic group phenomena that go beyond the Freudian model of the dual neurotic relationship.

Ruesch and Bateson in 1951 placed emphasis on communication in the understanding of mental illnesses. They considered that mental illnesses were mainly expressed through disorders in the interactions, or in what they called social matrices, which were characterized as structure, process and content. Ruesch and Bateson (1951, 1987) believe that communication exists whenever there is a mutual influence between people, and this communication constitutes a kind of matrix in which all human activities are inscribed, in different contexts, meanings, and values, thus referring to the notions of social network and social field.

The concept of the group matrix was subsequently adapted by Foulkes and Anthony in 1957 for group analysis (Foulkes & Anthony, 2014), with a focus mainly on the features of the communication that emerge in the group under different forms. In this sense, Foulkes took this concept from the perspectives inherent in communication theory and defined it as a relational and communication network.

In 1957 in a collaborative work with Anthony, Foulkes (Foulkes & Anthony, 2014) characterized the matrix as a network of all the individual mental processes, the psychological environment in which all these processes meet, communicate, and interact. It was only later, in 1964, that he elaborated the concept of the group matrix in its more complete form (Foulkes, 2002).

Kaës, in 1999 (Kaës, 2003), in his approach to the understanding of groups as an entity, integrated Foulkes's concept of the group matrix, which Kaës termed structuralist models. In these models, the group is conceived as a collection, with the members that constitute it bound by a law of composition, which is responsible for the structure of the group. Thus, in addition to the possible change of the members of the group, the structure of the group, i.e., the aspects of the permanent organization of the group, will be maintained. Ribeiro (1994) also focused on the concept of the group matrix. According to Ribeiro, the matrix expresses an invisible, although active, reality and is considered to be a construct and a process simultaneously. As a construct, it is similar to other concepts, such as social unconscious, group culture, group atmosphere, and group mentality. As a process, it is close to the Gestalt concept of figure-ground perception. Ribeiro views the matrix as being in constant change; whenever new members integrate into the group, the figure-ground perception is transformed.

Ribeiro (2007), when reflecting on Lewin's field theory, contends that the two fundamental principles of this theory are based on behaviour being a function of the existing field at the moment that it unfolds, and the importance of the situation considered as a whole, from which the components are differentiated. For Ribeiro, these principles are in line with Foulkes's basic positions, by which the group must be considered as a whole, and where there is an alternation between figure and ground (group-patient) in a here-and-now dynamic.

Ribeiro makes an interesting analogy between the concept of each patient's life space (as defined by Lewin) and the matrix. The life space refers to all the facts that may determine each subject's behaviour at a given moment and in a given psychological environment. The life space is therefore dynamic, as is the matrix, since it is responsible for all the processes that occur in the group.

Pines (2009) undertook a study on the concept of the matrix in the analytic group, envisioning it in both historical and social terms. Pines refers to Foulkes conceiving of this concept in a social and personal context, which allowed for this originality, in consonance with European thought at the time regarding the importance of the group in the individual sphere and in the different social spheres. However, according to Pines, Foulkes wasn't actually referring to the influences that the socio-cultural context could have had in his training, but indeed to the specific authors and schools that had influenced him, such as Trigant Burrow, Eric Erikson, Goldstein, Schilder, Huxley and Norbert Elias.

The groupanalytic matrix

The concept of the groupanalytic matrix developed by Cortesão (Cortesão, 1989) derived from the concept of the group matrix defined by Foulkes (Foulkes, 1964a/2002), and both these concepts have been addressed by various authors over time.

Worthy of note, and regarding the importance Cortesão attributed to the matrix concept, is a paper published in the first number of the journal *Grupanálise* by the then Groupanalysis Section of the Portuguese Society of Neurology and Psychiatry (Cortesão, 1977), in which Cortesão recalls an afternoon spent with Foulkes at Golders Green, during which they talked about various aspects of the work with groups, and about the transmission of knowledge. At a certain point, Cortesão mentions an intervention of his to Foulkes: "I'm thinking—I told him—how the concept of the matrix is as necessary as it is relevant in our groupanalytic work, on such diverse scales" (Cortesão, 1977, translated from the Portuguese).

Furthermore, Cortesão (1977, translated from the Portuguese) continues, stating,

> in this transfer of knowledge the significant links that some men have established in this transmission may be detected. It is as if they were nodal points in a complex matrix in which the renewal of scientific knowledge envelopes them and agitates them continuously.

Cortesão (1967a) states that the term matrix derives from Latin and has various meanings, namely it means a mother, in the sense of procreation, a breeding animal, and the uterus, and in the wider sense of propagation, as something which gives origin to something. He considered Foulkes's definition of the matrix to be insufficient, hence elaborating the concept of the groupanalytic matrix, by comprehensively integrating other concepts into his concept, which as a whole consubstantiate central aspects of the theory and technique of the Portuguese school of groupanalysis.

In 1977, Cortesão broached the concept of the groupanalytic matrix as

> the specific network of intercommunication, inter-relationship and interaction, which, through the integration of the groupanalytic pattern, stimulates the evolution of the groupanalytic process. (Cortesão, 1977/2004, p. 119).

Furthermore, Cortesão (1977/2004) states that he believes that the nuclear essence of this model may, to a certain extent, be transposed to larger groups, even to the national level, in the context of psychological and sociological policies.

Cortesão (1989, p. 111) subsequently assigned a more complete definition to the concept of the groupanalytic matrix, which he described in the following manner:

> The groupanalytic matrix is the specific network of communication, relationship, and elaboration, which, through the integration of the groupanalytic pattern, stimulates the evolution of the groupanalytic process within the theoretical and technical dimensions that shape it.

This definition clearly specifies the importance of elaboration, consistent with the psychoanalytic nature of the concept of groupanalytic matrix, as well as the reference to the theoretical and technical dimensions of the groupanalytic process.

As mentioned above, this concept has its roots in the concept of the group matrix, and according to Cortesão (1989) it was thoroughly explored by Foulkes and Anthony under the scope of communication in the group.

In 1964, Foulkes (1964a/2002, p. 292) presented the following definition of the matrix:

> The Matrix is the hypothetical web of communication and relationship in a given group. It is the common shared ground which ultimately determines the meaning and significance of all events and upon which all communications and interpretations, verbal and non-verbal, rest.

Concerning the functioning of the group, Foulkes (1964a/2002) states that the group has four levels at which it functions, from the superficial to the most profound. These levels are: the actual or current level (community, society, and public opinion), the transference level (the group represents the family, parents, and siblings), the projective level (other members as parts of the self and parts of the body), and the primordial level (the collective unconscious). The first two levels correspond to the macrosphere, the third corresponds to the microsphere and the last level to what Foulkes termed the autocosmos. The group matrix would then be the result of the constant interaction between these levels of communication present in the group.

In his work, Foulkes was greatly influenced by Goldstein's work on the nervous system and the brain's neuronal network. Goldstein considered the individual neurons as nodal points in a complex network of connections where the impulses pass through. Hence, the emphasis Foulkes gave to the group matrix and the communication processes that pass through it.

Nevertheless, there are differences between Cortesão and Foulkes. For Cortesão, the matrix is a place of elaboration in the sense of perlaboration, as detailed by António Guilherme Ferreira (1992), whereas Foulkes basically considers the matrix to be a network of relationship and communication. Cortesão introduces two fundamental concepts which are the groupanalytic pattern and the groupanalytic process, and integrates them with the concept of groupanalytic matrix.

The concepts of the matrix, pattern, and groupanalytic process constitute a specificity of the groupanalytic theory and technique of the Portuguese school of groupanalysis. For Cortesão (1989) the theoretical dimensions (mainly metapsychology and the object-relationship theory) and the technical dimensions (matrix, pattern, levels of experience, and of interpretation) converge towards the analytic objective, which is the installation and resolution of the group transference neurosis. This perspective constitutes the essence of Portuguese groupanalysis and confers on it a markedly psychoanalytic nature.

This author continues his explanation by resorting to a curious analogy concerning the network, the matrix and the pattern (Cortesão, 1989). The network is seen as if it were communication channels; here Cortesão clearly establishes an association with Goldstein's concept of the neuronal network of the nervous system, in addition to the network of blood vessels. In this analogy, the matrix would be more closely associated with the blood content, and with blood circulation, in other words, associated with metabolic processes. The groupanalytic pattern would be the heart, which pumps the blood; however, this would all be functioning in an inter-dependent manner.

Cortesão's conceptualizations enabled the integration of various concepts originating in psychoanalytic theory, in addition to concepts of Gestalt theory, field theory, organismic theory, and general systems theory.

The concept of groupanalytic matrix prioritizes the elaboration aspects, with an emphasis placed on the theoretical and technical dimensions of the groupanalytic process, and places greater relevance on the importance of the groupanalytic pattern. Foulkes, in his concept of group matrix, mainly emphasizes the communication aspects in the here-and-now, and has given greater prominence to this dimension, not evincing the psychoanalytic characteristics of group analysis as much as Cortesão, and moreover that which is preconized by the Portuguese school.

The group matrix plays an important role in the choice of the members, or members, for the group. To a certain extent the group matrix already exists, in an anticipated and imagined manner in the mind of the groupanalyst even before constituting the group, based on the knowledge he or she has of each of the members which might form the group. It should also be mentioned that the matrix of an existing working group is important as an indicator for the selection of new members. It might make sense to place a new member in a determined group by articulating the characteristics of his or her personality with the characteristics of a particular group matrix, with the aim of achieving stronger analytic integration.

It is also worth pointing out that the occurrence of phenomena such as resonance, scapegoating, mirroring, projective identification, levels of communication, as well as the perspective of the group as a whole, among other things, becomes more comprehensible from the perspective of a matrix that is already constituted. This circumstance is due to the fact that the matrix—in the matrix-pattern relation—provides the emergence of interpersonal movements and mechanisms that are conceptualized in an analytic perspective.

From the perspective of the Portuguese school of groupanalysis, the objective of the groupanalytic process is the resolution of the group transference neurosis. Foulkes, on the other hand, placed greater emphasis on the ego training in action technique and not on the resolution of the group transference neurosis, which, in his later writings, he stated should not be encouraged given that it provokes greater dependency and regression, which is not intended. For Foulkes, the group analyst also has an important function; however, the group has priority. Foulkes did not adhere to the concept of groupanalytic pattern, and this is not accepted as such in the English School.

Foulkes (1971) developed the concepts of the web and matrix. He introduced the concept of the foundation matrix, as the result of experiences, internal experiences, as well as the aspects that are common to all human beings, including their biology. The foundation matrix catalyzes different levels of communication which, during the group's interaction, constitute what Foulkes denominated the dynamic matrix.

In a certain manner, Foulkes's conception of the matrix establishes a bridge with his definition of the mind, as if these two concepts could be associated by their characteristics. According to Lavie (2005), Foulkes believed that in the group a multi-personal matrix is created, and that the individual mind of the group's members when in interaction is also a multi-personal mind. Foulkes, in 1973 (Foulkes, 2004) stated that the mind is not an individual belonging, but can be defined as the interaction process itself between a number of individuals, who are intimately connected, thus forming the nodal points of the web.

This characteristic of the mind as a multi-personal phenomenon becomes associated with the transpersonal process, also referred to by Foulkes, and is situated in his conception of the group matrix. To this effect, the concept of the matrix in Foulkes is different to that referred to by Cortesão, since for Foulkes, the group mind and matrix have faint borders. Cortesão (1989) stated precisely that the group is a structure, a matrix and a space of communication but that it is not a psychic entity or a mental apparatus.

Personal group matrix

Regarding the dimension of an internal matrix, the concept of the personal group matrix conceived by Maria Rita Mendes Leal (1968, 1994c, 1997) should be highlighted. This author considers that during development, the subject continuously structures this internal matrix based on multiple relational experiences, starting with the primary relationship with the mother, and continuing with experiences in other groups. Each individual's personal group matrix is transformed through the dynamic of the group matrix, where there are emotional exchanges, regressive movements, and other phenomena that extend to proto-verbal levels as well as the repetition of early childhood situations.

In 1968, Rita Leal stated that groupanalysts view human life as occurring in a life-death cycle and that within this cycle, the subject's experiences are located in a complex network of relationships, which may be designated as an internal interpersonal network, or personal group matrix, or even a matrix of individual relationship (Leal, 1968/1994c). According to this author, the individual's psychological disorders should be located in the relationships that they establish in groups throughout their development, which then appear in the present, in a repetitious manner, in the form of a communication disorder in the group. Rita Leal continues in this vein by saying that "When we describe this process of communication within the matrix of an actual (concrete) group we speak of locating the disturbance of the individual in his 'personal group matrix'" (Leal, 1968, p. 101).

Rita Leal makes reference to the importance of the mirror phenomenon and its repercussions that take place in the analytic group. According to this (Leal, 1968, p. 104), the emotional resonance of a multiple mirroring experience in a group is a very significant phenomenon for groupanalytic evolution. She states:

> The multiple mechanism of complementary reactions which we observe in analytic groups and which we call 'mirror reaction', following Foulkes, can then be understood as a 'here and now' repetition of primary (childhood) experience and stage of evolution wherein the child finds himself in the mirror of the important 'others' and to that same extent differentiates himself in relation to the 'matrix' so constituted. (Leal, 1968, p. 104)

Leal (1994c, p. 104) continues:

> In this perspective of a regressive experience, the concept of 'primitive group' is established for each participant: as an internal interpersonal network of relations, as a homeostatic system of mirror reactions, in which multiple feedback is organized as a stabilizing mechanism structured satisfactorily or not in childhood and repetitively re-lived and re-experienced in the 'here and now' of an analytical group process.

During this whole process, the revival of the relational phase of the mirror reactions, through regressive movements, could allow the adaptive ego to integrate emotions.

According to Rita Leal (1968/1994c), in the groupanalytic process the occurrence of regression is found, and experienced, by each element of the group, however this should be located in the here-and-now, in the intra- and inter-personal matrix or group network. This regression phenomenon is not merely interpreted in the various levels of libidinal fixation, but is described as multiple resonances, located in the group network.

Regarding Rita Leal's concept of personal group matrix, Cortesão (1989) did not personally conceive it as a structure, but more as a circumstance of the personality and which he designated as family and socio-cultural matrix. However, Guilherme Ferreira (2005), for example, does not share this perspective, and considers that this internal matrix corresponds in a way to the conceptions of structure, as developed by Hartmann, or in accordance with Rapaport's psychosocial perspective. Last but certainly not least, it is important to emphasize that this concept of the personal group matrix emerges as a reference in the clinical thought and practice of most Portuguese groupanalysts. Amongst other things, this probably has to do with the importance that these groupanalysts have given to the concepts of the partial and total objects which become objects of the self, in reference to authors such as Kohut and Fairbairn.

Pichon-Rivière's (1988, 2000b) work is also of note in that he makes mention of the concept of the internal group that configures the perspective and importance of bonds in psychoanalysis and of the relation between the intrapsychic and the interpersonal. According to Souza (2011) this concept, in turn, appears to have its roots in the concept of the internal group, around which George Mead's pioneering work in social psychology developed reflexion on the process of social interaction.

Kaës (2003) also broaches the subject of psychic groupality and that of internal groups, conceiving the model of the psyche of the individual subject as a group model, as well as referring to the importance of the internal groups as organizers of group bonds.

According to Kaës, the notion of psychic groupality refers to the characteristics of association and grouping of members by the psyche, but also to the de-grouping, as such, a fundamental activity in psychological and intrapsychic functioning. In this sense, the internal groups are a specificity of this psychological structure and activity.

This perspective redirects to the conception of the group as a whole, a place of formation and transformation of psychic reality, a space for the construction of new realities, produced by an open psychic apparatus of all of its members.

The psychological apparatus thus appears to have a matrix organization where the different psychological elements are interrelated in a dynamic operating system.

Other contributions by Portuguese authors

Various Portuguese authors have referred to the importance of the concept of groupanalytic matrix, and have articulated it within the perspective of internal matrix, as well as made reference to the relation of these concepts with the different phenomena that occur in the group (Marques, 2015).

César Dinis (2000b) highlights the emotional transactions that occur in the matrix, and states that these contemplate what is understood as the bond in the intersubjective dimension.

He holds an original position on this matter, which makes it possible to clarify how the personal group matrix updates itself and becomes functional.

According to César Dinis (2016, personal communication) the group's actual pragmatic network is constituted in the here and now and is predominantly constructed by conscious alliances/affinities or rivalries and discord between one member in the group and another. Another network with much more weight and determinative relevance superimposes itself on the actual pragmatic network: a complex network resulting from the re-actualization of the internal relational matrices of each of the group members which have a purely transferential, hence unconscious, nature.

It is from this complex (pragmatic network and transferential network, with naturally a greater influence of the latter) that the group matrix results. In his opinion, the group matrix is predominantly a transferential construction (the superimposition of each member's transferences) although it also contains, with alternative impact, the interventions by conscious choice of the group members.

By establishing this relation (between the internal relational matrix and the current pragmatic network)—conceptual and practical at the same time—César Dinis confers depth and dynamism to the concept of groupanalytic matrix, inasmuch as it goes beyond the more static territory where the concepts are merely defined, and he bestows on them a functional character.

Rita Leal (1997) with a perspective of groupanalysis based more on the influences of ethology and the communication theories, preconized that the groupanalytic matrix is an open structure, complex, and "dissipative" which can be characterized by regulation automatisms and by circular causality, and not by determinism.

For this author (Leal, 1975), what is considered important in the groupanalytic process are the communication aspects, at their various levels, which emerge from a transpersonal matrix, a term also used by Foulkes, and it is in the group matrix that the different group phenomena and their interpretation occur.

Cruz Filipe (2000b) stated that in a group-analytic situation the basic psychological dynamic processes are the relationship, the configuration, and the communication. These processes should be perceived by the whole group, in other words, in the conception of the group as a basic matrix in which its members are in interaction and in interrelation. According to Filipe (2000b, p. 21), the characteristics of this relational network depend on each of the members of the group:

> The matrix is therefore dynamic, a network at all times, a transpersonal tangle in which the nodal points are the individuals suspended within. It is specifically the relationship that the therapist works on.

During the course of the group's life, the individual internal experience of each event derives from the matrix and affects the group as a whole. The configuration will be the manner in which the group expresses itself through its elements, as if it were a "living being".

In turn, Filipe (2000b) considers that the communication is a structure, an active process, and that each communication is a world. It integrates conscious and unconscious processes and is expressed in different manners: verbal, non-verbal, and through symptoms. He believes that the therapist should be an authority in translating the patient's communication, leading him to the verbal expression of the conflict which is hidden behind a given situation. Therefore, for Cruz Filipe (2000b), the communication also emerges as a crucial feature of the analytic group's function, and the groupanalyst should interpret the conscious and transferential aspects of the communication which emerge from the matrix.

Azevedo e Silva (1971) emphasizes the microculture that is created in the group. He actually prefers the concept of a group microculture over that of the matrix, given that he believes that the former expresses what is happening in a groupanalytic group in a more complete manner. He states that the culture of the populace/population is a complex construct, in which racial, magical-religious, and other factors intervene, and still integrate the individuals' unconscious projections that reflect the dynamic of the psychic system. In the group, during the course of the interactions between its members, a certain group culture emerges, which integrates rational and logical factors as well as unconscious and magical factors. These aspects represent a means of appropriating external reality as well as internal reality. For Azevedo e Silva each group has a specific microculture, besides the universal traits that integrate it. The groupanalyst should mainly intervene on these symbolical-mythological constructs by means of interpretive action, with the aim of progressively making conscious the unconscious. All of the interventions that occur in the group will become an integral part of that group's microculture. We believe that this is an important contribution when addressing the concept of the matrix.

Cortesão (1989) also referred to the importance of the culture in the group, and stated that the communication should be understood according to the aspects of the culture that emerge in the groupanalytic matrix. In this regard, he (Cortesão, 1989, p. 45, translated from the Portuguese) mentioned that "the roots of the culture germinate in the group-analytic matrix and take on *nuances* that have to be taken into account for the understanding of the communication...." Cortesão (1989, p. 97, translated from the Portuguese) continues:

> The groupanalytic research propitiates the clarification of certain group phenomena, as well as social phenomena, although these phenomena may be better elucidated in the meta-psychological and object-relations perspectives that occur in the groupanalytic matrix.

The importance of the object relations theory (Cortesão, 1989, p. 45, translated from the Portuguese)

> results, amongst other factors, from repetition, in the group transference neurosis, of primitive phantasies, which are internalized in the groupanalytic object relations.

Communication, in its entire spectrum, is constantly present in the groupanalytic dynamic. According to Dinis (1994), groupanalysts should pay close and constant attention to their verbal and non-verbal communication, so that they are not unconsciously manipulated by the analysands through the interactive part of projective identification (as conceptualized by Ogden, 1992). What is important is being more conscious of the possibility of being in countertransference than favouring the interactive part of the transference. This counter-transferential scrutiny may allow for the groupanalyst's adequate interpretation, in and about the transference, aimed at the objective which is the resolution of the transference neurosis.

Any interpretation to a member of the group is founded on the group matrix, and consequently echoes in the other members (Dinis, 2000b). Subsequently Dinis (2002, p. 12) refers to the group matrix and the groupanalyst as follows:

> Everything happens in the group matrix, this highly complex web of inter- and trans-subjectivities, where teeming meteors of regressive intra-subjectivities circulate, so often at risk in their collision course. It is mainly up to the groupanalyst to be the signalman, the organizer of this unstoppable traffic, transmitting with clarity, and discernment the signs which avoid serious accidents and allow the journey to continue.

In this aspect of communication, empathy, as an attempt to comprehend the other, has a fundamental role. Dinis (2005) alludes to its importance, and states that one cannot change that which one does not understand. In this manner and from his clinical experience, he determines that, at times, the group functions in a way that he usually calls the empathic resonance box, creating the opportunity for narcissistic reformulation, and consequently, personal development. This aspect is discussed elsewhere, primarily in Chapters 3, 6, and 7.

Aucíndio da Silva (2012) also refers to the importance of the groupanalytic matrix, emphasizing the way that projective identification, in its diverse dimensions, may be lived in the groupanalytic process, thus contributing to a better understanding of the matrix concept. According to Aucíndio da Silva, the group members' propensity to receive certain types of projection is lived by the members themselves in interaction in the group matrix. Each and every member in the group may have this function, besides also being projectors, thereby the group would become a kind of focal point, and all the members in the group would become each other's echo points, or points of resonance. In this sense, it is not by chance that one member in the group chooses another member to interact with and to project parts of himself in the other. This choice depends, to a large extent, on the receptiveness of the other member (e.g., scapegoat, spokesperson, etc.) for such interaction.

According to Isaura Neto (1999b), the matrix gradually integrates the pattern, and this is the result of identification with the groupanalyst's groupanalytic function.

Etelvina Brito (1992) also highlights the role of the groupanalytic pattern and states that the group appropriates the pattern and incorporates it, which in a certain way is equivalent to the internalization of the mother, with the establishment of object constancy. In this way, by integrating the groupanalytic pattern, the matrix transmits particularities to the groupanalytic process, given that the matrix is an instrument that is necessary for the organization of the transference neurosis and for therapeutic elaboration.

Thus, the concept of groupanalytic matrix appears to be of great relevance for all Portuguese groupanalysts, who emphasize its importance on various levels: from the communicational and relational perspective; in the close connection with the personal group matrix of each of the group's elements; in the organization and elaboration of the group's transference neurosis; in the specific aspects of the group's culture and microculture; in the diverse phenomena that occur there; and in the integration of the groupanalytic pattern.

The groupanalytic matrix appears as an open concept, with its own identity and a space where different phenomena take place. It is the matrix's dynamics that enables the Gestalt figure-ground process, by constituting a space where the visible and the invisible, the part and the whole, and unity and plurality, cohabit.

Clinical practice

All of these aspects have implications in clinical practice since they allow the comprehension of the groupanalytic process as the result of the interactions between the matrix systems; in other words, the internal matrix of each of the group members and the groupanalytic matrix are both in progressive transformation. This also results in the possibility of understanding the different roles that the group members play in the groupanalytic matrix and its relation to the group's transference neurosis.

Clinical vignette 1

The following practical example, based on a groupanalysis session, allows an illustration of the performance of the groupanalytic matrix and the internal relational matrix of each of the group members:

In a groupanalysis group that has been running for about a year with twice weekly sessions, and which is composed of six members, four females and two males (besides the groupanalyst), in a spirited manner, the members share amongst themselves ideas and experiences about the various possibilities of each one starting a physical activity and the inherent health advantages. They dialogue between themselves without addressing the groupanalyst, who does not intervene in this phase. The group matrix is constituted, and the different communications occur in a free-floating discussion. At one point, it becomes clear that Luis never seems to know as much as the others, and is always asking questions, almost as a child would, with little experience and knowledge (which was disproportionate with reality). Luis was unconsciously placing himself (in transferential terms) in the position of a younger brother who depended on the opinions and decisions of the "older brothers"; recreating in the groupanalytic matrix the internal experience he had actually had in his family history with his two older siblings. Luis wasn't even the youngest member in this analytic group, but he played this part in the group, which corresponded to one of the objects in his internal relational matrix. The progressive evolution of the members in the group and the groupanalytic matrix made it possible that this facet revealed by Luis, during this phase of his analysis, could be elaborated and transformed, in a progressive movement of individuation of the self.

Clinical vignette 2

Another example, taken from the groupanalytic practice, refers to what could be designated as "Ana's silence" in the group. In effect, in this group, also with a twice weekly frequency, Ana at a certain point in her analysis practically stops talking about herself and is limited to reporting facts that had occurred. Her communication was deprived of personal internal experience, besides the fact that she refrained from speaking about more intimate issues. However, what was verified was this occurred only when the male members weren't present (not considering the male groupanalyst, in whom Ana invested in a different way). The alteration of the figure-ground perception in the groupanalytic matrix brought about by the sporadic absences of the male elements, made Ana change the quality of her communication in the group. During analysis, it became clear that during that phase of the groupanalytic process, the male members of the group represented for Ana her difficulty in "becoming close" to the male figure, who was perceived as dangerous, referring this to facets of her genetic-evolutive and her internal relational matrix. When Ana became aware of this aspect it enabled her to progressively communicate more in the group, in the presence of all, and as such, transform facets of her personal group matrix. Thus, the dynamics of the intersubjective lead to the transformation of the intrasubjective.

Clinical vignette 3

One last example also serves to illustrate the way in which the personal group matrix of the elements in the group may be expressed in the groupanalytic matrix. This example refers to the role represented by a member in the group, who will be used as a projection by the other members of their aggressive impulses and various anxieties. This is a role with a masochistic nature.

In a groupanalytic group, with a duration of about two years and with a well-established matrix, Maria, who was part of the group for less time than the other members, clearly attempts to establish a preferential relationship with the groupanalyst, usually addressing him directly, whether through verbal or non-verbal communication. This contextual situation, as well as Maria's sadomasochistic disposition, made the other group members verbally aggressive towards her, at times in a very expressive manner, or made them ignore her. They would talk to each other, but not to her. For her part, Maria tended to disqualify some of the group members through her words or attitudes. Throughout the groupanalytic process, not only did the group members come to understand the aspects of envy and jealousy, which were inherent in this attitude towards Maria, but Maria herself also became aware of the fact that she derived some pleasure out of being attacked, and from how she provoked this behaviour in others, and how this had roots in her genetic-evolutive, namely in the position she held in her family, in which she had placed herself, wanting all the affection of her father-figure for herself and deprecating (and attacking, in her sadistic part) her siblings. Her internal matrix was organized in this manner and that's how it was represented in the groupanalytic matrix, by projecting her network of internal objects in the different elements in the group. When all the members in the group became aware of these aspects, it enabled a progressive change in the groupanalytic matrix, with transformations in the personal group matrix of both Maria, and the other elements.

Concluding remarks

The concepts of groupanalytic matrix and of personal group matrix contribute to the understanding of the groupanalytic process, which for the Portuguese school of groupanalysis, can be characterized as being a process with a significant analytic nature. In concert with the concept of the groupanalytic pattern, it is also worth noting the importance these concepts may have in the conception of a groupanalytic meta-theory (Ferreira, 2015a, 2015b, 2004).

The concepts of the groupanalytic matrix and of personal group matrix broached in this chapter emphasize the importance of the interactions and relationships on the level of the external and internal objects, which constitute, in an analytic framework, the primary material of groupanalysis.

Both the concept of groupanalytic matrix and of personal group matrix found their roots in previous formulations, not only in the psychoanalytic and group-analytic domains, but in other areas, such as group dynamics, social psychology, and communication theories.

In an interactive movement, both concepts may be understood in an integrated manner, in a continuum between two entities with dynamic and systemic characteristics which mutually transform in the groupanalytic process.

This results in the progressive evolution of the way the group functions as a whole, but even more importantly, results in the personal evolution of each of the elements in the group, which constitutes the objective of groupanalysis.

Chapter 5

The pattern

Isaura Manso Neto and César Vieira Dinis

Introduction

The Portuguese school of groupanalysis, founded by Eduardo Luís Cortesão, has been structured upon a strong psychoanalytic influence interacting with the small group dynamics conceptualized by Foulkes and followers.

This psychoanalytic influence includes:

- Psychoanalytic concepts per se from the metapsychology, the intrasubjective areas to the intersubjective relational perspective.
- Foulkesian concepts' reformulations.
- Psychoanalytic understanding of some Foulkesian group-analytic concepts.
- A personal groupanalysis in small mixed groups, without a previous defined ending, usually of long duration on that basis of two or three sessions a week. This is the most important part of the tripartite training.
- New concepts.

The pattern is precisely one of them. It highlights the importance of the groupanalyst in the groupanalytic process whose main aim is to treat and analyze each individual, each member of the group within the group matrix.

This way the SPGPAG (Portuguese Society of Groupanalysis and Analytic Group Psychotherapy) considers that psychoanalysis and groupanalysis have similar objectives. Cortesão introduced the concept of the pattern in 1967(a) in London at a workshop on research in group analysis. Groupanalysis was a recent discipline which deserved definition and clarification so that it could acquire scientific identity. The pattern was the way to conceptualize the definite importance of the groupanalyst interacting with the matrix as a seed or a catalyzing factor.

The concept—history, controversies, and debate

This concept—pattern—has been unfamiliar to most group analysts outside Portugal. We think it may have provoked a defensive reaction amongst Foulkes and his followers at the time it was presented by Cortesão in the London Workshop in 1967.

This may have been a consequence of the socio-political context at the time: the recent and devastating events that led to World War II: Adolf Hitler had been a leader who manipulated a large group. *Führer* is the German word for leader and the pattern was associated with the importance, thus power, of the group conductor.

As Foulkes remarked (Cortesão, 1967a, p. 34):

> The word "pattern" is misleading here. We would have to look for another designation. "Pattern" in the usual sense would refer to a repeated and typical psychodynamic constellation observable in the analytic group and many other groups. Besides this, pattern has a meaning which may stand midway between the two above mentioned namely: a privileged or established way of reaction nearer to that of a model.

Foulkes (1990b) was careful to underline in his later writings the importance of using the name conductor instead of leader. In those papers he also wrote that the group analyst is in a responsible position as leader (p. 289) in the sense that he or she lays down certain conditions, makes the decisions, selects the members of the group, and has the responsibilities. "… this leadership responsibility is inseparable from the analytical function of the conductor" (p. 290).

Nevertheless, in a 1968 paper he called the conductor a "group analyst" and not a conductor. In 1970, he stated (1975, p. 210):

> When I say 'the group', I mean in this case the group-analytic group—that is to say, a group of patients under specific conditions set by us, with therapeutic intention, and under the specific leadership of a group analyst.

Foulkes was ambivalent towards the influence of the conductor/therapist/group analyst in the group process. He was also ambivalent about whether group analysis was a setting where true analysis could occur. Therefore he was also ambivalent on how to refer to the group analyst, using several names such as conductor, therapist, group analyst. He had suggested the term conductor even though in his last papers he spoke of the "analytical function of the conductor" (1975, p. 290), making it very clear that one of the main tasks of the conductor/group analyst was to analyze transference as a resistance.

Of the conductor, in 1970, he wrote (Foulkes, 1990a, pp. 217–218):

> The conductor needs a thorough knowledge of psychoanalysis. Ideally he should be a fully trained and experienced psychoanalyst, provided he keeps an open mind and flexibility so as to approach the new task in an analytic group with the necessary freedom.

Nevertheless, in the immediately preceding paragraph, Foulkes wrote: "I am not so much concerned with the objective functions, knowledge, skills, which the conductor should have, as with saying something about his personal involvement, his own hygiene, as it were" (1990a, p. 217).

In addition to the above reasoning, the group-analytic community usually says that Foulkes strongly suggested the name "conductor" instead of group analyst. We think this perspective is somewhat incomplete and not sufficiently rigorous.

Foulkes had also a strong identity as a "convinced Freudian psychoanalyst" (Foulkes, 1990b); he belonged to the IPA (International Psychoanalytic Association) through the British Society of Psychoanalysis (BSPA) where he faced a difficult fight against group analysis. Psychoanalysis was very much influenced by the Freud's "Group Psychology and the Analysis of the Ego" (1921). We believe that it might be interesting to trace its steps: Freud acknowledged that human beings have always lived in groups and been under their influence. It seems that it was impossible for Freud to deny the importance of groups to the functioning and survival of human beings. He was trying to understand how the group could be so regressive, destroying human individuality and yet also be creative, and he questioned which psychology came first: that of the group or the individual. He tried to find a solution for that contradiction. Freud reflected on this issue based on scientists of his generation—Le Bon, McDougall, Trotter. He conceptualized the importance of the group, recognizing that there were several kinds of groups: short-lived and long-lived; homogeneous and heterogeneous; natural and artificial; primitive and highly organized; with and without leaders. All these variables should condition the group's psychology. Strong libidinal, emotional ties are the essence of the group mind, whose main mechanism is identification; idealization and suggestion are natural consequences of the psychology of groups. In the aforementioned work, Freud (1921) quoted Trotter's concept of "gregariousness" as innate in human beings, which was conceptualized as another expression of libidinal ties.

Finally what we would like to emphasize is that Freud was very curious and preoccupied with group life and psychology, recognizing that groups cannot be split off from humankind. Moreover they are part of a human's primitive needs, starting with the family. Freud could not give strong opinions on this issue; he merely made many observations or highlighted questions and hypotheses. Indeed, Freud could be thought of as a "weak" leader on this matter by the psychoanalytic community, which is an artificial, long-lived, well-structured group, since he appeared to be threatened by the de-idealization of its leader who was unable to formulate strong, rational concepts to solve the issue of what a group's mentality is about.

Moreover, psychoanalysts have resisted something new that could also have had psychotherapeutic potential, and have introduced possible rivalry between psychoanalysis and group analysis.

For all these reasons, we think that their prejudice on this topic has been institutionalized, and rationalized through a distorted and incomplete understanding of Freud's text on "Group Psychology and the Analysis of the Ego".

This might, therefore, have inhibited Foulkes to defy Freud's writings, pointing to other ways of looking at groups. We imagine that he might have tried to hide the psychoanalytic identity of many group-analytic concepts giving them more or less metaphoric names and expressions such as: conductor, matrix, resonance, ego training in action, and mirroring. This could have been the way he chose to avoid some conflicts with those very powerful institutions. In the DVD edited by GAS (Foulkes, 1964c) Foulkes was asked about object relational theory in group analysis. He replied that everything was in the matrix.

Even though it seems that Foulkes's way of looking at group analysis was not that different from the Cortesão perspective, Foulkes and his followers overlooked the groupanalytic concept of pattern introduced by Cortesão.

Cortesão was also a psychoanalyst member of the BSPA and the IPA. Moreover, Eduardo Luís Cortesão was a Portuguese living in Portugal. Foulkes was, by contrast, an immigrant in England. In Portugal at that time, the Portuguese Society of Psychoanalysis was dependent on the French Society of Psychoanalysis. Cortesão was already an IPA member and was therefore perhaps freer to defend his own ideas about groups or even a more relational/intersubjective perspective of psychoanalysis. Cortesão was trained by Foulkes. He belonged to the same small group as other Foulkes followers—and rivalry is a universal aspect of the human condition.

We think that Foulkes's ambivalence about the importance of the group conductor in the group process may have contributed to the outcome of groupanalysis being viewed as a less credible form of personal analytic psychotherapy. Lessening the importance and responsibilities as well as the required training skills of group conductors could well have paved the way for group analysis as a form of powerful personal analytic psychotherapy to be called into question. This has served to have group analysis pushed on to national health services institutions as a cheaper form of psychotherapy or have it applied to working groups. That is what has happened in countries/cultures very much influenced by Bion's contribution to understanding groups and/or by societies with a very strong psychoanalytic bias.

We would like to comment on the metaphor of the conductor of a group as the conductor of an orchestra that still prevails in many group analysts.

We do not agree with this comparison, even though, of course, the orchestra conductor must know the musicians, the instruments as well as the music itself quite deeply. Everything is settled and controlled to ensure that a specific musical score is played as well as possible. Therapeutic group conductors should know their patients/members of the group, ideally choosing them, but unlike a conductor of an orchestra, they never know what is going to play out in each session, nor who the players of each part or communication will be. It is a free-floating discussion and, therefore, the opposite of a well-trained and well conducted orchestra.

We would like to add that we consider the members of a groupanalytic group perform what we are accustomed to calling a supervising function towards the groupanalyst. (Dinis, 2000a; Neto, 2010a).

Pattern—current definition (Portuguese school of groupanalysis)

This concept was introduced by Cortesão in the conceptualization of groupanalysis to highlight the extreme importance attributed to the groupanalyst in the group's processes of each member.

Generally speaking, many Foulkesian group analysts consider the definite importance of the group analyst's functions. However, this topic is not sufficiently highlighted in their books and other writings. There are exceptions such as Morris Nitsun (1991, 1996, 2006, 2009, and 2015) who makes a claim for this in his several writings; the same applies to Garland (2010a), and Steinar Lorentzen (2014). It seems that group analysts have a tendency towards adopting a kind of faith in groups, a kind of idealization of the group.

The groupanalyst is the one who selects the group members. The groupanalyst is also the ultimately responsible for the group; and it is the groupanalyst who settles the contract with each member (Dinis, 1994).

In our view, groups conducted with too much passivity lose their healing power. They may become settings dominated by primitive, primary mental functioning, and eventually become destructive of individuality. We must add that we are not supporting intrusive group analysts. We will come back to this topic later in this chapter.

This concept is particularly relevant as the groupanalyst will convey an analytic attitude and culture to the group, which is going to allow the subsequent development of that therapeutic net—the matrix.

We all know that any communication can be understood, highlighted, and eventually developed in countless ways. It is therefore up to the groupanalyst to choose which meaning or perspective is chosen in every "present moment" (Stern, 2004b) of any psychotherapy.

The thinking behind Cortesão's (1989) coinage of the term for his concept of pattern could be thought of as somewhat idiosyncratic, if partially erroneous as to its earliest known etymological origins. He set aside the

Latin etymology of *pater* (father), whence *patronus* (defender, protector, former master of a freed slave; advocate), preferring to dwell on the secondary meaning acquired in the Old French *patron* meaning a model, pattern or template, something which can be imitated, drawn or prefigured. To this idea he added the mistaken supposition that an even earlier antecedent was the Sanskrit *pa* (प), which has multiple meanings, one of which is rooted in the idea of the seed, giving rise to connotations of sowing, nourishing and promoting—thus—because the groupanalyst should not offer himself or herself as a protector, or a role model, nor should he or she guide either actively or didactically.

As for an interpretation of the concept presented by Foulkes, Cortesão explains that it is not really about the imprint which the therapist makes but rather the imprint he conveys.

In this sense, the analyst is a conveyor, that is, a transmitter, a catalyst, and is not, in any way, a causer and certainly cannot be a leader with whom one identifies, not even a standard for purposes of adaptation and conformism (Cortesão, 1989, p. 115, translated from the Portuguese).

The pattern is integrated by the group, stimulating the communication and, specifically, the interpretation promoting the regression inside the groupanalytic matrix.

Cortesão (1989) defined pattern as the specific attitudes sustained and transmitted by the groupanalyst with an interpretative function that fosters and develops the groupanalytic process.

The groupanalyst will act as a seed or a catalyst. Progressively the other group members will integrate those functions and attitudes, that is to say, the pattern is integrated in the matrix; we may say it in another way: the members of the group identify themselves with the analytic function of the groupanalyst, developing the analytic function of their personalities, i.e., the groupanalytic function of their personalities.

The Pattern has three main dimensions: Nature, Function, and Objectives:

1 The nature is related to the groupanalyst's personality and worked through by his or her own personal groupanalysis as well as by his or her theoretical continuous education and supervision.
2 Function is related to the selection of patients, the set of rules, specific conditions, clinical attitudes, and interpretative activity during the sessions.
    We think that this issue includes what Foulkes called "dynamic administration" and the "therapeutic activity". Malcolm Pines (2000, pp. 277–278) called both "the functions of the therapist".
3 The objectives were defined by Cortesão as the establishment and development of the groupanalytic process within the matrix promoting the working-through signification and differentiation of the self of each member, promoting insight and self-reconstruction. In other ways, the

objectives of the pattern are closely related to what we might call the results, the benefits (Wallerstein, 1995, p. 491), or "the cure". This may be defined in several ways, depending on the theoretical psychoanalytic model applied. We will come to this issue later.

Nature

a **Personality**

There is no question that psychotherapy is remarkably effective. The more complex question is what factors make psychotherapy effective. The research evidence is not altogether clear, and there is much debate about certain issues, but there appears to be sufficient evidence to indicate that the psychotherapist is instrumental in producing the benefits (Wampold, 2011).

The evidence that there are small or negligible differences among treatments that are intended to be therapeutic for particular disorders and the evidence that some therapists consistently achieve better outcomes than others, in clinical trials and in practice, raises the unmistakably important question: what are the qualities and actions of effective therapists? (Shedler, 2010).

We must also take into account that these small differences may be attributed to the fact that the "active ingredients" of therapy are not necessarily those presumed by the theory or treatment model. For this reason, randomized controlled trials that evaluate a therapy as a "package" do not necessarily provide support for its success. For these reasons, studies of therapy "brand names" can be highly misleading. Studies that look beyond brand names by examining session videotapes or transcripts may reveal more about what is helpful to patients. Such studies indicate that the active ingredients of other therapies include unacknowledged psychodynamic elements (Shedler, 2010).

Bruce Wampold (2011), who belongs to the American Psychological Association, describes "Fourteen qualities and actions of effective therapists":

The fourteen qualities and actions of Effective Therapists (ETs), based on theory, policy, and research evidence, can guide therapists toward continual improvement. Various therapists, delivering various treatments, in various contexts, will clearly emphasize some of these more than others.

In summary:

Effective Therapists have a sophisticated set of interpersonal skills, including:

a Verbal fluency
b Interpersonal perception

c   Affective modulation and expressiveness
d   Warmth and acceptance
e   Empathy
f   Focus on the other

They should be authentic, never avoid difficult material, trustable, coherent, flexible, and recognize the positive skills of their patients. They should monitor the patient's progresses. They must be attentive to their countertransference and should try to continually improve.

Otto Kernberg (2003) highlights the personality features of social and political leadership; he proposes that, "ideally, functional leadership combines 5 characteristics: 1—high intelligence; 2—sufficient emotional maturity and human depth; 3—solid and deep moral integrity; 4—sufficiently strong narcissistic tendencies; 5—sufficient paranoid features." We agree with these characteristics, adding: 6—empathy; 7—authenticity and coherence; 8—sense of humour; 9—capacity to acquire and sustain auto-analysis; 10—open minded attitude towards updating knowledge; 11—tolerance to what is different and unknown; 12—tolerance of the paradox every scientist might have to work with: belief in a model being able to criticize it or even abandon certain paradigms in the event of unsuccess. Thus, psychotherapists/group analysts should be able to transmit hope (Hopper, 2003), being always attentive to unsuccesses, changing diagnosis, technique, and suggesting therapeutic alternatives whenever necessary. This mental attitude is actually the most difficult task for analysts/group analysts/group therapists as we do not have rigid and formal ways to experiment.

We deal with many variables which make research an incredibly difficult task. We do think that research is necessary, though. And that we should pay attention to the results.

Guntrip (1975), writing about his analysis with Fairbairn and with Winnicott, speaks of the bonding capacity/capacity to establish a relationship, which he believes is independent from his theoretical competency. It is also important to note that the group analyst/group therapist should feel pleasure when working with groups. The group-object relation by Nitsun (1996) is the way individuals characteristically perceive and relate to groups; it should predominantly be motivated by positive feelings towards groups.

Group analysts should feel at ease working with difficult feelings such as: shame, envy, jealousy, several forms of aggression including the several forms of the anti-group (Nitsun, 1996) as well as to deal with sexuality. None of these themes should ever be avoided; on the contrary, they deserve the group analyst's special attention. These topics are developed in other chapters of this book, mainly in Chapter 8.

Group analysts have some basic references based on scientific information which should be differentiated from prejudices. Group analysts/psychoanalytic therapists should be permanently aware that there are always blind spots in their minds. The unconscious/non-conscious is always there.

Therefore, to be a good enough groupanalyst we must pay most of our attention to the other side of the nature of the pattern: the training.

b **Training**

As is the case at every training institute belonging to European Group Analytic Training Institutions Network (EGATIN), SPG has a tripartite training programme.

We attribute the most important part of the training to the personal groupanalysis in small mixed groups without a fixed end, on a 2 or 3 sessions per week basis. Our main objective is to deeply analyze our character. In this way, we are able to acquire the skills described above to reduce to a minimum the blind spots which might act as pathogenic resistances of the groupanalysts and interfere negatively in the understanding of the group and its members. In our groupanalytic process, we must analyze our primitive object relations, our internal conflicts and anxieties, defence mechanisms, pathogenic and pathologic ego-syntonic character traits and their powerful consequences in other people minds mainly those who most depend on us.

Groupanalysts should also have in their background education deep knowledge in psychiatry, psychopathology, and basic notions of an interest in mathematics, physics, philosophy, and history. They should have an open minded attitude towards updating their knowledge.

The theoretical training course will give the information about psychology, psychoanalytic and group-analytic theory and technique, giving a solid and coherent basis to the continuous study of those subjects; the training at the SPG will be detailed in another chapter of this book. The theoretical training course covers four main areas: updated psychoanalytic concepts, updated group-analytic theory and practice, psychopathology, and applied groupanalysis in several settings and with a number of different objectives. The course lasts four years, with two two-hour sessions each week. SPGPAG also holds monthly seminars open to every member. We believe that the theoretical course is just the beginning. Continuous study is a must. The SPG suggests and informs members about new trends, and new challenges but cannot be substitute personal efforts and activities to keep abreast of developments in the profession. The basic theoretical course should provide and develop a critical integration or rejection of the several concepts and theories.

International and national conferences are other forms of opening one's mind.

Training institutes should be spaces for free thinking and creativity. It is not that easy. It may be difficult for seniors to tolerate new ideas as they may feel threatened by the younger trainees' questioning. Misunderstandings are the sand traps of life. Training institutes must be careful avoiding the 30 methods to destroy the creativity of psychoanalytic candidates mentioned by Kernberg (1996).

Supervision is the other vertex of the training. Supervision is an intersubjective learning-teaching process which occurs in a predominantly positive affective relationship. Its main and direct goal is the better understanding of the patients' minds as well as the group's dynamic which includes the conscious and unconscious relational perspective, and transference and countertransference.

Moreover, supervision protects patients as well as therapists, being a detoxifying space where difficult feelings, doubts, and conflicts may be shared and discussed, eventually relieving the therapist.

A bibliographic search on this topic in 1999 published in Portuguese (Neto, 2000) highlighted supervision as the second most important part of the psychotherapist's training being useful for each patient, the group, the psychotherapist and the supervisor, and paving the way toward the self-development and autonomy of every participant. It is another way to reach our own unconscious, our biases, and our blind spots.

> Supervision can be seen as the integrating point in training: bringing together theoretical understanding and personal, subjective development; helping empathically to identify the trainee's anxieties, projections and blind spots; and bridging the all-important theory-practice divide (Nitsun, 2006, p. 266).

We believe supervision helps and complements the working-through of the last period of the personal group analysis. It is quite usual that blind spots become manifest in the clinical material brought to supervision.

Supervision is focused both on the understanding of each member of the group and on the group functioning. As a compulsory activity, it lasts six years. The material is presented verbatim in writing during the initial phase when trainees are more insecure. Progressively oral presentations take place, using reported speech.

Peer supervision is a very useful method of continuous training.

We think that each analytic society should formulate training that includes guidelines for every member. However therapists/analysts do not integrate the various aspects and theoretical formulations in the same way. We adhere to some authors and theories more than we do others. The way analysts internalize their own analysis and supervision may be quite different for many reasons. Therefore, we think that we should become more explicit about our way of understanding and working in a group.

We have noticed that the better the training, the greater the capacity of groupanalysts to be flexible, to adapt and create fresh solutions to new situations using the groupanalytic model without losing their identity (Neto, 2009/2010).

This topic will be further developed in Chapter 9.

Function

The function of the pattern includes the selection of group members, and the establishment of groupanalytic rules and attitudes so that the objectives may be achieved. There are differences according to the several kinds of groups as discussed in Chapter 2. In this part, we will focus exclusively on small therapeutic groups.

a **Selection**

Conscious and unconscious motivations are the basis of choices we make as regards friends, spouses, profession, ideas, work or social groups, psychoanalysts, groupanalysts, etc. We have noticed this both in our private and professional experience over the years. And being a question of interactions and relationships, those who are chosen, also choose. (Neto, 1999a). To some extent, these choices may be determined by compulsive repetitive mechanisms, having their roots in childhood, in an attempt to find a bad object in order to transform it into a good one, and hence, in adulthood, transform the traumatic past, or, on the other hand, they may correspond to attempts at finding good objects once more.

And what about our clients/patients? I believe that even in an institutional setting, choices are made; even in an emergency, we choose to invest more in certain situations than in others, in the same way that some people allow themselves to be helped more than others.

It seems there is a general agreement when it comes to the constitution of a group. This determines whether its functioning will be predominantly constructive or destructive. And the one who chooses the group members is the groupanalyst! Cortesão (1967b), Hopper (1982), Graham (1984), Raymond Battegay (1986) Ronald Sandison (1987), Zender (1991), Zimerman (1993a), César Dinis (1994). Morris Nitsun (1996) considers selection as the "obscure object of desire of group psychotherapy" (p. 161), as so little is known about this vital and highly complex area of the process.

Neto (1999a) summarizes some guidelines on this topic:

1   Before a new member joins a group, we hold several individual sessions with two objectives: (i) to gain a better knowledge of their personalities (ii) to establish a therapeutic relationship/alliance

which may prevent some potential narcissistic threats during the initial phase in groupanalysis.
2   We believe that we should choose on the basis of our empathy, in order to achieve a countertransferential empathic balance in the group (Dinis, 2000a).
3   To like is not to idealize, and beware of idealizing our patients! There will appear other areas of their personalities with which we will empathise with more difficulty.
4   We also have to choose a new member according to the already existing group. We should foresee whether and how the new member and the group will interact, mainly in the initial phase during which relationships and alliances are still weak.
5   In situations of acute destructiveness and aggression in the group, we should try to analyze to what extent we are contributing or even introducing into the group unresolved conflicts of our own internal reality, through the selection of a particular patient (Neto, 1999a).

b   **Rules**

These have not introduced significant disagreement among the several group-analytic perspectives and have been generally accepted by the whole group-analytic community.

The therapeutic contract should be made before the patient joins the group. The following should be explained:

- Complete and bilateral confidentiality is required. Supervision is an exception, being a setting also protected by strict confidentiality.
- Contact among the elements of the group is forbidden outside the sessions.
- No group analyst will get emotionally involved with their clients outside of the therapeutic framework.
- Group analysts shall not talk to the patients' families and other significant people.
- Verbal communication is privileged in the group, and by no means is physical contact allowed (for example, verbal expression of aggressiveness or affection is allowed, but any physical acting out is not).
- The patient will have to renounce the attainment of secondary gains in the group.

c   **Setting**

This is another issue that has not given rise to any significant disagreement, being generally accepted by the whole group-analytic community.

The group analyst has the obligation of ensuring the physical space, the frequency, and duration (1 h 30 m) of the sessions. He or she is also responsible for the regularity and punctuality of the sessions. He or she should provide the group-analytic setting: the patients should sit in a circle, all facing each other, and the groupanalyst should stimulate free-floating discussion of the ideas without any social censorship.

d **Attitude**

There are some attitudes that are generally accepted while others are not. The following are generally accepted:

- The analyst shall have several attitudes in order to initiate the groupanalytic process which is itself a purpose that will achieve the results. This statement is shared by every group analyst. Disagreements may arise when defining what the results will be and how to evaluate them.
- There are other attitudes that provide no cause for disagreement and that are also generally accepted.
- The conductor/group therapist/group analyst shall promote free association and free-floating discussion.
- The main task of any analytic therapist is to promote free thinking as well as the free expression of emotions and conflicts.
- Empathy is an important skill to any analyst. Empathy does not mean a symbiotic relationship.
- Analysts shall pay constant attention to their countertransference, to their relation towards each patient as well as to the different forms of transference.
- It is up to the analyst to abstain from trivial interventions and opinions if they are not relevant to the therapeutic process. That is what we call analytic reserve.
- The conductor/group therapist/groupanalyst shall pay attention to each member, to the group as a whole and to its dynamics. The appropriate proportion of each of these perspectives is often discussed and triggers different attitudes.
- The conductor/group therapist/groupanalyst should pay attention to both verbal and non-verbal communication.

e **Analytic interventions and interpretations**

The interventions take the form of questions, clarifications, confrontations, analogies or metaphors, and interpretations. This issue is discussed in Chapter 3 in particular.

The topic of attitudes gives rise to divergent thinking that is the source of quite different ways of approaching groupanalysis. It seems important to highlight the five main controversial issues:

1. how to address and refer to the conductor
2. neutrality versus activity of the therapist/conductor/groupanalyst
3. how to deal with the individual and the group as a whole
4. the dichotomy between the here-and-now and the there-and-then (Hopper, 2006, p. 136); the here-and-now as a concept on its own is generally accepted
5. the therapist's/conductor's/groupanalyst's "trust in the group".

These five issues are deeply connected to other much-discussed issues such as the different perspectives between Foulkes and Bion, apparently acted out through the rivalry between the Tavistock and the IGA models of group-analytic psychotherapy. These issues also bring up the old discussion about how active or passive group analyst should be as well as what they should be called (e.g., conductor, group analyst, etc.). "Many believe that had Bion done more group therapy, he, like Foulkes, would have found a way of using the totality of the group's interactions" (Hume, 2010, p. 127).

Bion (1976) was asked if he still worked in and was still interested in group work. He said he was interested in group work, but no longer doing any group work. We agree with Brown (2006b, p. 230) that settings such as well-functioning therapeutic groups which promote genuine contact prevent the emergence or persistence of basic assumptions. For groups with other tasks, e.g., committees, institutions, wider social groups, basic assumptions more often offer a way of keeping the group together, according to Brown, who thinks as we do, that basic assumptions may be viewed as group defences against primal anxieties. Some authors think that the more passive the leadership is, the more regressive the group functioning is, since this way, groups are prone to work at the level of basic assumptions. In practice, in the Tavistock model (Hume, 2010, p. 126),

> there exists a flexible integration of Bion's theory of group process and his psychoanalytic approach to understand the material, with a clinical style that owes more to Foulkes. Thus, when a group is getting on with its task and the individuals in it are facing their problems and allowing themselves to know and be known by each other, we do not seek to dig out and identify basic assumptions activity.

Garland calls our attention to the fact that we cannot only be attentive to the group as a whole and the group dynamics; interpretations to individuals are necessary. She talks about the supposed rivalry: "Although there is a mythology that the "Tavistock" approach ignores the individual in favour of the "group", in reality our approach is pragmatic" (Garland, 2010a, p. 126).

Richard Billow (2003, pp. 41–42) goes in the same direction:

> I value the interpretative mode in group as well in individual analysis, but do not limit myself to group-as-a-whole interpretations, as did Bion. To be effective, group-as-a-whole interpretations should be made sparingly, couched in conversational language, and without sounding or being definitive. [...] A curious, empathic, and emotionally responsive leader secures an environment in which more can be said and examined, and thereby averts unnecessarily provoking anxiety and exaggerating basic assumptions defences.

We believe that these five main controversial issues are the basis of whether we should consider group analysis as analysis or not. If we avoid the analysis of each member, being attentive just to the group as a whole, and if we assume the dominant attitude of just making interventions in the here-and-now, we cannot consider groupanalysis as an analysis neither can we call the conductor a groupanalyst. The same applies to the "trust in the group" issue which, in some way, seems to run contrary to the conductor's responsibility to analyze each member: "Although whole group interpretations provide a powerful instrument in the therapeutic task, they are not on their own sufficient if patients are to feel noticed and valued as individuals, as well as being valued as part of the group" (Garland, 2010b, p. 40).

Behr and Hearst (2005, p. 109) comment on this issue:

> Group therapists are sometimes urged to 'trust the group'. But what does this mean in practice? It is unwise to embrace this slogan in the innocent hope that somehow the collective wisdom of the group can justify a technique of neutral non-intervention on the part of the conductor. The trail of group therapy is littered with people who have dropped out or have been rendered more disturbed after having felt neglected or put at risk of being scapegoated by a well-intentioned, but passive conductor nursing the belief that the group process should be allowed to run its natural course and that the wisdom of the group would prevail in the end.

Is the here-and-now opposed to the there-and-then? We think that both are necessary. Harold Behr (2011, p. 455) considers that the past is as important in Group Analysis as it is in any other form of psychoanalytic psychotherapy:

> Past is important as a therapeutic instrument and as a means of throwing light on psychopathological processes. […] When we introduce people into groups, we aim not only to foster communication but also to bring the past alive, to re-create in the group, so to speak. This happens in two ways: unconsciously, through re-enactment of past relationships scenarios and … through individual narratives … the act of telling one's story is itself therapeutic, mobilizing emotions which have been repressed …, taking the necessary time and finding their own language; eventually these troubling thoughts and emotions from the past are shared and tested with the others, lessening guilt, shame or any other negative feeling.

Harold Behr (2011) also points out that one reason for the bypassing of Group Analysis as a treatment of choice is that group analysis has paid less attention to the study of individual psychopathology.

Pines (1994. p. 56), quoting Dennis Brown:

> ... for each person, there are two personal narratives, the here-and-now in the group and there-and-then in the past, and it is the dynamic juxtaposition of these two stories that gradually fits the two together.

We agree with Zimerman (1993a), Billow (2003), Garland (2010a), Hopper (2009), and Lorentzen (2014), who are also basically in accordance with this perspective. However (Lorentzen, 2014, p. 11) writes,

> many are of the view that it can be important to keep the focus on patients and their relationship to the therapist in the here-and-now in the treatment situation, rather than on the patient and his significant others outside the treatment situation in the there-and-then.

Some are ambivalent or, we might even say, split on this issue. We believe that if we consider the basic importance of psychoanalytic concepts in groupanalysis, such as transference, we cannot deny the necessity of genetic-evolutionary interpretations, i.e., the there and then.

We would like to say that it seems to be easier for the conductors to focus just on the here-and-now as, this way, they do not need to memorize and work with the immense variables of the object relations and important main anxieties and important life events of each of the patients/members of a group. The links between all these issues are definitely important to understand and eventually interrupt the vicious circle of the transference repetition compulsion, thus paving the way to emotional corrective experiences or, in other words, to the development of the self and the transformation of the internal relational matrix.

Clinical vignette 1

Silvia, a 32-year old woman, intelligent and attractive, had been in group therapy once a week for almost two years. Her attitude in the group was sometimes ironic. It was easier for her to express herself using humour and irony. She was protective over others whenever she considered that they could be feeling vulnerable and humiliated. Due to her work commitments, she had to change to another group, which met twice a week.

From the very beginning, she had complained about the difficulty in connecting with this second group. Her humour disappeared and a strong feeling of not being accepted by the group showed up. From time to time, she pointed out the feeling of being left out within the group. She begun with symptoms, such panic attacks and generalized anxiety.

Prior to group psychotherapy, she suffered from generalized anxiety disorder, and had had several major depressive episodes. She had been medicated with an antidepressant for a period of ten years. Only after joining the new group, did the symptoms start to fade away leading to total remission.

Silvia was always very resistant to every expression from the groupanalyst, and she hardly accepted the group analyst interpretations on her transference. Nevertheless, she managed to stay in the group. One year later, she allowed herself to cry. For the first time, she felt safe and trusted the group's capacity to hold her.

She was able to compare the difference between this group (twice a week) and the first one (once a week) and express how she didn't feel safe enough, and was always trying to control herself not allowing to become closer to the new group, using humour rather defensively.

At the same time, the other members had started to display some perplexity towards her self-image. They confronted her frequently with affection, questioning how it was possible for her to see herself in such a devaluated manner. She strongly reacted with anger saying that their perspective was not necessarily the truth. Like other members, the groupanalyst also shared her feelings towards Silvia. Silvia also doubted the groupanalyst.

The situation was only possible to overcome after the acceptance and recognition of her own child suffering of having felt guilty and devaluated by her parents. Her low self-esteem and fears of being rejected had been compulsively repeated on transference for almost one whole year.

In this vignette, we highlight the definite importance of the frequency of the sessions to foster transference and its understanding and eventually discovering the development of the true self. We also point out that the here-and-now as well as the there-and-then belonged to the groupanalyst pattern, thus were introjected by the group.

Could the way of facing the groupanalyst's attitudes, avoiding the there-and-then, be a therapists' defence? We must add that child development research and neurosciences have given groupanalysis an added value as a setting that favours psychic changes. "The information proceeding from the investigation and observation of infants emphasize the importance of the analyst as a person and of intersubjectivity" (Schain-West, 1998). Paparo and Nebbiosi (1998) state that through new relational experiences with the analyst, with several individuals in the group, and with the group, the founding and consolidation of alternative principles is facilitated by broadening each individual's relational patterns, through the internalisations of positive, consistent and empathetic interactions. "Groupanalysis is an especially rich environment for the observation of the non-verbal; authenticity, affect, and coherence are easily and clearly transmitted when you see and are seen, as is the case of groupanalytic psychotherapies" (Neto, 2002). Mirror neurons research is also crucial in supporting empathy as well as the changing the potentialities of face-to-face psychotherapies.

We would like to introduce a little of the experience of the Boston Change Process Study Group (Stern, 2004b, p. 226):

> The distinction between the cognitive understanding of experience and the enriching of experience is vital. Of course there must be a search for meaning so that a psychodynamic understanding can be constructed, and a life narrative created. For this, a verbally explicit account of the patient's experience is paramount. But, there must also be a process of appreciating the experience more deeply, of feeling his experience and sharing it with him so that there is an enriching of who he is, what it is like to be him, and what it is like to be-with-him.

Objectives

We think that we should try to separate objectives and results although we consider this a difficult and somewhat confusing task.

It is not enough to accomplish the rules and attitudes leading to the development of the groupanalytic process which is the objective; results should also be taken into account. Are objectives somehow different from results? We might have objectives that might not have concordant results, or the ones we expected. Results should be observable objectively and subjectively, being a consequence of the analytic processes.

This topic introduces another controversial issue in the psychoanalytic community: Is psychoanalysis a way of treatment or mainly a way to achieve self-knowledge? What are the goals of psychoanalysis and group analysis? Are they a means to investigate mental and group functioning or are they primarily therapeutic ways to achieve healthier ways of living? We agree with Joan Coderch (2010), who discusses this topic in a very clear and courageous way affirming the therapeutic vertex as the most important. He defines the objectives of psychoanalysis as the establishment of the psychoanalytic process, i.e., the development of transference, interpretation whether transferential or not, past reconstruction, and the establishment of a strong therapeutic alliance based in an emotional therapeutic relation. These will give rise to observable changes—the results.

Cortesão (1989) wrote that the nature and the function of groupanalysis convey the groupanalytic process paving the way to working-through and self-reconstruction. The groupanalytic process was defined orally by Cortesão in 1970, at the 1st GAS Symposium: it is "the mode through which the various theoretical and technical dimensions that contribute to giving a framework and form to groupanalytic therapy are structured, organized, and perform a function" (Cortesão, 1989, p. 31, translated from the Portuguese).

We would like to emphasize here that the groupanalytic purpose or the objective of groupanalysis, as defended by the SPG is to work with three central concepts: the unconscious, transference, and their analysis. Group analysis is a kind of applied psychoanalysis in a group setting, using its countless dynamic potentialities. Cortesão always sustained the links between psychoanalysis and groupanalysis. The SPG has considered them as different, though not contradictory, settings. They are both methods of research and therapy with common theoretical bases and results but different operating procedures.

We would like to add that we may have groups and members working according to group-analytic processes and, as with psychoanalysis, we think that in groupanalysis some people develop groupanalytic processes; however, not all of them achieve what we could call a cure. Wallerstein (1995, p. 491), reporting a research study on this issue, wrote: "some patients treated by psychoanalysis develop an analytic process and achieve therapeutic benefit, while others achieve therapeutic benefit while not apparently developing an analytic process".

Mark Leffert (2013) speaks about a study of therapeutic action supported by the narratives of analysts of their own personal psychoanalysis; levels of satisfaction were related to the emotional bond established with their analysts. We think this is an objective of groupanalysis too.

Jonathan Shedler (2010, p. 100) in his paper about the efficacy of Psychodynamic Psychotherapy writes:

> The goals of psychodynamic therapy include, but extend beyond, symptom remission. Successful treatment should not only relieve symptoms (i.e., get rid of something) but also foster the positive presence of psychological capacities and resources. Depending on the person and the circumstances, these might include the capacity to have more fulfilling relationships, make more effective use of one's talents and abilities, maintain a realistically based self-esteem, tolerate a wide range of affect, have more satisfying sexual experiences, understand self and others in more nuanced and sophisticated ways, and face life's challenges with greater freedom and flexibility.

The results may be "benefits" and "cure", which Zimerman (1993b, p. 141) called analytic results.

Therapeutic benefits concern three levels:

- Acute crisis overcome
- Symptom remission
- Adaptable, although still unstable, ameliorations/improvements

The analytic results concern structural and permanent changes. We can conceptualize them according the several authors and schools of psychoanalysis. Zimerman (1993b) mentions a list of skills and psychic changes based on Freud, Klein, Bion, Kohut, Lacan, Mahler, and general systems theory that can be summarized as follows:

- Lessening of primitive (paranoid and depressive) anxieties
- Capacity to communicate and interact with the others without losing one's limits
- Lessening projective and splitting defence mechanisms
- Adequate use of projective identifications developing empathy
- Tolerating differences
- Development of the capacity to be alone as well as to be with others, without fear of abandonment and rejection
- Equilibrium between the individual and the group identity
- Capacity to elaborate and overcome new situations
- Abandon old pathogenic identifications, beliefs, and roles
- Development of the psychoanalytic function of the personality
- And, of course, all the above imply a better self-knowledge, a development of insight

Dennis Brown (2006a, p. 107) speaks of "self-development through subjective interaction" as a concise way to what is experienced in well-functioning small stranger groups. He thinks this way of talking of ego training in action, a Foulkesian expression, is more specific. Brown highlights the importance of the concept of intersubjectivity.

> I will argue that in groupanalysis, the achievement of awareness of intersubjectivity with a range of other personalities, not restricted to the analyst, and in their presence, powerfully promotes maturity and a capacity to engage in mutually validating relationships.

Pines (1998) explains the objectives speaking of "process of healing" linked with three principal needs: cohesion, firmness, and harmony (p. 82): "the cure is essentially the filling of defects of self-structure that have arisen during faulty development". The working-through, termed 'transmuting internalization', takes place through the repeated optimal frustrations that are an inevitable part of any analytic, or of any human, relationship: "the aim of therapy as well as of healthy development is the attainment of attunement and consonance, harmony, fitting together" (p. 83). He strongly supports Kohut's self psychology to speak about healing. "The way in which the therapist helps the patient to attain that level of normality is through the technique of self-psychology" (p. 84).

Like the authors above, the SPG identifies in many ways with relational psychoanalysis paradigms. Foulkes and some followers seem to think the same way. However it was Cortesão and his followers who first expressed it clearly.

Thus, our objectives are mainly therapeutic. Insight and working-through are elements of the mechanisms of change leading to results that should be subjective and objective (recognized by others), i.e., internal changes as well as changes in disturbing both ego-dystonic and ego-syntonic behaviours.

In 2008, a survey was conducted among SPG members to investigate several variables (Carvalho, Galamba & Neto, 2008). Concerning the results after the end of their personal group analysis, 70% answered that they almost achieved the expected results; 20% answered that they achieved just part of their expectations; 10% did not answer to that question; and 90% attributed the most important benefits in their personality changes and/or in their professional development to the personal groupanalysis, followed by supervision and third, to the theoretical course.

Although almost every groupanalyst considers the importance of the groupanalyst/conductor/therapist/group therapist in the development of the group and of each member, sometimes this fact is not made explicit enough by all authors. Generally we may say that this topic—The importance of the conductor/group therapist/group analyst—is rather dispersed or even not enough valued.

The pattern is very complex, introducing the whole theory and practice. Organizing the issues of this subject may facilitate research.

The SPG has worked for the past 50 years highlighting the definite importance of the groupanalysts, as we call the conductors, or therapists of groupanalytic groups. The analysis of the individual is their main objective, using the dynamic of the group matrix. The cure is its aimed-for result.

Our groupanalytical theory and practice is what we could call a neo-Foulkesian one, integrating direct followers of Foulkes, as was the case with Cortesão, both British and international followers as well as information and concepts coming from contemporary psychoanalysis, child development research and the neurosciences.

We think that groupanalysts should have in-depth training in mixed, small groups, after a period in a dual setting.

We value both the here-and-now and the intersubjectivity of working together as well as the there-and-then. In this kind of being in therapy, the interpretation is what we would call interpretative activity, which includes much more than the classic types of interpretation.

Leadership, as parenthood, is responsibility and not a way to exert power. At the initial stages of a group or a recent joining of a new member the groupanalyst should be more active in their interpretative activity. This will be progressively internalized by the group members, i.e., the groupanalytic pattern will be internalized paving the way to the development of the groupanalytic part of the personality, achieving autonomy and freedom.

Clinical vignette 2

Rudolf told the group two dreams which were named by him as "No Escape" and "The Wedding".

No escape

He described a series of terribly difficult situations which he was continuously accused, incriminated in several ways. In each of them, he tried to find a solution by running away to avoid the dangers; however, another dangerous and threatening situation arose. He wasn't safe anywhere!

He was systematically followed by his enemies who wanted to incriminate him. He tried to run away from the country where he was in his dream to another country, but the passport would give him away. No escape!

Dream work

Niel, another member of the group: "At last you are thinking that your country is safer, has more advantages ... You've stopped idealizing the USA!"

Groupanalyst: "Rudolf, what do you think and feel about your dream? You haven't told us yet. Niel has given his interpretation of it; however the dream is yours."

Rudolf: "I have felt these kinds of feelings all my life. I have always felt alone, solving difficult situations; there has not been anybody there to help me; I've survived but it has been very difficult. I understood my dream almost immediately."

The wedding

Rudolph: "I was invited to a wedding. I had been told that the bride loved me for several years. But I didn't know. She approached me in a very sad mood. However, suddenly she married the groom and looked very happy with him. I stayed at the party and all of a sudden, the bride approached me. She was very sad which made me terribly anxious. I tried to help her. But she disappeared again and again."

He looked very sad, stopping his dream narrative.

Groupanalyst: "What are your feelings about?"

Rudolf: "It has always been the same: when my father left us, my mother became very sad; I felt that I should fill my father's empty place. And suddenly, that other man came once or twice a week! I heard them having intercourse frequently. Afterwards, my mother became sad again."

Rudolf was talking with tears in his eyes, his voice was tremulous: "These two dreams ... it's the only way to reach emotionally my childhood sadness and solitude! Now I can understand that I have chosen sad women as girlfriends, instead of looking at smart and happy women; I always get near those who have a sad look—" At this point, the comment "and … children" was added by another member of the group. Rudolf, crying silently, said: "I want to avoid these memories and suffering. I needed to dream them first, though".

In this case, we can say that the pattern was introjected by the group members of this three-year-old small group run on a frequency of three sessions per week.

Beginning of the 21st century: is "pattern" still a useful concept?

The usefulness of the concept of the pattern has been demonstrated during the course of this chapter. We believe that the pattern of any therapist is of definite importance in any kind of psychotherapy; the way one feels and behaves in any kind of human relationship is similarly important. However, we cannot avoid the importance of the framework of psychotherapy which also belongs to the concept of the pattern according to our (SPG) definition. Hence our contention that the personality of the therapist and their psychotherapeutic framework are equally important.

The "pattern" as we use it clearly points to the complexity and responsibility of our profession.

Chapter 6

Foulkes, Cortesão, and beyond
Other specific concepts of the Portuguese school of groupanalysis

João Carlos Melo and Paulo Motta Marques

Introduction

Nowadays, several decades after the introduction of group analysis, it is difficult to point out the clear differences between Foulkes and Cortesão, and their respective schools. We are of the view that it is useful to trace the historical evolution of the concepts and point out what, even today, the differences between the two are, and also to consider their similarities.

Main differences between group analysis (Foulkes) and groupanalysis (Cortesão)

Designation

Sigmund Foulkes attributed the designation of "group analysis" and "group-analytic psychotherapy" to his technique, while Eduardo Luís Cortesão chose the term "groupanalysis", to accurately translate in a precise manner the analytic character that constitutes the specificity of his technique. Choosing to unite and integrate both terms—"group" and "analysis"—instead of maintaining a space between them, is intended to create one unique word which corresponds to his specific concept.

Hence, these different designations are not idiosyncrasies of their authors, but rather a reflection of the different nature of the techniques they advocated. However, it is not only this designation that is different. There is another, subordinate to the first that is also significant: the term "conductor", adopted by Foulkes and disseminated by his followers, which reflects the absence of an analytic character, contrary to what happens with Cortesão who, by using the term "groupanalyst", clearly assumes that character. Chapter 5 fully discusses this issue in relation to the pattern.

Duration and frequency

Group analysis, as practised by Foulkes, had an average duration of two–three years, with a weekly frequency, in which each session lasted 90 minutes. In the rare cases that the frequency was twice-weekly, the length of the sessions was only one hour. Groupanalysis usually has duration of four to 11 years, and is frequently longer. As a rule, the number of weekly sessions is three, however recently, after the last revision of the Statutes of the Portuguese Groupanalytic Society, in 2012, it was determined that the number should be "at least two" sessions per week.

Influences

Foulkes was a psychoanalyst and never renounced this appellation. Furthermore, when he conceptualized group analysis, he considered it to be group psychotherapy with analytic inspiration that took into account phenomena such as regression, fixation, resistance, and transference, as well as interpretation as a therapeutic procedure. However, he did not confer on them the same importance that they have in psychoanalysis. In fact, the influences that ended up having preponderant roles were sociology, culture, communication theories and Gestalt therapy.

In determining psychopathology, it was the social and cultural factors that he considered most important, relegating each individual's genetic-evolutive factors to a secondary level.

Cortesão, on the other hand, put an unequivocally psychoanalytic stamp on groupanalysis, which is its distinctive mark. The influence of psychoanalysis on the groupanalytic process may be found in metapsychology, ego psychology, object relations theory, and self psychology.

Nonetheless, he also acknowledged other influences, namely those of Foulkes himself, the general systems theory, Kurt Lewin's field theory, and Goldstein's organismic theory. Therefore, he considered the most significant factors of psychopathology to be the genetic-evolutive ones.

Theoretical foundations

Foulkes made an attempt to theorize his work, conceiving a "general dynamic theory" and a "metatheory". However, he considered them to be over-ambitious and ended up reviewing them and replacing them with mainly technical and pragmatic considerations.

By contrast, Cortesão attempted to construct solid theoretical fundamentals and a theory of the technique.

The high esteem in which he held Foulkes was well known and always assumed, yet their divergent thoughts in respect of theory and technique were clear, as was revealed in the testimony of a conversation between the two (Cortesão, 1989, p. 36, translated from the Portuguese):

> Therefore, once again, I conveyed to him my apprehension that the empirical and natural merit of the process would not be sufficiently completed without the strengthening of a valid body of theoretical knowledge.

Thus began his conceptualisation of the following theoretical and technical dimensions (further developed in other parts of this book):

- Matrix
- Pattern
- Levels of Communication
- Levels of Interpretation.

A concept that reflects these differences is that of the "mirror reaction". As a process, it is from a phase of development which is conceived as a fundamental mechanism of the organization of the personality and enables the differentiation between the self and the non-self through the affective confrontation with "others", immersed in a global network of relationships.

Maria Rita Mendes Leal (1968/1994c) considers that in groupanalysis, it is by means of regression that an emotional reactivation develops and is processed, and is therefore a repetition in the here-and-now of experiences found in previous phases of development. Hence we can say, in other words, that the mirror reactions which are observed in a group-analytic group correspond to a reactivation of the mirror reactions that take place in the initial phases of individual development.

Cortesão (1989) offered an important contribution to the theoretical body of work in groupanalysis, but he also asserted that the "concept of the mirror reaction, inasmuch as it may be of interest for a phenomenological, descriptive, and explicative understanding, with special focus on the groupanalytic situation, it encases a more analogic value in the context of object relations than it does as a significant analytic concept" (p. 109).

On the other hand, Grinberg, an Argentinean psychoanalyst who worked with groups, upholds that what Foulkes referred to as mirror reactions was the "final and manifest expression of a phenomenon, whose essential and profound mechanisms may be found in the projective and introjective identification processes" (Grinberg, Langer & Rodrigué, 1957).

The subject in the group versus the group as a whole

For Foulkes, the group as a whole prevails over each of the elements that constitute it. The group is the figure and the individual is the ground. The group is the basic instrument of action: it is an agent and a patient. The group is the main vehicle and therapeutic instrument.

As such, group analysis is a form of psychotherapy through the group, and of the group, including its conductor.

The group's task is to communicate freely and spontaneously, and that of the conductor is to interpret these communications, predominantly in the here-and-now and for the group as a whole.

Cortesão has a different understanding. Even though he considers the group to be a privileged therapeutic means, he argues that the object of analysis is not the group in itself, but the individual. Not the isolated individual, but each individual in the interpersonal context that constitutes the group matrix.

In this sense, the purpose of groupanalysis is the personal analysis of each of the elements in the group, through the resolution/working-through of the transference neurosis of each one, in the relational context of the group.

Therapeutic factors

For Foulkes, the main factor that leads to therapeutic change in group-analytic psychotherapy is ego training in action. As a therapeutic instrument, interpretation has a less significant role.

In the group-analytic situation the whole group interprets, in concert, the communications that develop. As to the interpretations of the conductor himself, they may be aimed at the group as a whole and, less frequently, to one or the other individual in particular.

The main areas of interpretation are the content of the communication, the behaviour and the non-verbal language of the individual and of the group, as well as the interpersonal relationships.

In Cortesão's groupanalysis, the main therapeutic factors are interpretation, insight, working-through, and the analysis and resolution of the transference neurosis.

Transference neurosis

The transference neurosis assumes a very significant role in groupanalysis, as Cortesão (1989, p. 37, translated from the Portuguese) conceived and developed it, and constitutes a major determinant in the analytic dimension that characterizes it:

> The crucial point, the passing of the border that determines the territory and the scope of psychotherapy on one side, and the terrain and environment of analysis on the other, is distinguished by the establishment, or not, of transference neurosis and its interpretation. This border, that enables the distinction between psychoanalytic orientated

individual psychotherapy and psychoanalysis, also satisfactorily enables the demarcation between psychoanalytic orientated group psychotherapy and groupanalysis.

Foulkes, on the other hand, held a different point of view, as Guilherme Ferreira (1990) pointed out: after having started out from a position in which he purely and simply denied the possibility of establishing transference neurosis, he then stated that its formation and working-through were possible, and ended up taking a stance that, although it was possible, it created a significant situation of regression and dependency, therefore it should not be encouraged.

The groupanalytic process

Groupanalysis, as conceptualized by Eduardo Luis Cortesão, and later developed by him and his followers, is based on three pillars: a well-defined and well-founded theoretical framework, a specific technique, and long and consistent training.

It was within this context and with the purposes outlined above that Cortesão found it necessary and useful to formulate and structure a groupanalytic theory and technique as well as elaborate his definition of the groupanalytic process. It was both necessary and useful in order for the empiric and natural merit of the process to be sufficiently strengthened with a valid framework of theoretical knowledge and in order to securely enable the definition of the technical procedures involved.

To begin with, we shall consider the expression itself and the words that make it up.

"Process", in this instance, contemplates two dimensions: one implies the idea of movement, the act of progressing, of going forward, while the other comprehends a series of acts and procedures that are carried out in order to attain an objective.

Cortesão intentionally wrote "groupanalytic" as one word to denote the unified, integrated character of the conceptualization he elaborated. His purpose in doing so was to do away with the distance between the words "group" and "analysis". By joining the two words thus to reflect his unique concept, he aimed to highlight the analytic character of groupanalysis.

Now that these preliminary ideas have been introduced, let us consider the definition of the groupanalytic process that Cortesão (1989, p. 31, translated from the Portuguese) proposed:

> The groupanalytic process is the manner in which the various theoretical and technical dimensions—that contribute to giving a framework and form to groupanalytic therapy—are structured, organized, and carry out a function.

Following this, with the aim of clarifying his idea, Cortesão (1989, p. 31, translated from the Portuguese) added that his description was predominantly formulated within a therapeutic perspective, although one should not exclude it from a research perspective.

> In this sense, the groupanalytic process includes the entirety of the psychoanalytic process and presupposes its technical and clinical management in a specific group situation "although different from, but not contradictory to, the dual psychoanalysis situation".

Psychoanalysis and groupanalysis are thus conceptualized and described as research and therapeutic methods with common theoretical bases, but different operational procedures.

The concept of the groupanalytic process seems to have points of contact with the broader concept of the analytic process. However, and as referred to previously, it presents with its own inherent theoretical and technical groupanalytical characteristics.

For Santos and Zaslavsky (2007), the concept of analytic process concerns the set of characteristics that will define what the analytic treatment is per se; it became a universal concept in the literature and one of the main concepts of clinical theory and practice. Santos and Zaslavsky (2007), referring to various other authors that reflected on the analytic process according to Freud's perspective, concluded that Freud characterized it as a process of change of the subject; whether as a process with a certain autonomy within the dyadic analysand and analyst; or even, as consisting of four elements which are free association, resistance, interpretation, and working-through.

For Cortesão (1989) the term process refers to the implicit movement in groupanalysis and to the need to bring awareness to the scientific methods and procedures that are used. According to this author, the term process should be outlined as such, owing nothing to other perspectives and discussions as is the case for example, with the controversies between the theory of the process and meta-psychological theory.

Now that the subject is in place, we will focus on it in greater detail, by taking into account the three pillars of theory, technique, and training mentioned above.

The **theoretical framework**, in its essence, derives from the psychoanalytic theory, and, more specifically, from the fundaments of metapsychology, and object relations theory, although ego psychology and psychology of the self are equally considered.

We shall consider the case of regression, a basic concept of metapsychology, as an example of the specificity it may take on in groupanalysis. Although regression always has a hallmark of individuality, the groupanalytic situation promotes a global regression, which may operate down to very early developmental levels, even though it assumes different depths in each individual.

In the case of object relations theory, it is equally significant, inasmuch as, going beyond the mainly intrapersonal dimension of metapsychology, it enables the establishment of a bridge between the intra and the interpersonal, between the individual and the group.

Of the authors who contributed to building the framework of the theoretical dimensions referred to above, we would like to cast emphasis on Sigmund Freud, Melanie Klein, Bion, Balint, Winnicott, Fairbairn, Guntrip, Kernberg, and Kohut.

More recently, the Portuguese groupanalysts, on the path towards updating knowledge and maintaining the "contemporaneity of scientific information" preconized by Cortesão himself, have incorporated into the theoretical framework of groupanalysis dimensions such as bonding, mentalization, intersubjectivity, and the neurosciences, and the ideas of authors such as Peter Fonagy, Daniel Stern, Jaak Panksepp, Marc Solms, Giacomo Rizzolatti, António Damásio, and Allan Schore, to name a few.

The **groupanalytic technique** is inextricably linked to the dimensions and the concepts which embody it. The elements to consider in groupanalytic technique, discussed elsewhere in this work, are as follows: matrix, pattern, mutable levels of communication and interpretation, transference/countertransference, group transference neurosis, commutative interpretation, and working-through.

Groupanalytic training in Portugal is a comprehensive, lengthy, and rigorous training process, often distinguished from others that are carried out in other group-analytic Societies around the world because of its demanding requirements. It contemplates five components:

- Dual analytic psychotherapy, previous to personal analysis, during a period that can last anything from a few months to one or two years, is undertaken with the groupanalyst with whom, at a later stage, personal groupanalysis will be conducted. This work, besides functioning as a preparation for the entrance into a group, constitutes the experience which will give the candidate the necessary practice so that he or she develops the competence to practise individual analytic psychotherapies.
- Personal groupanalysis with a Training Member, in a mixed group, with a frequency of two to three sessions per week, usually for more than four years. This experience is fundamental in the training process, because it is through this personal process that candidates improve their ability to deal with the different regressive, conflictual, and aggressive situations, with which they will have to deal as groupanalysts; they acquire a more profound knowledge of themselves and gain the ability to make healthier relationships with themselves and with others.

- Training course lasting four academic years and consisting of theoretical and clinical seminars, with weekly two-hour sessions, covering psychoanalytic theory as well as group-analytic/groupanalytic theory and technique.
- Supervision may be individual and/or in group with a Fellow Member. The supervision work unfolds through a relationship where the supervisor, based on the description of the sessions or of fragments of these, offers new perspectives about the patients, as well as about the groups and their analyst, in other words, the supervisees. The supervisor helps the supervisee to identify and clarify the difficulties that the supervisee feels in the comprehension and management of difficult situations, many of which are ingrained in his or her countertransferential features. This work allows the supervisee to become a more experienced and autonomous analyst, in addition to enhancing his or her own identity as an analyst.
- The Eduardo Luís Cortesão Seminars are theoretical and clinical seminars held monthly. Other scientific sessions take place periodically at which communications are presented, which range from research work to personal reflections, and which are considered to have foremost conceptual and scientific expression.

Interchangeable levels of communication and interpretation

Levels of experience

In a groupanalytic group, the interaction is established through experience, communication, and the sharing of emotions, opinions, conflicts, anxieties, and fears. These contents may become the object of verbal exchange, dialogues, suggestions, advice, orientation, logic argumentation, encouragement, and directive therapeutic objectives.

Although all of these means of communication can be presented as a free-floating discussion, they can be systemized into levels of communication, termed "levels of experience" by Cortesão.

Three levels may be considered when characterizing the content which is communicated and the manner in which the communication unfolds.

When one of the elements in the group conveys a concern, anxiety or a conflict, for example, or shares a significant experience or perception, the level addressed is that of the **individual subjective experience**. The group is functioning on this level when the other elements, each one for themselves, share their communications without establishing a relation and interaction between them.

However, if in the sequence of a communication, another or more elements in the group align on the same subject, and communicate their own experiences on the same matter, the group will be functioning on the **multiple subjective experience** level. In this case, each one communicates their own experience, but there is a subject that unites them, and that enables the creation of an interaction between some or all of the group members.

However, if other members comment on that which was communicated, ask questions, attempt to clarify the content, propose suggestions, give advice or offer propositions into the meaning of the communication, then, the group is functioning on the **associative experience** level.

In group psychotherapies (and in the most diverse techniques and orientations), the therapeutic function works its way towards this level.

During the period of time in which communications are being established, it is possible to observe that these three levels of experience are mutable, meaning that the communication may oscillate between one or another of these levels, thus enabling the form and the content of the communication to become accessible to interpretation. The associative experience level is the one that best puts to evidence the groupanalytic process at work and that is very clear in supervision.

Levels of interpretation

Interpretation, according to Cortesão, consists in translating the face value and the manifest content of that which is expressed through ideas, chains of thought, attitudes, and both verbal and non-verbal behaviour into new and more elaborate constructions.

An interpretation may be considered an active interpretation when it translates and proposes more differentiated connotations and meanings than previous ones, and passive interpretation when the subject receives a communication or proposition to which he attributes a meaning that does not alter the previous proposition, or even when he or she does not understand it (but which can be understood at a later date). A particular type of passive interpretation is that which Cortesão termed "spurious interpretation". In this case, the proposition is not understood in its context but will trigger and stimulate affective constellations or prevailing ideas in the receptor, which may become the target for work, through active interpretation, thus leading to an improved insight.

Cortesão conceptualized the following levels of interpretation in the group:

- Genetic-evolutionary Interpretation
- Developmental Interpretation
- Meaning Interpretation
- Creativity Interpretation
- Transference Interpretation
- Commutative Interpretation

An interpretation is a **genetic-evolutionary** one, when its focus accentuates the genesis of the personality and the self. It investigates the structure, the growth, and the function of the self as a whole. It is situated in the territory of causality.

The interpretation is **developmental** when an attempt is made to correlate the different phases of development and the way the self is inter-related with the family and social matrices. An effort is also made to assess the manner in which the self reacts to change, frustration, and conflicts in different life phases. It foments new significations/meanings and new conjectures of creativity.

These two forms of interpretation may coincide and overlap.

The idea of **meaning** interpretation presupposes that the symptoms and the behaviour have a meaning and that these may be interpreted as actions and a means of communication. Here, the interpretation becomes a mechanism used for the quest of new meanings and creative findings.

Even so, Cortesão adopted Rycroft's formulation, according to whom **creativity** consists in the ability to attain innovated but valid solutions for the problems. Groupanalysis does not "generate" creative abilities, as stated by Cortesão; however, when the levels of interpretation expand their horizons, they take on and include new multidimensional perspectives that ensure more expansive therapeutic and research objectives. In this sense, causality, meaning, and creativity are not antagonistic or separated from each other.

The level of **transference** interpretation operates when a member in the group, or more frequently the groupanalyst, may interpret that the latent content, which is expressed in one or more levels of communication, has a more specific meaning (whether in the ideative contents, or in the affects invested in these contents) in the current relational situation, which is experienced, tried out and acted out in the group itself.

The **commutative** interpretation is an interpretation in transference which immediately changes the levels of communication to such an extent that the group members' loose, partial, and isolated communications, are integrated and assimilated, with an increase in insight, which leads to a partial gain by the group of the consciencialization and modification of forms of behaviour, attitudes, metapsychological elaboration, and reformulation of the subject-object relations.

Empathic resonance box

The concept of the empathic resonance box, formulated by César Vieira Dinis (2001), is of enormous significance for groupanalysis, as it is understood and practised in Portugal. Furthermore, its clarity, comprehensibility, and pertinence become evident if we consider it within the specificity of Portuguese groupanalysis, and, more so, due to one of its distinct and specific characteristics: the importance of the individual in the group context.

It is within the group that the groupanalytic process occurs, and it is in the group setting that these significant interpersonal phenomena emerge and are updated, namely triangulations, fraternal rivalry and alliances, as well as maternal and paternal transferences. It is natural that this should be so. After all, we are born, develop and live integrated in multiple groups, and we hold the representation of all of these groups inside of us, which become progressively updated in the groupanalytic process.

Thus, the group is a privileged therapeutic environment. However, the object of analysis is not the group itself, it is the individual. Not each individual isolated, as if various individual analyses were occurring at the same time, but each individual within the interpersonal context which constitutes the group matrix. The meaning of "the individual in the group context" is similar to that which Ortega y Gasset ascribed to it with the term "Man" (Carvalho, 2009): an isolated self does not exist; however, what does exist is the self and its circumstances. It is true that there are many moments in which the group's regressive state is very evident, and in various circumstances, common anguishes and phantasies emerge, but, within the group matrix, the analytical processes developed are as many as the individuals that constitute the group. In this sense, to speak of "group transference neurosis", for example, may only be justified as a reference to the context where the individual transference neuroses emerge and evolve.

Thus, the objective of groupanalysis is the personal analysis of each of the elements in the group, through the resolution of each one's transference neurosis, all of this within the relational context of the group. Therefore, due to the fact that the groupanalytic situation induces a regression in the matrix, at a certain point it becomes evident that each of the elements in the group is functioning at their own regressive level. Foulkes, in 1957, named this phenomenon "resonance": "each of the members of the group will display a distinct tendency to reverberate with any group event, in accordance with the level in which they are functioning" (Foulkes & Anthony, 1957b, p. 152). Taking this circumstance into account, the manner in which interpretations are made becomes relevant for groupanalytic technique (and also for the theory). Interpreting the group as a whole, or elaborating interpretation for each of the members and considering these in the group's context and experience are different procedures and have different technical and therapeutic implications as well.

The analyst's interpretation directed to a member, but taking into account the relational context of the group, will reverberate in a different manner in each one, enabling the emergence of phantasies, representations, and conflicts which were latent, and allowing the realization of how a set situation may affect each one in a particular manner. Furthermore, it allows the correspondence with the desire that each individual has and seeks to satisfy in their relationship with the others, both in their analysis and in their life: being unique, being special, and being recognized in their specificity. According to César Dinis (1994, p. 15, translated from the Portuguese):

> the interpretations directed to other members will help foment each member's rational insight, and overcome the ego's resistances, however, only each member's own interpretations, during the transference and at the exact timing, will promote the acquisition of emotional insight, and the removal of the id's resistances by means of working-through.

It is in this context that the phenomenon that gives body to the concept elaborated by César Dinis arises. The empathic resonance box consists in "the precious empathic amplification that the group offers when the interpretation directed towards someone who accepts it leads to the communion of all the elements in the group concerning the meaning of the suggested hypothesis" (Dinis, 2001, translated from the Portuguese). As we can see, when the group functions as an empathic resonance box, it participates actively in the construction and validation of an interpretation directed to one of the group members. The interpretation of a phenomenon is the attribution of a meaning which is shared by those whom are involved in this phenomenon, the group, which due to its contribution with true analytic work, is profoundly and indissociably implicated in each individual process.

The importance of the group, both as a matrix where the process unfolds, and as a co-constructor of a meaning, is not therefore annulled by the importance of each individual—the "empathic resonance box" allows us to see how it is possible to reconcile them. In conclusion, "strengthening the individuality in a context of plurality will be a major intention of groupanalysis, and compatibilizing 'N' singular interests, at the same time preserving and increasing the group's cohesion, will constitute one of the most fascinating challenges posed to human virtue and to the groupanalyst's technical expertise" (Dinis, 2001, p. 23, translated from the Portuguese).

Inner space of optional doubt and metadramatic communication

João Azevedo e Silva (1971, 1994) is the author of the concept of inner space of optional doubt, which presupposes two attitudes on the part of the group analyst: a general attitude and a specific one.

The general attitude consists of free-floating listening, which is inclusive, non-biased and non-defensive. It is an acceptance of that which is different, unpredictable, and of the unknown. It is also an attitude of reflexive maturity considering the existential phenomena that the groupanalyst reformulates in the therapeutic group.

The specific attitude emphasizes the importance of the countertransferential attitude of systematic doubt regarding knowledge, and involves continuous attention towards countertransference.

In that sense, the concept comprehends the importance of the balance of power within the group, safeguarding the idea that the relational asymmetry by no means justifies any omnipotence or arrogance of the groupanalyst.

The groupanalytic group setting, with its various members, who are seeing and being seen, with the interactive and relational mirror phenomena that it provides with the different representations, opinions, and reflections, offers the permanent confrontation and sharing of uncertainty, which has the potential of transforming the object and self-representations of each member.

Azevedo e Silva (1971, 1994) also conceived the idea of metadramatic communication which features a verbal communication process where someone tries to express their life experiences to someone else that arises from the subconscious (poorly defined dreams, unspeakable anxiety, *saudade* [deep yearning] for primary identifications, etc.), a place where only thing-presentations circulate following the principle of pleasure and logic of the affective chain, connecting them, through a link with the word, where the principle of spoken reality imposes itself, yet without the underlying affections fading.

Concluding remarks

Groupanalysis as it was designed and is practised in Portugal possesses specificities that give its own identity.

Its highly analytic nature, the importance of the individual in the group context and its long and demanding training are the main characteristics that define it.

Eduardo Luís Cortesão used his theory of technique as a starting point from which he formulated his concepts of the groupanalytic process, interchangeable levels of communication, and interpretation. These, in turn, gave rise to his followers developing concepts such as the empathic resonance box, the inner space of optional doubt, and meta dramatic communication, which have been defined and discussed in this chapter.

Chapter 7

Transference and countertransference in the Portuguese school of groupanalysis

César Vieira Dinis and José de Abreu-Afonso

Introduction

This chapter focuses on the peculiarities in the establishment and progress of the individual transference within the groupanalytical context, since the original psychoanalytic concept refers to the dual relationship. Indeed, in groupanalysis, transference, and transference neurosis are developed and solved in a group setting. It is this specific nature that triggers new challenges to analysts and group members. Patients are agents of cross transferences. For the groupanalyst, object of multiple transferences, and not being the only transference object, countertransference also takes on some specificities.

In short, in the groupanalytic process, the individual takes to the group his personal group matrix (Leal, 1968; 1994c) which will be modified throughout the process, by the groupanalytic matrix in its interaction with the groupanalytic pattern (Cortesão, 1989). This matrix-pattern interaction will lead to the transference neuroses resolution of group members and to the individualization of the subjects' selves (Cortesão, 1989; Ferreira, 1989).

The concept of personal group matrix refers to the object and object relations representations' inter-active complex, coined from the individual experience in the original family group, that the individual will tend to reproduce in his or her successive collective experiences throughout life (Leal, 1970) by adding successive complexities to it. It is this personal group matrix, different for everyone and enabled by regression, that is at play in the analytic group and blends dynamically with those of the other members. Thus, the conditions for the establishment of simultaneous N transference neuroses are gathered (Dinis, 1994).

The complexity of transference neurosis in groups

Group therapy, more so than the dual setting, evokes the patient's first group—the original family—and is where transference lies. In the dual setting analysis, several object relations are revived with the analyst, ranging from the relationship with the father or mother, both parents, to sibling, and other significant relations. Analysands fantasize about analysts' lives and relationships including those with other patients.

In the group, the several matrix components serve, for each other, as figures of investment and transference of multiple object relations. Being multilateral, the transference configuration focuses on the group objects: analyst, group members, and group. For each individual such transferences are connected with each other and it is the analyst's job to clarify those links and, eventually, interpret them from a meta-psychological and object relations point of view. The situation of the group elements is different from what it would be in psychoanalysis; transference is divided among—and not diluted by—the members of the group. "For each subject considered in its singularity, the group device allows transference object links constituted diachronically to play in the group synchrony" (Kaës, 2003, p. 46, translated from the Portuguese).

The group setting conveys the understanding of the relationship that individuals establish with their internal objects and the relation between them (Kaës, 2003). The simultaneous transferences towards several individuals unfolds into several transferences, either by displacement of internal objects for different people, decomposing different parts of the ego, and appearing to be independent objects, or by the displacement of internal persons which will appear to be reincarnated. Therefore, there are not only partial objects or people, but also recomposed elements of the family network that can be transferred into the group (Rouchy, 1982).

In these complex dynamics, lateral transference of a group member towards another, or others, is one of the unconscious processes by which one patient replaces someone of his/her childhood with another patient, in the presence of the analyst, transferring not only the chain of interactions, but perhaps also reconstituting lived family scenes. In other situations, there are obvious references to the analyst, often with erotic and aggressive charge (Kutter, 1982; Rutan & Stone, 1993). British and often North American group analysts use the notion of "horizontal transference" referring to the transference of a group member towards another, or others. As Hopper (2006, 2007) clarifies, Foulkes used the spelling (T)ransference and (C)ountertransference with regard to members of the group and the conductor, as distinct from (t)ransference and (c)ountransference, concerning relations among the members of the group.

The group may also transfer as a whole, as well as coexist with the individual transferences, which the groupanalyst must take into account. In our opinion, however, the predominant view of the group as a whole excludes much of the transference materials inherent in the groupanalytic process.

We would like to underscore that the interpretation of lateral transferences acquires major significance concerning the relationship with the analyst. Sometimes this is obvious: fraternal struggles focused on the analyst and triangulation movements in which the analyst is one of the vertices. The analyst is the elective receiving entity of the transference neurosis of everyone in the group, and the transference dynamics agglutinant (Cortesão, 1989). Therefore, because of the instinctual intensity of transference movements, displacement to another member occurs which mitigates the internal conflict and makes its expression easier.

Considering the concept of the personal group matrix (Leal, 1968/1994c; 1970), any member of the group may have, in relation to any other, a transference dimension—transference in a broad sense—different from the transference neurosis, the "artificial neurosis" established in the relationship with the analyst. Thus, the other members are used mainly as displacement objects, allowing the individual to work out their problems without the possible disruptive intensity of parental transference towards the analyst (Dinis, 1994; Rutan & Stone, 1993). Nevertheless, it should be noted that an exclusive focus on the analyst would also be reductive and necessarily devaluates the transference multiplicity mentioned above.

In groups, eye contact is global and always present, imposing external reality. Thus, for example, with a male groupanalyst, it may occur that maternal transferences (conveying intense conflict) are displaced to a female group member, reducing their anxiogenic potential. Clearly, a symmetrical situation happens in respect of paternal transferences in the presence of a female groupanalyst.

During the life of a slow open group, the displays of lateral transferences vary, according to the composition of the group. Moreover, the same participant may play or enact substantially different transference roles depending on the other participants, and also they may change these roles as the therapy progresses (Kadis, Krasner, Winick & Foulkes, 1963).

Zimerman (2003, p. 6, translated from the Portuguese) wrote:

> I believe that what the group loses in the depth of transference neurosis that characterizes the level of depth of many individual analyses, it gains in breadth, because the projective identification game, which is the raw material of the transference-countertransference phenomenon, is much more visible and intense.

Clinical vignette 1

After his divorce, F, a 35-year-old man, sought individual therapy because he had developed an anxious and depressive condition which was having disturbing effects on his professional life and on his parental function as a usually available and dedicated father. After a short dual psychotherapy period face-to-face, which he found very gratifying, he was admitted to a group composed of three women and two other men. He integrated well, and always valued communication and relationship with the other males.

Two years later, by which time F had successfully stabilized his professional and parental functions, the other two males in the group ended their groupanalysis, making F the only man left in the group. Quickly and progressively, his way of being in the group changed. He stopped talking about himself, as if abdicating his space in favour of the women, repeatedly referring with nostalgia to the time he had been alone with the therapist in a face-to-face therapy.

F's mother was described as a pragmatic woman, who exercised great restraint in expressing affection. F's father was experienced as emotionally effusive, but constantly requiring his son attention and company, indicating a role reversal during F's adolescence. His only sibling, a sister, was two years younger than F.

The understanding of the sibling relationship helped to clarify that since an early age, F felt that his sister monopolized all parental attention and care; moreover, he also felt responsible for her whenever their parents were absent, even at the school they both attended.

F's transference neurosis in the group matrix led him to enact his childhood situation. From the moment he became the only male group analysand he felt, once more, that he did not have his own place in the group which, of course, hurt him and caused him resentment, triggering nostalgia for the "only child" situation idealized in the dual relationship experienced with the therapist before joining the group. The working-through of the transference neurosis in the group allowed F to unblock the situation thus reformulating the representation of fraternal object relation by accessing a harmonious and parity relationship with his "sisters" in the group.

The group transference neuroses

In the groupanalytic process, the transference objects and the quality of resistance create different object relations of those in dual psychotherapy, but the transference does not appear because of the group. The group is like a framework for a specific communication mode. We agree with Cortesão (1989) when he says that the group is neither a psychic entity nor a mental apparatus. Thus, the group transference, as well as the group transference neurosis or the group resistances, just refer to their context.

According to the Portuguese school of groupanalysis, we face a triangular structure (individual/group/groupanalyst) which contributes to the working-through of the Oedipus complex. In this structure, the groupanalyst takes a parental representation. This is equally valid for investments in the group. Moreover, the patient in group transference neurosis may identify himself as a mother in relation to a group-child and a father-analyst, or as father to the group-child and a mother-analyst.

However, in the group, in addition to Oedipal repetition, earlier object relationships are also revived, making the group a facilitating and holding environment where, for example, the analyst is invested as a mother figure that can satisfy oral needs as well as relieve anger and destructiveness. This decal of the mother-baby relationship is due to the reproduction of the original object relationship that arises in transference neurosis (Cortesão, 1989). Thus, if patients can experience the analyst as a whole person, a parent, then the transference neurosis develops. The interventions of the analyst, when necessary, help the recognition of the issues at stake; they facilitate the working-through of transference conflicts in which the groupanalyst is experienced as the beloved (or feared and castrating) father or seductive (or rejecting) mother. Throughout the analytical work, transference will change and can be sometimes erotic, sometimes full of aggressiveness (Kutter, 1982).

The transference neurosis of each member is combined with other transference neuroses in a "multidimensional and multifaceted" context. In the group, the patient's transference neurosis is contoured differently than it is in psychoanalysis: "It is different in form and structure, but it differs little in content and function. It is different, but not contradictory" (Cortesão, 1989, p. 228, translated from the Portuguese).

Personal analysis, theoretical training and supervision will provide the groupanalyst with the ability to be empathetically available without getting into an unconscious neurotic relationship with the analysand, nor mingling with him or her. In the group, members may be neurotically involved with each other, but the inputting of the pattern by the analyst enables this relationship to be therapeutically elaborated in the context of group transference neurosis. A difference of the dual psychoanalytic model is that the primitive internalized object relations will return more spontaneously to be re-experienced in the group matrix (Cortesão, 1989).

> The groupanalyst must recognize and dissect the transference neurosis concerning each analysand, isolating, and using it in conjunction with countertransference in order to remove the resistance it represents, chasing the patient 'cure' (Dinis, 1994, p. 11, translated from the Portuguese).

The transference neurosis resolution, by the effort and knowledge involved in working-through, conveys a growing insight, leading to permanent character and behavioural changes (Dinis, 1994).

The groupanalyst will be confronted with several transference neuroses, multilevel regression, differences in object relation models, libidinal investment, and psychic apparatus instances. An interpretation directed to an element will reverberate in a unique way in each of the others, according to their idiosyncratic features (Dinis, 1994). Furthermore, the interpretation can enhance individuality, distinguishing the analysand-groupanalyst relationship in the group, or enhancing the group, emphasizing the group-groupanalyst relationship. Dinis (1994) considers the latter less interesting with regard to the resolution of transference neurosis. He also underlines the difference between making an interpretation for the group as a whole and an interpretation for the whole group, naming each element. He favours the latter because it includes personhood.

The therapeutic contract is previously established by the groupanalyst with each element *per se* and therefore a basic trust and therapeutic alliance will be structured between them *ab initio*. We cannot see how the analyst ethically and deontologically can escape from this commitment and consider the group a holistic entity in which individuality is diluted. The groupanalyst cannot act as a football coach, where the purpose is the collective performance at the expense of individual interests. He or she will, on the contrary, reconcile as many individual interests as there are group members. Matching individual needs with a global function that makes them possible, is indeed his or her delicate and demanding purpose (Dinis, 2005).

Therefore, we understand that whenever someone is selected to join a group, the analyst should be particularly rigorous in his countertransference scrutiny, in order to avoid obvious asymmetries in the empathic relation with the different group members. It is only by doing so that he or she will be able to encourage in each patient the precious sense of belonging, despite the inevitable and necessary conflicts that will arise. The analyst will also expand the group's opportunity to work as an empathic resonance box (Dinis, 2001) when the interpretation directed to one patient receives the contributions of others and its profound meaning is shared not only by the groupanalyst and the person to whom the interpretation is addressed, but also by his or her peers.

Research in cognitive psychology led to the construction of a multisystemic model of memory: the long-term memory is the explicit or declarative memory that allows evocation of the past in terms of a narrative; the other is the implicit or non-declarative memory referring to experiences prior to the acquisition of verbal competences; therefore, they cannot be narrated. In this type of memory, there will be nothing to be explicitly recalled, although it influences, inevitably, subsequent experience and behaviours (Davis, 2001) are enacted in the transference.

As Peter Fonagy (1999, p. 218) stated, "repression removal no longer will be considered as key to therapeutic action. Psychic change ... will occur in implicit memory, causing the person to change the way of living with the self and with others."

The above will lead to a more general and comprehensive approach of the classic concept of transference neurosis.

Daniel Stern et al. (1998) found how baby and mother, in their interaction since the pre-verbal stage of child development, are gradually able to decode each other's emotional expressions. He called this initial communication system "implicit relational knowledge" which means a baby has a pre-verbal ability to anticipate interaction and have expectations regarding the interaction with the caregiver, expressing pleasure, surprise or displeasure, depending on whether these expectations are met or frustrated. This implicit knowledge, registered in non-symbolic form, will continue to operate throughout life. The bigger or smaller overlapping area of the implicit relational knowledge of both partners will constitute the "shared implicit relationship".

We can consider two areas in the interactive process of the therapeutic relationship: one concerning the classical interpretation in, and of, transference, making use of declarative memory, the other belonging to the implicit relational knowledge, and not subject to memory evocation as there has not been repression in the formal sense of the concept. Therefore, it is called non-conscious. "The shared implicit relationship and classical transference relationship are simultaneous and connected. They are complementary processes, but using different changing mechanisms in different experience areas" (Dinis, 2003, p. 33, translated from the Portuguese).

The concept of moment of meeting (Stern et al., 1998) introduced by the Process of Change Study Group of Boston showed how these two dimensions may actually be inextricable. Dinis (2003, p. 33, translated from the Portuguese; 2006) describes the connectedness:

> The moment of meeting implies that each party contributes to its construction with something authentic about himself or herself ... There will be moments of mutual adequacy occurring in the field of the shared implicit relationship and leading to changes in implicit relational knowledge. It may, sometimes, be mediated by an interpretation, but more than that has to happen. It is not enough to say the right thing; one needs to say what needs to be said. In an analytic group, the other members of the group may also participate in the construction of these privileged moments, by reason of their own authenticity or by genuinely echoing them, thereby increasing the shared intimacy.
> These are the legitimate moments when we would use the term empathic resonance box [...] we would say that they [...] 'are moments of multiple empathic adaptation'.

In the meantime, countertransference is complex and is related to various forms of group members' transference as well as to several collective phenomena such as the group-as-a-whole, its subgroups and counter-groups. Ormont (1970, 1991, cited in Hopper, 2006) suggests that group analysts should be observant of group members as possible assistants in the resolution of pathological countertransference (in the sense of it being derived from the analyst's pathology). Likewise, they should use normal countertransference (in the sense of it being caused by the patient's condition) in the resolution or working-through of the group resistances.

Therefore, we should consider this supervisory function of the group as a unique, very interesting aspect, since it promotes the ongoing research of transference-countertransference interaction in group settings

(Abreu-Afonso, 2010; Dinis, 2000a). The following is an account of a countertransference situation that happened to one of us as an example.

Clinical vignette 2

Analysand A defended himself against the groupanalyst's attempt to analyze his narcissistic deficit, making increasingly grandiose defences. In the session, the groupanalyst X felt increasing difficulty and discomfort in the countertransference. Realizing that he was possessed by intense irritation, he decided to refrain from intervening, trying to be aware of the cause of his distress. The session continued until another member of the group, B, said to A: "You would never have chosen Y (which both patients had known professionally) for your groupanalyst". It happened that Y had been X's groupanalyst too. Then, everything became clear for the groupanalyst X: the circumstances of this group made him review a painful event of his own analysis when he intensely felt misunderstood by his analyst trying to analyze his narcissism. The awareness of the disturbing countertransference allowed the Analyst X to restore his empathy towards Analysand A. The way this happened was only possible because they were in a group setting.

Groupanalysis and analytic group psychotherapy

Another issue concerning the subject of this chapter is the difference of transference management in analytic group psychotherapy and in groupanalysis. However, this important topic has been neglected.

The approach to (neurotic, narcissistic, psychotic) transference not only distinguishes psychoanalysis from psychoanalytic psychotherapy, but it also differentiates groupanalysis from analytic group psychotherapy.

In analytic group psychotherapy the therapist, only by exception, interprets the transference neurosis, although whenever it seems appropriate, he or she may suggest a possible link between the present and the past, thus reaching the genetic-evolutionary level of interpretation.

Group-analytic psychotherapy has less ambitious goals, being directed to faster, although less profound, results. That is the reason why it is usually shorter (but not less than one or two years) and with less frequent sessions (weekly or fortnightly). Its main purpose is to eliminate or mitigate disturbances experienced by the patient as ego-dystonic and to promote self-knowledge, aiming at some adaptive changes in personality and behaviour.

Groupanalysis as practised by members of SPGPAG has a frequency of two or three sessions per week, usually for a period of four or five years. The procedure that fundamentally distinguishes it from the analytic group psychotherapy is the establishment, interpretation, and possible resolution of the transference neurosis. As for its goals, it intends to overcome the level of relief or symptomatic remission, aiming to structural and long lasting changes in the character and personality.

Quoting Neto and Centeno (2006):

> Comparing the processes, [...] what seems to differentiate them is that the transforming capacity in Groupanalysis mainly occurs due to the analysis of the transferences and resistances of each member in the group. Whereas in Analytic Group Psychotherapy, the analysis is mainly focused on the mirror phenomena, on the interaction and relation between the group members and of each of them with the objects in their actual lives. In analytic group psychotherapy, ego training in action is, in fact, the factor with the greatest therapeutic capacity ....

Group-analytic psychotherapy works at a level where the patient experiences affections related to his childhood conflicts and the analyst seeks to elucidate the nature of his or her attitudes. The transference neurosis with its level of regression is not desirable because its resolution requires a different setting. Therefore, the therapist limits and controls the transference, focusing on the more conscious level, related to the here-and-now material, and does not stimulate patients' regression, especially with the most fragile or rigid personalities. His or her attitude is generally softer and more gratifying, more active than in groupanalysis. Anxiety is maintained at tolerable levels. Consequently, this form of intervention allows us to work with a broader range of pathology. The patients' personal characteristics are, however, very important in determining their therapeutic evolution. In fact, some of them in psychotherapy have a progress close to the one of an analysis, while others in a formal groupanalysis, due to structural constraints, may eventually develop a more psychotherapeutic path.

The transference and other therapeutic factors in the group-analytic treatment

As we have stated throughout this chapter, we believe that in groupanalysis, work on transference and with countertransference is vital. We support Cortesão's (1989) view of the process in terms of pattern, matrix, changing levels of experience, communication, and interpretation. We agree with the psychoanalytic essence of groupanalysis. However, we also find, as already noted, that some patients seem to benefit more from group dynamics themselves, the sense of belonging and the ego training in action, than from the intense experience of transference with the analyst in the group setting. Nevertheless, we believe that the group-analytic potential is still fulfilled, fostering significant changes in members' lives and those of the people with whom they have significant relationships. Communication and interaction within the group will undoubtedly enable the development and modification of the psychic apparatus structures, promoting the improvement and adaptation of the individual to reality. From our point of view, groupanalysis offers several levels of treatment determined by specific patients' features, although the groupanalyst pattern must be consistent.

Despite the high level of regression that can be achieved, we know that the group holding potential allows intervention with weaker structures, traditionally excluded from the psychoanalytic treatment. But this openness inevitably means that the traditional path "clinical neurosis/transference neurosis/resolution of the transference neurosis" is not easily achieved by all. It is precisely in these circumstances that the interaction in the group matrix, fertilized by the analyst pattern, can be valuable for the possible analysis within the patient's own constraints.

Others, though, follow a track similar to the classic sequence: clinical neurosis/transference neurosis—elucidation of infantile neurosis/resolution of the transference neurosis. This will be the most desirable way that drives to major and long lasting changes in personality structure.

As we have stated, the groupanalyst role is very demanding, much like that of a caregiver with a large number of offspring: continued attention and intervention at the appropriate time combined with the ability to create space for all participants to express themselves freely, are essential prerequisites for any groupanalyst, even if under stress (Abreu-Afonso, 2010).

In our opinion, a groupanalyst runs the risk of making countertransference mistakes because of the exuberance of projective identification phenomena brought into play. We also believe that in this context, the variety of relational objects available and the fact that all meet face-to-face, offering themselves to reciprocal observation (physiognomic expression, body language, etc.) are factors that favour the appearance of pathological projective identification phenomena, even in neurotic structures. The groupanalyst will therefore have the opportunity to detect these phenomena in the group members' interaction. Above all, groupanalysts will choose not to intervene and anticipate that sooner or later they will appear in the transference relationship of one or another analysand with the analyst. They should, thus, be well prepared for it whenever this happens, which will avoid them falling into the trap of unconscious manipulation of the interactive part of projective identification. This will be one more argument in favour of self-requirement of a very rigorous and ongoing countertransference scrutiny that the group analysts have to confront (Dinis, 1994).

It is time to clarify that the way we understand and operationalize the countertransference resembles what Louise de Urturbey (1994, cited in Dinis, 2000a) states in her comprehensive work on the subject of "The theory of countertransference as part of the analytic space". We will briefly say that this theory highlights the inseparability of transference and countertransference. Both can only be understood in interaction being a cohesive and irreproducible binomial in its uniqueness, contributing to a final solution (Dinis, 2000a). Obviously, as in the parent-child relationship, the asymmetry of the responsibility of the parties is immense when it comes to a final result. Therefore groupanalysts can never decline or even lighten their caregiver responsibility.

It is very rewarding to review groupanalytic sessions where the analytical engagement of the group members takes place and contributes to a further step in the development of all participants, including the groupanalyst.

Chapter 8

Group analysis and group-analytic psychotherapy as favoured settings to deal with conflicts and difficult feelings

Isaura Manso Neto and Ana Bivar

Introduction

Eduardo Luís Cortesão left his followers a huge theoretical and practical legacy. He looked at the past concepts and theories with new perspectives by recent authors coming from psychoanalysis, group analysis, and other areas of science. He also applied psychoanalysis and groupanalysis to further understand and treat severe mental illnesses.

This chapter is the result of several identifications with Cortesão (as a groupanalyst, as a physician, and as a human being) and of our own perspective, giving us a new and thrilling way to be, understand, and interact in a group setting. Some of us worked in psychiatric units having implemented psychoanalytic and groupanalytic frameworks in their therapeutic and training programmes (Neto, 2010b; Neto & Dinis, 1994; Neto, Fialho, Godinho & Centeno 2010a, b).

Small therapeutic groups are settings where members should feel safe enough to be able to share every kind of ideas and feelings, whether positive or negative: love, desire, anger, guilt, envy, jealousy, and vengeful wishes. Most of these experiences are felt as difficult to be expressed, as may anticipate conflicts evoking fears of retaliation, shame and guilt, even though they are ubiquitous within humanity.

Clinical vignette I

Claire, a 25-year-woman, with a personality disorder, was admitted to a psychiatric unit after she made a violent suicide attempt when she discovered that her boyfriend and her best friend were sexually involved. Claire felt betrayed and humiliated.

Only after being in group therapy three times per week for ten months, was she able to express all her anger towards her boyfriend. The group enabled her to talk about the humiliation and shame for her vengeful wishes: she truly wanted to kill her boyfriend and her friend, but did it to herself instead. During her teenage years, she used to cut herself badly, especially after having arguments with her parents. These arguments were always more violent with her mother. Claire used to deny anger. It was common hearing Claire tell other group members that they shouldn't be so angry, especially with their parents.

Only months after being in group, she was able to talk about the rage and anger that she felt when her mother accused her of being "a bad daughter and a selfish little girl". The group was empathic with her complaints and for the first time Claire felt sufficiently secure to express herself truthfully: "I used to be so angry with my mother that sometimes I imagined myself hurting her (she starts to cry), the way she hurt me."

Reacting to the betrayal by her boyfriend and best friend by attempting to drown herself was the consequence of feelings of not being good enough for them, similar to what she felt regarding her mother.

This case belonged to a psychiatric unit with a groupanalytic framework implemented in 1977 by four psychiatrists and groupanalysts: João França de Sousa, César Vieira Dinis, Isaura Manso Neto, and Sara Ferro (Neto, Fialho, Godinho & Centeno 2010a, b). The group-analytic framework continues to be used in this psychiatric unit to this day. This vignette reflects how the failure of the primary object caregiver in understanding and responding to primary narcissistic needs paves the way to injuries that do not preserve the integrity of the core self, leading to shame, jealousy, anger, aggression, and vengeful wishes, which, in turn, lead to shame and guilt. The group worked as an empathic resonance box (Dinis, 2001) making it possible for the authenticity of the self to be supported and understood by the empathy of the other members of the group.

Aggressive feelings and positive affects regarding love, pride, sexuality, and gratitude, may be difficult to mentalize and verbalize, although they are part of life's engine. Seeking (expectancy), fear (anxiety), rage (anger), lust (sexual excitement), care (nurturance), panic/grief (sadness), and play (social joy) (Panksepp & Biven, 2012) are basic affective systems that suffer change, being strongly influenced by interpersonal relations. The mind-brain/brain-mind equivalence is a strong conviction for many researchers, such as Damásio (2010), Panksepp and Biven (2012) and Cozolino (2014, p. 278):

> Early interpersonal trauma in the form of emotional and physical abuse, sexual abuse, and neglect, shape the structure and functioning of the brain in ways that negatively affects all stages of social, emotional, and intellectual development.

Therefore, even positive effects may be felt as conflictual and painful. We assume that this information is correlated with the ways chosen by certain authors to talk about basic human affects and emotions, being more or less adequate. Bion referred to these as L+-, H+-, and K+-.

Angela Molnos (1986) makes an interesting differentiation: "anger that destroys and anger that heals", and the most important difference between them is the displaced target of the aggression; destructive anger is towards a displaced target. The same was said by Aristotle (4th century BC in Panksepp & Biven, 2012, p. 145):

> Anybody can become angry, that is easy; but to be angry with the right person, and to the right degree, and at the right time, and for the right purpose, and in the right way, that is not within everybody's power, that is not easy.

Concerning shame and guilt, Cozolino (2014, p. 282) suggests that we must distinguish between adequate forms of both, and inadequate ones:

> Appropriate shame and guilt emerge slowly during childhood along with an understanding of others' expectations, an ability to judge one's behaviours, and the cortical control required to inhibit impulses.

By contrast (Cozolino, 2014, p. 282):

> Core shame develops earlier in childhood as a function of overwhelmingly negative attachment experiences [...]. Children and adults with core shame come to experience themselves as fundamentally defective, worthless, and unlovable: the polar opposite of self-esteem.

Phil Mollon (2002, p. xi) wrote a very interesting book. He writes:

> Shame and jealousy are both hidden turmoil that pervade human life, exerting their secret terror and control from within.

He states that they may have adaptive functions or, conversely, become destructive forces. They are both interrelated with sexuality. "Shame and fear of shame are amongst the most powerful of human aversive experiences [...]" (Mollon, 2002, pp. 19–20). Furthermore, "the cure for shame is the empathy provided by an other" (p. 142).

Both shame and jealousy are connected with rage and guilt.

Miriam Berger (2013) writes that modern societies have a tendency to ignore and suppress the right to vengeful wishes. She argues that there is a pattern, or culture, of forgiveness, and there is an attempt to eradicate all aggressiveness. From her perspective, this leads to more aggressiveness and sometimes to brutal conflicts. Modern societies could be considered as "guardians" of the culture of unconditional forgiveness, supporting their belief on the need to see only the positive side of the aggressor. Vengeful wishes (Berger, 2013), p. 73) are a reflex of one's disrupted internal relational matrices; reciprocity, recognition, and mutual respect are absent:

> Victims might thus feel twice discredited: once because of what has been done to them, and once again for having the "wrong" feelings about it. "Thus, forgiveness, reconciliation, and acceptance are the prescribed states of mind that accord social approval and legitimacy" (Lansky, 2001, 2005 cited by Berger, 2013, p.73); vengefulness, along with other ways of protesting one's lot, is proscribed.

We agree with Miriam Berger in Berger (2013)

> All those feelings should appear in any kind of psychotherapy, either dyadic or group, otherwise the psychotherapeutic processes may remain incomplete. If there is an adequate groupanalytic pattern, those feelings can be worked through and overcome, that is to say, groupanalysts should be at ease in themselves with dealing with those situations. This is one the reasons why the Portuguese Society of Groupanalysis and Analytic Group Psychotherapy has sustained deep analysis of their members' personalities.

Nevertheless, we have noticed that some analysts have difficulties with patient's complaints about reality, about their families as well, about their analysts, and analytical processes. That is to say, the abovementioned feelings—mostly aggressive feelings, are too often interpreted as resistances.

Phenomenology and meaning

Conflicts, destructivity, anger, and aggression

Anger can have multiple origins, but the most common are irritations and frustrations. They develop from events that restrict freedom or from very frustrating life events. Of utmost importance is childhood maltreatment or neglect, which can engender anger that lasts a lifetime (Panksepp & Biven, 2012).

Hostility and conflicts may be clearly expressed or dissimulated, in a verbal or non-verbal manner. They can be expressed by anger, rage, violent words, and behaviour with strong emotions, or hidden by powerful defence mechanisms: rationalization, reaction-formation, splitting, and denial. Conflicts can be intrapsychic, interpersonal or transpersonal, conscious or unconscious, and they usually cause some kind of frustration and anger, whether real or mainly of a transference nature (Neto & David, 2017).

Dealing with conflicts and difficult feelings 141

The phenomenology of destructivity, i.e., the ways it appears in small psychotherapeutic groups and in group-analytic groups may be summarized as follows:

1. Hostile attitudes (verbalizations, mimicking, and behaviours) towards the group as a whole or towards any of its members including the group analyst, being recognized as aggressive, subjectively and objectively. These are easily diagnosed.
2. Inadequate and hostile attitudes objectively recognized by most of the members of the group but denied subjectively by the aggressive communicator.
3. Lengthy and uncomfortable silences.
4. A worsening of symptoms.
5. New symptoms.
6. Absences or repeatedly arriving late.
7. Delays in payments.
8. Negative Therapeutic Reactions (NTR).
9. Drop-outs.
10. Actings-out.
11. Scapegoating.
12. Long lasting idealization of the groupanalyst.
13. Erotic Transference.

All these phenomena should be understood within the transference-countertransference interactive process.

1 and 2—The first two—**hostile behaviours and attitudes**—are easily identifiable as aggressive phenomena unlike the rest. They are correlated with misunderstandings which are mainly consequences of distorted mirroring. Aggression and conflicts may also be felt as the only way leading to separation and autonomy. It is easier to separate while one is angry than in a loving and grateful mood.

3—**Silences that are too long and uncomfortable**: most often, they indicate that something is being unspoken; to speak about it may cause conflicts, raising fears of retaliation, shame or guilt. Occasionally, to be silent is a way of being absent.

4 and 5—**Worsening symptoms and new symptoms** are more difficult to understand and interpret: unconscious processes are definitely more active. Groupanalysts should think that something is happening that cannot be mentalized and communicated in a more overt way. We should also consider that we might be facing an NTR.

6—**Absences or repeatedly arriving late** may be omnipotent and efficacious ways of stopping time and evolution. To be absent from the analytic space may be felt as a safe way to avoid thinking and feeling. Sometimes it may also be a way to conceal rage, avoiding fears of an anticipated retaliation from the groupanalyst or the group members. Additionally, we learned from our groups and patients that absences may have other meanings: the repetition-compulsion of past abandonments searching for better answers and solutions as well as ways to confirm one's existence and belonging. Patients who have patterns of non-secure attachments, having suffered huge experiences of abandonment and rejection, usually confirm this hypothesis and progressively overcome this resistance, as long as it is interpreted this way. These patients feel that they are useless to others. From a countertransferential point of view, absences may be felt as threatening to the groupanalyst, raising abandonment fears and anxieties.

7—**Delays in payment** are usually strong resistances defended by powerful reasoning based on reality that are difficult for the groupanalyst to approach. Many times groupanalysts are not sufficiently at ease with their own aggressiveness, becoming guilty, and/or ashamed whenever this issue—which may be a relational symptom—is raised.

8—We should bear in mind that we might be facing an **NTR (negative therapeutic reaction)** whenever a patient suddenly and unexpectedly begins to feel worse. Synthetically, we understand this psychopathologic situation as resulting from the Fairbairn's moral defence concept (Neto, 2001): patients feel worse, devaluating their psychotherapeutic relationship, in spite of it being experienced as much better than the previous and current object relations with their primary caregivers or parents; patients feel that they are empathically recognized and understood by foreigners (the group members, including the groupanalyst), as opposed to what had occurred within their families, submerged in a conflictual situation that conveys more anger against their parents, paving the way to frightening reactions and guilt. The solution seems to be to get worse again or even to abandon the psychotherapy in order to avoid these difficult feelings.

9—**Drop-outs** may be resulting from an NTR as mentioned above but there are many other situations that might be at the root of this kind of symptomatology. We often find their roots in transference and countertransference frustrations and anxieties (Neto, 2003). Dropping out of therapy seems to be the only exit to the patients. Drop-outs are usually felt as narcissistic menaces by the therapist, which may lead to irritation and guilt.

10—**Actings-out** are difficult to identify and analyze as they are also conflictual situations for any psychotherapist. As groupanalysts, we should think of them whenever we feel in our countertransference that there are too much splitting in the behaviour of a member outside the group setting, contrasting with too much silence and passivity inside the group matrix.

11—We believe that **scapegoating** is one of the major risks in group psychotherapy/groupanalysis. Our approach to scapegoating is illustrated in Clinical Vignette 6. We must think of it whenever we are facing a conflictual situation between one member of the group and all the others. The isolated member is perhaps saying something that the others do not want to feel or think about. Of course, there are usually certain character features of the scapegoated member that facilitate these kinds of situations.

12—**Long lasting idealization of the groupanalyst** may be a primary narcissistic need of the patients, demanding time as well as continuous attention of the groupanalyst to slight signals of de-idealization, which must be identified and recognized. This issue is usually a sign of avoidance of conflicts within the group, including the groupanalyst; conflicts and anger must occur in any human relationship, including psychotherapies; if these aspects are systematically denied, the analytic process and the personality development may be blocked, performing a destructive psychopathological situation. Another risk is that idealization of the therapist may be also a narcissistic need of the therapist, in this case pathological, paving the way to severe wounds in the group-analytic process with deleterious consequences in the patient's development.

13—**Erotic transference**. We will approach this issue later as one of the most difficult situations in any kind of therapy, including group-analytic psychotherapy/groupanalysis. It is a way of blocking the group-analytic process.

As in any of the above-mentioned psychopathologic destructive features, groupanalysts should be at ease with their own narcissism, aggressiveness, and sexuality, being able to identify those features stimulating their verbalization through the open free-floating discussion.

Clinical vignette 2

A man, member of a groupanalytic group, said that he had to leave. There was a painful reaction from others. It was a precocious interruption, as he had been in the group for four years and was feeling much better. He said he had no more problems to overcome. He preferred to spend his money travelling. Some years later, he asked for help again but did not want a group setting. The groupanalyst tried to understand his resistance. Joking, he said that it was not tolerable to dream and deal with the sexual attraction towards the female members of the group anymore.

Actually, he didn't talk about his phantasies in the group because of shameful feelings.

Leffert (2013) highlights the guilty and shameful feelings analysts have been suffering through the psychoanalytic ideology. Is love a curative factor in a psychotherapeutic relationship? Does love belong just to the transference and countertransference relationship, or are such feelings real in therapies? How much love should an analytic process have? Neuroscience has contributed more and more to the idea that the "presence of loving feelings are [sic] required for the therapy to be maximally effective" (Leffert, 2013, p. 110). Nevertheless, psychoanalytic education went in the opposite direction, producing guilty and shameful feelings.

We would like to remind the reader of the nature of the parent-children relationships as a paradigm of therapeutic love. Human beings should love their children, being conscious of their psychological and physical charm, intelligence, as well as negative traits. Therefore, love should dominate in functional families. Of course, incest does exist, but we may consider it as a relational symptom. Good enough parents may notice and be proud of their children's success as women or men, as objects of desire. Do healthy parents feel desire towards their children? We don't think so. We all know that incest and other forms of power abuse, including infanticide, do exist, but we must leave this issue in order to avoid writing one chapter inside another. We think that this topic should be much more developed in writing, over and above being discussed as a topic at scientific events, where we have found ourselves fighting our own fears, shame, and guilt.

Conflicts, Destructivity, and Aggression

Self psychology considers the angry patient as a person with a narcissistic injury. From the Kleinian perspective, envy is not understood as a consequence of narcissistic injury but rather as arising from instinctual drives. Stone (2009) considers that envy may be inhibited, displaced, and transformed, sometimes into idealization or it could be focused as malignant envy with one destroying the other. This can only be surpassed if envy is empathically understood.

Mollon (2002, p. xi) writes:

> Shame is where we fail. And the most fundamental failure is the failure to connect with other human beings—originally, the mother. Jealousy lies in our perception, that there is another (originally the oedipal other, or a sibling) who might succeed in connecting where we have failed.

Mollon (2002, p. 50) continues in a similar vein:

> There could be complicated spirals of interaction between shame and guilt as shame leads to rage and aggression—the wish to do actively to others what was suffered passively (vengeful wishes)—which leads to guilt, to a retreat to passivity and shame again, and so on.

We may synthesize thus: empathic failure of the primary objects towards the primary narcissistic needs lead to shame, which may develop in two main directions: admiration, or envy and jealousy. The last two pave the way to feelings of rage and desires for revenge, which lead to guilt. The passive and silent repression of these feelings closes the vicious circle with shame. All these feelings and mechanisms may be more or less conscious, belonging to the dynamic of sibling relations (Wellendorf, 2014) which may be very clear in groups.

Concerning vengefulness, we agree with Berger (2014) who thinks that one of the central curative elements that group therapy provides is the very arena it creates for the act of "telling in" including the "telling on them", namely the vengeful, punitive act of naming offenders in public (the group therapy), being part of a culture of reciprocity. Thus, the understanding of vengeful wishes as coded information about ruptures in the self becomes an essential constituent in a transformative process towards nonviolence.

Triggers

We think that conflicts and difficult feelings may be caused and triggered by several factors: group features, individual and relational psychopathology, transference and countertransference. All these factors interact within the groupanalytic matrix. In order to be clearer, we will separate them; most of the time, however, they cannot be disentwined from one another.

Paradoxical group features

It is difficult to ask for therapeutic help in a group. Usually it feels easier when in psychotherapy in a dyadic setting. Nitsun (1996) wrote about the reasons that might cause such difficulties, which are very frequent upon joining a group and when a person has a fragile personality, triggering drop-outs. These may also justify the difficulty of some group analysts to suggest group analysis as an adequate therapeutic setting to treat their patients. Groupanalysts could be afraid of their patients' drop-outs. The author refers "10 obvious characteristics of psychotherapy groups that may contain hidden paradoxical elements which may worry participants" (Nitsun, 1996, p. 48), making the initial phases of their group-analytic processes difficult. We also believe that these features are partially responsible for some of the resistance young group analysts have when forming groups to treat individuals. However, these characteristics in themselves also contain curative factors. Groups are more prone to evoke fears of past suffering as they may quickly enact the family's imago and conflicts; the group analyst is idealized but not the other members; free-floating discussion is perceived as much more dangerous than free association as we cannot control others' free associations; therefore, there is always an unavoidable element of surprise; suspicion about breach of confidentiality, fears of retaliation and shame whenever free expression of conflicts and all those difficult feelings occur; plurality and diversity may be felt as threats at the beginning.

We would say again that the group is a continuous de-idealization setting, much more than a dyadic setting. Uniqueness does not exist; there is always another; we need to share time and availability of the caregivers, and challenge the confusion between time and availability. The conflict between groupality and individuality is always present in a therapeutic groupanalytic group, and it appears in its deepest meaning: the conflict between autonomy and symbiosis.

To overcome those difficult situations, Portuguese groupanalysts and group therapists keep their patients in a dual setting for some time to strengthen the therapeutic alliance before they join a group. They also add another important factor: frequency. Sessions held two or three times per week are considered by SPGPAG to be one of the main contributing factors to overcoming difficulties and working through conflicts, thereby reducing the drop-out rate.

Finally, we would like to highlight that in well-selected, structured groups, those paradoxical group features are important ways to achieve change, leading to what we can call "cures", overcoming the inherent difficulties when they become conscious, and are even overtly discussed, understood, and interpreted. Thus, they can become accelerative curative factors.

Individual and relational psychopathology

We contemplate individual psychopathology as the symptoms and conflicts strictly related to oneself, and think of relational psychopathology as a disturbed relational pattern, based on the prevalence of projections, projective identification, splitting, and denial. We are thinking of misunderstandings, distorted and malignant mirroring, and ego-syntonic pathogenic character traits.

Each member's personal group matrix (Leal, 1997) will interact with the group's dynamic matrix through transference (Neto, 2014). Thus, we think that the group setting is a stage where all those representations will be enacted, becoming available to be worked through. Therefore, the group setting is an excellent one to observe and distinguish normal and pathological communication, whether verbal or non-verbal, coherent or chaotic. Acts of communication (that are more or less pathological) could lead to misunderstandings (that if not worked through could lead to intense suffering). Zimerman (2000) defined psychoanalysis as the science that studies misunderstandings. Their analysis will lead to their being understood and eventually achieving healthier forms of connecting with oneself and others.

Clinical vignette 3

TATIANA: "I wasn't here when you said that Rudolf ..." looking around.
Rudolf didn't answer her. The other members insisted that Rudolf told them about his experiences again.
Rudolf addressed Tatiana, ironically but vaguely irritated: "Do you actually want to know about it?" Tatiana: "Not anymore!!"
RUDOLF: "Okay, you will never know about it! In fact, you never cared about it!"
GA (GROUPANALYST) ADDRESSING THE GROUP: "What do you think it is going on here?"

There was a short silence, felt in the transference as uncomfortable, and anticipating a possible conflict.

GA: "Tatiana, were you really not interested in knowing what had happened to Rudolf? Do you agree with Rudolf's last comment?"

TATIANA: "No; if I weren't interested in it, I wouldn't have asked!"

RUDOLF: "But you didn't ask me directly!!"

TATIANA: "Yes, I did, and you didn't answer!!"

RUDOLF: "You asked them! Not me! So, you were not that interested."

GA: "Rudolf, would you consider another possibility to understand Tatiana's reaction?"

RUDOLF: "No, I wouldn't. I need to feel that people are really interested in me!!"

GA: "And what does Tatiana need?"

TATIANA: very tense, with tears in her eyes. "I don't know ..." (whispering).

GA: Tatiana was the most recent member of the group, with very low self-esteem; the groupanalyst decided to help her stimulate her own mentalization by suggesting an interpretation to her difficulty in addressing Rudolf directly: "Tatiana, were you afraid that he wouldn't answer you?"

TATIANA: "I am always afraid that people won't care about what I say!"

GA: "It seems rather clear what's going on in your lives all the time. Rudolf, you have some difficulties in noticing what you trigger in others; you usually need others to communicate exuberantly and explicitly with you before you believe that they are paying attention to you. Tatiana, you have always been afraid that people don't like you, don't care; so you are not clear enough about what you feel and think. This way, both of you end up confirming your beliefs from childhood."

Both of them told the group that they had never noticed these relational patterns before.

There are several kinds of misunderstandings from the mildest ones like the previous example, to more severe instances which we can include in the category of malignant mirroring phenomena.

All interactions and relationships established in an analytic group include more or less realistic mirror phenomena. Mirroring may become extremely distorted because of transference and primitive defence mechanisms, leading to destructivity. The concept we are referring to is the one that Zinkin (1983) called malignant mirroring. Malignant mirroring is very frequent among human beings, and is responsible for multiple destructive behaviours in many circumstances and it can be a frequent trigger of anger in groups. Every time we need to get rid of parts of ourselves, or parts of our internal objects, we may use splitting and projective identification. Sometimes these situations are not easily identifiable which contributes to the difficulty in managing, interpreting and working through them. That is part of what we call the "pathogenic character traits in action".

Distorted and malignant mirroring and ego-syntonic pathogenic character traits may be thought as relational psychopathology; they may be clearly observed in groups thus eventually worked through, paving the way to stop the vicious cycles of intergenerational and transgenerational psychopathology. Psychological inheritance (Badaracco, 1986) may thus be prevented (Neto, 2014).

Clinical vignette 4

Tina had been in a group that met three times per week for approximately nine months after having had psychotherapy in a dual setting on a weekly basis for four months.

The relationship with her three adolescent children was a very unpleasant and tense one characterized by silences, firm opposition, passive-aggressiveness, and occasionally there were moments of explicit verbal and physical violence.

Part of the therapeutic work was focused on the development of empathy using the stimulation of mentalization about what she could imagine concerning her children's reasons to behave in such ways.

The groupanalyst asked the group and her, in particular, about their phantasies about Tina's children's feelings towards her. Several possibilities came up after the classical "I don't know": Tina's sadness as well as orders, rules, and preaching constantly imposed. Tina commented that she had done to her children precisely what had been done to her (identification with the aggressor). The group asked her many times why she was imposing so many rules on her children. Tina insisted that it was a matter of discipline, and they must help her do some domestic tasks.

The groupanalyst asked her once she felt that her daughters were helping her or if she preferred to do those tasks herself.

Tina: "I definitely prefer to do them myself! It's much more difficult to have them around me!" The other members of the group remarked that bringing up comes out mainly from identification.

In fact, punishment, preaching, and guilty telling-off had progressively been replaced by caresses and compliments.

About nine months later she said that her children had changed, approaching her in a friendly way, and had started to help her spontaneously.

Even though it is difficult to make these processes conscious, during our years of clinical practice, we have come across several examples that prove that patients will accept hard truths as long as they are said with affection.

Transference

Conflicts in groups are mainly of a transference nature. Transference phenomena are rooted in past primitive object relationships, and may be triggered by several causes, more or less determined either by the reality of each member and/or by the group as a whole.

We consider that most conflicts are related with the groupanalyst, either expressed in a direct way or displaced towards other members of the group. The other becomes the deposit of the rejected negative parts of oneself. The other loses their independence and individuality, becoming the enemy to be destroyed or from whom one must run away. In case of idealization, the "other" becomes the saviour.

Cortesão (1989) spoke of the hostile transference as a resistance mainly based on envy of the power of the analyst or of any other envied member of the group. We would like to add that power can be viewed from many perspectives: the groupanalyst is the one who chooses the group's members, decides about rules, holidays, and other interruptions, as well as the one who deals with each member and the group, understanding or not, being empathic or not, protecting or not, having the power to love and destroy. This could lead to frustration and several rage reactions.

Among these transference phenomena, we highlight the sibling dynamics that have not been conceptualized enough by psychoanalysts and by groupanalysts. A therapeutic group setting is a favoured setting for the enactment of sibling dynamics in its four main dimensions: "1—siblings have a definite influence on self-development; 2—siblings are inherently rivalrous; 3—utility of having a sibling; 4—the analytic endeavour is useful for understanding sibling phenomenology" (Kahn, 2014, p. 41).

Sibling rivalry has been included in the Oedipus complex. Some groupanalysts in SPGPAG have written on this theme (Salgado & Pinto, 2000). Sibling Rivalry is deeply dependent on the way parents deal with the group of their children as well as with the ubiquitous need of the human baby to be the one uniquely and unconditionally loved by the primary caregivers. Ashuach (2012) maintains that siblings could be considered as self-objects of one another thus reflecting their inner world. According to this author, that is another reason why sibling relations could be complex and filled with conflicts, since they appear quickly and clearly in groups. "The groupanalyst may be felt consciously or unconsciously—as treating one or several group members 'better' than the member who feels jealous" (Neto & Dinis, 2010). This kind of conflict may be felt in a vivid way just with the analyst or totally displaced towards the other members.

Clinical vignette 5

Barbara, a 30-year old woman, in group therapy for five years, twice a week, felt angry with her groupanalyst, after the groupanalyst pointed out that unlike Barbara, most of group members had difficulty in being spontaneous. Some members started talking about their own experiences and what they associate with that difficulty.

For Barbara, that comment felt like an exclusion and not as a compliment. Barbara immediately asked: "and what about me?"

The groupanalyst told her that she didn't have that difficulty; for her it was easy to be spontaneous. Horacio, surprised by her reaction, asked her why she was feeling excluded. Barbara replied: "I'm ashamed, I feel like a little girl, but I think it's the feeling of being put aside. I've always felt that my brother was my mother's favourite. I've always felt excluded from that love [...] I felt exactly the same here today!"

When a new element joins a group, situations of this kind might be triggered, which could enhance the levels of anger and aggressiveness based mainly on jealousy and envy. These are painful situations that can be analyzed and overcome with healthy consequences in other areas of one's family (husbands, wives, and children) and professional life. This way, chronic dysfunctional relational patterns may be stopped or restructured.

Countertransference

Countertransference may obviously be a source of conflicts, aggressiveness, or other difficult feelings in a group-analytic setting. Adherents to the Portuguese school of groupanalysis believe that a "good enough groupanalyst" should be at ease with conflicts, anger, and all the above difficult situations that may occur in a group. Blind spots should be reduced to a minimum. Stone (2009) states that the ability of a group to talk and discuss difficult issues like envy or aggressiveness and the possibility of interpreting them depend on how conscious and at ease a groupanalyst is of his or her own similar feelings. SPG's followers consider that the way groups are conducted, particularly the groupanalyst's own consciousness of his or her contribution to the emotional climate in the group, definitely influence the capacity of the group to mentalize and transform anger and aggression. Groupanalysts must detect their own contribution in the triggering of conflicts and aggression within a therapeutic group, should they be more or less due to transference. Delays, holidays, conferences, and many other situations may provoke frustration and rage among the group. They are the usual triggers of aggressive communication and behaviour and may also be a form of acting in by the therapists.

Attentive of the particular psychopathology of each member, groupanalysts must be aware of their countertransference when communicating pragmatic situations to the group which may contribute to the aggressive phenomena, namely the possibility of not having been empathic enough towards aggressive reactions as well the possibility of amplifying peer jealousy, which is a major risk in group analysis.

Moreover, countertransference is also important in the way the groupanalyst deals with the conflicts or other difficult feelings that arise in the group due to transference. Gans (2010) highlights the importance of the leadership in dealing with hostility: "Hostility in group psychotherapy is inevitable and potentially constructive; its understanding and management are crucial to successful group leadership". A groupanalyst able to deal with conflicts will not force anyone to forgive, or be tolerant and kind. We should promote free discussion and thinking about the present and the past. Complaints about the here-and-now as well as the there-and-then should not be avoided. Otherwise, countertransference may become a kind of poisonous influence avoiding the development of the group members' selves. If for some reason a groupanalyst avoids verbalization of aggressive feelings towards the primitive object relations, aggression may be introverted, be transformed into psychosomatic symptoms, or displaced towards current objects, paving the way to intergenerational and eventually transgenerational aggression.

Dealing with difficult situations in therapeutic groupanalysis

To begin with, we must identify difficult situations is therapeutic groupanalysis. Most of the time, this is not a simple job. It implies the risk of de-idealization of the patient as well as of the group analyst, amplifying rage, leading to fears of breaking the relationship, paving the way to separation and rejection anxieties.

Whenever faced with a difficult situation, the groupanalyst must think about its several causes, including the auto-analysis of his or her countertransference. Only after that, will one be able to name the aggressive communication, highlight it and begin any possible interpretation activity. It may be difficult to find an empathic and creative way to point out the aggressive communication. Sometimes, it takes a long time between the process of diagnosis, naming it, highlighting it, and beginning the interpretation activity.

We believe that the most difficult situations to be handled are those which raise countertransference uneasiness; groupanalysts are touched in some of their main internal conflicts or blind spots. Those situations may also provoke fears of hurting their patients evoking in them previous experience of humiliation, thereby repeating the traumatic past. Another difficulty comes from the fact that these situations are defended by strong rationalizations based on objective reality.

We would like to mention some of the most difficult situations we have faced in groupanalysis: envy, erotic transference, malignant mirroring as well as the de-idealization of the groupanalyst, frequent absences, chronic delays, and difficulties in payment.

Erotic transference towards the groupanalyst, either directly or displaced to other members, with other members, is extremely difficult to overcome. In order to be able to stress these situations bringing them for discussion in the group, groupanalysts should be at ease with their own sexuality. Moreover, the rule of asepsis must be introduced very clearly and all group members (including the groupanalyst) must understand its aim, taking care to avoid the mere imposition of the rule, which could be felt as being in an autocratic relationship.

Rules are important to protect the group-analytic process and not for the sake of according power to the groupanalyst.

In our experience, envy is the most difficult feeling to deal with within a group. It leads to drop-outs very often, even when we try to be empathic and careful. Patients that usually react with envy to try to avoid mentalization. They feel ashamed and afraid as it uncovers narcissistic vulnerabilities that provoke intense suffering. Therefore, they react with rather more aggressiveness. The mentalization of envy is the first step to overcoming this feature of narcissistic psychopathology. Just afterwards we may reach and understand the roots of the narcissistic wounds and overcome this invasive personality feature that is so disturbing in all areas of life.

Clinical vignette 6

Wyona is a 30-year old woman, who began individual psychotherapy after a psychotic episode and pursued therapy once a week for five years.

Her psychotherapist suggested she follow treatment in a groupanalytic setting three times per week; her groupanalyst thought that the group setting could be a useful tool to analyze her aggressiveness particularly denied and displaced towards her husband and children. Her therapist was persistently idealized.

She became very angry when another member of the group made an important scientific work, acknowledging with special thanks to every member of the group, mentioning each of them by their first names in the acknowledgement. She justified her anger saying that confidentiality had been broken. The others reacted with astonishment, replying that she wasn't right because there had not been any violation; their names were very common names and the group had not been mentioned. The groupanalyst was also surprised by her reaction, trying to listen to what the group was saying, and to her own feelings about this sudden reaction. The groupanalyst kept silent while evaluating what was going on. It could be a scapegoating phenomenon. The group members became angry with Wyona, who was being stubborn in her reaction. Wyona became more and more furious. The groupanalyst told her that what she was feeling towards her colleagues (the other members) could be a displacement of the jealousy and envy she had felt towards her sister and mother all her life. She had always had an enormous difficulty in being contradicted. Her mother had repeatedly humiliated Wyona. She came from a poor, humble family and studied mainly because of pressure from her teacher and the community priest. She achieved a high position in her profession. Her mother compelled her to be grateful to God, to make promises she would have to keep if she met with success as a student. Effectively, this meant that her skills were not recognized at all. God performed "miracles", and therefore, she must be grateful.

Wyona idealized her mother as well as her groupanalyst and religion. She was incapable of admitting that sometimes she wasn't right. She felt all criticism as humiliations, attacks on her narcissism. She was very authoritarian towards her husband and daughters, systematically denying the rationale of others. She was a survivor in a very dysfunctional family.

Once the groupanalyst had pointed out Wyona's displaced jealousy and envy, it was possible to talk and discuss her intolerance facing others' reasons and differences of opinion. It was the first time it was possible to identify this personality feature, and for it to be observable so that it could be mentalized and analyzed. Some insight developed, and it was possible to be angry with her groupanalyst without fearing humiliation.

Malignant mirroring is built upon powerful projections and projective identifications; as mentioned above, after identifying it silently, we are used to highlighting the situation which we identified. Normally, we say that it seems that something that we don't fully understand is occurring; we ask the group what they all think about what is happening. We ask the member who is being aggressive what kind of past life events were similar to what is happening at that precise moment. Sometimes the groupanalyst must be very active while trying to achieve the reminding of the repressed memories. This way, the "enemy" becomes correctly identified. The current enemy becomes progressively recognized as different from the past objects and the transference nature of the frustrating situation becomes clear enough so that it can be worked through. It gradually becomes possible to internalize the elements projected, and overcome the conflict and the aggressive behaviour.

Although jealousy and de-idealization may be causes of intense rage, they are easier to deal with as they are more prone to be accepted and mentalized, within the concept of group discussion, thereby suggesting that interpretation could induce change.

Chronic absences, delays, and difficulties in payment are dissimulated forms of aggressive communication and very difficult to transform. Those behavioural symptoms are organized in a very rational way. External reality colludes with inner resistances. We normally do not discuss the patients' lives or demands. We avoid promoting intellectual and concrete discussion of the problems that, although deserving empathy may hide unconscious resistances or unspoken conflicts with the groupanalyst and previous expectations regarding the analytic process, not to mention ancient patterns of relationship that lie behind psychopathology and character traits. We are interested in finding the unconscious forces that could lead to those symptoms. We commonly consider it important to ask the group to speak about what they feel about others' absences and delays. For example, chronic delays may be interpreted as a way to avoid waiting for responses from the current objects, which are felt as the primary object(s) that had always been too late to meet the patient needs.

We think it is important to mention by name those who are absent in any group session. Many times we have noticed that absences diminish after we systematically nominate the absent patient(s) suggesting the interpretation that they may feel useless to the group.

These behavioural symptoms are more frequent in group settings than in individual ones. What we have experienced is that often these forms of communication are reduced when members who communicate this way become emotionally convinced that they were missed by the others. The most important thing is that the groupanalyst and the group do not give up trying to understand hidden unconscious reasons.

Concluding remarks

- The conflicts and difficult feelings (shame, envy, jealous, vengeful wishes) we have been discussing can be either natural and healthy reactions—based on the reality principle preserving life, or destructive and unrealistic reactions. They should therefore appear in any relationship, whether therapeutic or not.
- The group setting is a much more effective facilitator of the appearance of these phenomena than the individual setting. They will appear spontaneously and reactively to triggers that are more or less of a transference nature.
- They must be neither avoided nor denied. They must be understood in order to be transformed, deprived of the displaced transference mechanisms into more realistic and creative attitudes towards oneself and others. Empathy is the key to approach them.
- We must point out and name the difficult and/or destructive phenomena in the group as soon as they become explicit.
- In terms of causality, they are mainly of a transference-countertransference nature.
- Groupanalysts should understand the several meanings of these phenomena in the context of the group's evolution, each member's mental organization and life history, transference and countertransference. Having ensured that, they may interpret.
- Groupanalysts should stimulate associative communication about the memories that might be responsible for the repetition compulsion of the traumatic past in the here-and-now of the group.
- The working-through of destructive and aggressive phenomena are fundamental to achieve insight and self-differentiation which are the bases of personality changes which pave the way to autonomy, freedom, and reciprocity with others. This way, intergenerational destructivity (relational psychopathology), which contributes to lessening or even stopping transgenerational transmission of psychopathology, can be reduced.

Chapter 9

The groupanalyst as a patient and related training issues

Margarida França and Isaura Manso Neto

Why talk about training?

The very important topic of training is probably not pursued enough in the literature on group analysis. Most of the articles published in *Group Analysis—International Journal of Group-Analytic Psychotherapy* in the last 20 years concern block training, training in other cultures, non-therapeutic applications of group analysis, and supervision. Only a few approach the way group-analytic training is conducted within group-analytic societies and institutes. It seems group analysts in general feel ambivalent when connecting problems they observe in training with the current moment we live in analytical societies, i.e., the crisis psychoanalysis and groupanalysis have been suffering for the last two decades. We will try to relate these two aspects.

While comparing the SPGPAG training programme with others from abroad, including those of EGATIN members, we have noticed that despite the premise of tripartite training, many differences exist, and we believe that our attempt to stress the most important ones and their hypothetical motivations might be of interest. Therefore, we will approach the way groupanalytic training has developed in Portugal over the years and we will discuss the advantages and disadvantages of our programme according to our conception of groupanalysis.

Crisis in analytic societies?

Some years ago Neto and Centeno (2005) approached the theme "crisis" pointing out the decrease in the number of candidates training in analytic societies. They made reference to Garza-Guerrero's (2002a) article about the crisis in psychoanalysis and his statement that the crisis arises from within analytic societies because of the organizational and relational issues behind training programmes. Garzza-Guerrero pointed what he calls "compulsory treatment" referring to the personal analysis one must complete to become an analyst and Neto and Centeno (2005, p. 7) elaborated further on this matter:

the promiscuity and lack of asepsis, since the same analysts are simultaneously evaluators, interviewers, and supervisors, in addition to the fact that they attend the same congresses, and the same places as their analysands.

Some authors align themselves with the view of Thomae (1991) quoted by Robert Marten (1999, p. 209):

> Everything points to the fact that the present crisis in which psychoanalysis finds itself is an indirect consequence of a training system which over the last 40 years has been prolonging the training analysis more and more, and given it a central position in the training process.

In 2008, three colleagues conducted a survey among the Portuguese members of the Portuguese Society of Groupanalysis (Carvalho, Galamba & Neto, 2008) which explored a set of questions about training and the groupanalyst's identity. The aim was to find hypothetical causes for observable facts such as: fewer candidates undergoing training over the last 20 years and fewer groupanalysts conducting groups—although groups are one of the strategies the Portuguese national health services use to deal with current economic and social demands. The survey results led them to question whether these facts are related to a lack of conviction amongst groupanalysts about the efficacy of groupanalysis as a psychological treatment procedure. They produced a comprehensive questionnaire with over 60 questions covering themes ranging from the personal groupanalysis to supervision and the theoretical training programme. Their conclusions were presented at the 2008 EGATIN Study Day in Oslo. They point out the importance of the results of their personal group-analytic experience. Most of the answers indicated that is the most valued part of groupanalytic training. We think this suggests that, at least within the Portuguese Groupanalytic Society, the root of the challenges facing groupanalytic training does not seem to be the central position of the personal analysis in the training process.

Another author, Douglas Kirsner (2000), quite distant from groupanalytic societies, has written about American psychoanalytic associations. He states that analytic societies collude with the current state of affairs as they take refuge in themselves by constituting what he terms "ecclesiastical societies" with a group of "blessed" people (the training analysts) dictating their destiny (Kirsner, 2000).

Lorentzen (2010) addressing the problems group analysis faces, is reluctant to see it only as a victim of external circumstances and he thinks that it is of the utmost importance to discuss what the essentials of group analysis really are, otherwise group analysts may be perceived as preferring a marginalized position, not having to deal with their own idealizations and narcissistic fears. Neto and Centeno (2005) are of the same opinion saying how crucial it is to clarify concepts in order to avoid preconceptions which will ultimately arrive at a general lack of faith in analytic treatment.

The word treatment is here on purpose as we at SPGPAG believe that "treatment" is an issue when we discuss what we do and what our goal is. We will address this theme as it is one of the aspects we perceive as splitting group-analytic societies and obviously interfering with the design of each training programme.

We have been watching a wide spread of group analysis mainly through what we are calling group analysis' applications, from the organizational environment to learning settings and areas of social concern such as people affected by epidemics or natural disasters. We see this perspective as a search for the wider applications of group analysis. Nevertheless, we see group analysis mainly as a psychological treatment option. In the face of the difficulties analytic therapies are confronted with, should therapeutic groupanalysis persist in aiming for an "analytic cure"? If so, what must we focus on in order to achieve this objective?

We believe that unless we look carefully at the most important tool of the therapeutic process—i.e., the groupanalyst—we will fail to maintain the therapeutic essence of group analysis.

Programme structure: theory, personal groupanalysis, and supervision

The Portuguese Society of Groupanalysis took its first steps as the Groupanalytic Section of the Portuguese Society of Neurology and Psychiatry in 1960 (Pinto & Salgado, 2001). The original Constitution had the following as its first three objects: "a) the study of psychoanalytic theory and its application to groups; b) the study and research of groupanalytic theory and technique; c) the holding of scientific meetings, courses, conferences, and seminars to provide information and training for the advancement of individual and collective entities interested in the technical, theoretical and practical issues related to groupanalysis and group psychology" (Articles 3a) to c) of the Constitution of the Sociedade Portuguesa de Grupanálise e Psicoterapia Analítica de Grupo dated 31 March 1960).

The only amendment to these three primary objectives when compared to the recently approved and current version dated 30 April 2012 (available online at <https://grupanalise.pt/wp-content/uploads/2015/07/ESTATUTOS-SPGPAG.pdf>), is that article 3a) became article 3b) and vice versa. This serves to illustrate that in spite of almost 60 years' work, groupanalysis in Portugal deeply relates psychoanalytic theory to the way groupanalysis has grown.

The psychoanalytical influence is visible in the three areas of the tripartite training: in the personal groupanalysis as the most valued and lengthiest part of it; in the first two years of the theoretical course which are dedicated almost exclusively to psychoanalytic theory; and in the discussion about the supervision model each candidate should undertake.

We will discuss these three issues separately.

Nevertheless, we would like to stress that Portuguese groupanalysts tend to endure this training from six to 11 years (Carvalho, Galamba & Neto, 2008) and many times it does not end with a trainee running his/her own group of groupanalysis. This is also a subject of our concern and we consider that it might be related, at least, to the following aspects: the length of the whole process; the fact that the theoretical programme and supervision may be held separately in time and the consequences that follow; the high cost, both financially and in terms of time consumed, of being in a therapeutic groupanalytic group for a several years in succession, as these groups are only taking place in private practice and with no prior commitment of involvement with the SPG; and, finally, with the sometimes mysterious ways of transferential and counter-transferential processes that occur among all those involved.

Regarding this last issue, Nitzgen (1999, pp. 235–236) illustrates, in his article entitled "From demand to desire: what do we offer when we offer group-analytic training?" the influence and implication of transference (and, we would add, countertransference), in the process of training:

> However, the 'tendency to compliance and conformity cannot be ascribed to repression alone. [...] submission to the ruling, conscious and unconscious, opinions and value systems of training institutions is also based on transference reactions, leading to excessive idealization and (self-) induced dependency of candidates on training institutes and their representatives.

The author preconizes the increase of large groups within each training institute/group-analytic society as a way to ensure that the dilemma between the transference as "the libidinal motor force of the training process" (Nitzgen, 1999, p. 236) and the necessary democratization of analytic institutions may be solved/diminished. We tend to agree with his opinion.

We will return to these considerations later, when explaining some features of the personal analysis and supervision in the Portuguese Society of Groupanalysis and Analytic Group Psychotherapy. For now, we will continue describing the model of training employed by the SPGPAG.

Discussing the theoretical programme

Theoretical training takes four years, comprising a total of 432 hours. Candidates are accepted to the programme after presenting a letter of intentions, their *curriculum vitae*, being in personal groupanalysis for at least one year and being interviewed and approved by six training analysts, none of which may be their analyst or their supervisor. A large number of senior colleagues are responsible for lecturing the seminars and there is an annual evaluation focusing on assiduity, oral presentations and participation during seminars as well as one written paper per seminar.

The clinical written work candidates have to present to a jury about conducting a group at least a twice a week for two years is the final test that determines whether one should be accepted as a full member of the society. Another possible path to qualification is to gain access to affiliated member status, for which one must conduct a psychotherapeutic group once a week, for at least two years and present a clinical paper about it. The theoretical training programme and the final clinical written work are the parts of the training in which the SPGPAG has direct intervention, and consequently offers itself as a transferential object to the candidates. Usually this part of the training occurs simultaneously with the personal groupanalysis. In those cases when this does not occur, we suspect that the candidates have a difficult task: that of confronting themselves with perhaps a de-idealization of the institution, without the proper setting to elaborate on these emotions.

It is possible that the large number of interviews in this initial phase, the subjectivity of the evaluators, and the absence of defined criteria to take these interviews into consideration are pushing potential candidates away. The SPG's Constitution has undergone some amendment aimed at shortening the procedures and the time taken to become a full member of the society and achieving the title of groupanalyst.

Psychoanalytically influenced—justifications and controversy

As Cortesão stated (1989, p. 36, translated from the Portuguese):

> The groupanalytic process [...] includes comprehensively the whole of psychoanalytic theory and therefore the technical and clinical procedures—from the metapsychological formulations to the details of the object relations—in a specific group situation. Different from, but not contradictory to, the dual psychoanalysis situation.

This statement is still relevant today when we look at the first two years of the theoretical training programme. The first year deals with the works of Freud and the foundation of the psychoanalytic method with the emphasis on the birth of "the talking cure" that allows access to the unconscious.

The "discovery" of the unconscious and the way it manifests are very important: the programme follows Freud's pathway with the dreams interpretations and the myriad of other unconscious manifestations.

This is still the "golden" aim of groupanalysis as practised in Portugal: the access to the unconscious, as it is the cradle of conflicts, narcissistic flaws, impaired identities, and so on. This differs from the Foulkesian perspective of the unconscious in group analysis (Nitzgen, 1999). From Cortesão's perspective, and also that of his followers', the aim is to reveal the unconscious in the metapsychological sense, and not the group's unconscious deriving from the group's free-floating discussion.

The Freudian conception of the Oedipus complex as the basis of neurotic states is studied from an historical point of view. The texts in which Freud anticipates the importance of the object are studied in a critical and actualized perspective, resorting to contemporary authors with Bionian influences such as Carlos Amaral Dias (2005).

Only after the fundamentals of Freudian psychoanalytic theory are sufficiently assimilated are the other main authors lectured: Klein, Fairbairn, Guntrip, Balint, Winnicott, Kohut, Kernberg, Mahler or Racker mostly from the Kleinian and ORT perspective and Kohuts's self psychology are some examples. Recently, authors from the developmental (Bowlby, Stern, Fonagy) and neuropsychoanalytic (Panksepp, Damásio, Solms) perspectives have been introduced. This is the second year.

Foulkes and group-analytic technique are studied in the third year. Cortesão and the contribution of contemporary authors, mostly Portuguese, are addressed thereafter and there is a series of seminars in the third year that are lectured by training analysts—we are given to believe—as a way to ensure the depth of the discussion on the controversy surrounding Cortesão's groupanalysis and Foulkes group analysis and their followers.

The French perspective of group therapy is not included in the programme and is merely touched upon by some of the teachers. This is probably related to the fact that Portuguese authors generally disagree with the idea of a group mental apparatus and the concept of the group-as-a-whole (Dinis, 2002). Latin American authors have been recently included in the programme: Badaracco with multifamily psychoanalysis, that Isaura Neto and colleagues adapted in a Day Hospital creating multifamily groupanalysis (Neto, 2017); Waldemar Fernandes with his perspectives on groups conducted from a Bionian perspective; he has been invited several times to lecture seminars in Lisbon or via Skype. The language factor obviously facilitated this interchange: Brazilians speak Portuguese and therefore we have easier access to authors from South America. David Zimerman has been another strong influence in both our theoretical and clinical conceptions.

The fourth-year seminars are about groupanalytic technique. These are not lectured in a classical teaching-learning relationship: they are mostly practical seminars with clinical presentations and role playing methodology. As all the trainees have quite an extensive experience of being in a therapeutic group at this stage of the training programme, their personal experience is always present in the seminars dynamics and may be integrated with the theory and the technique that are under discussion. This will be crucial in developing what Cortesão termed the pattern and in helping each trainee to acknowledge their own.

Year-round course

Another important aspect of the theoretical programme is that it runs throughout the year. This is feasible because Portugal is relatively small and groupanalysis has evolved mostly in Lisbon. We accept that this cannot happen everywhere and that the need to develop groupanalysis in other countries or in a large country necessitates other methods. Nevertheless, we feel that our ability to hold seminars every week enables trainees to contact each other and work together in the interim, consolidates knowledge, and, for the most part, it facilitates the reflexive task and integration of theory with the clinical and relational experiences occurring during this extended period.

Block training, even if it is only theoretical, creates a focus that may also be productive, albeit less 'organic' in the sense that it may be more rational than experiential (Hilpert, 1995). This also has to do with the importance of the pattern in Cortesão's conceptualization and the idea of the authenticity of the analyst. In our view, the theory and what Bion so fortunately called the psychoanalytic function of the personality must be 'lived' otherwise the secure base of a relationship cannot happen in therapy, since the analyst as a whole person may be absent, substituted by, perhaps, a great scholar with very well studied and opportunely applied theories and techniques, but without the real relation that we believe induces the transformation and the analytic cure. In other words, the time should matter when training an analyst whose main tool is his or her personality and the capacity to be empathic in an authentic way.

The importance of supervision

In Portugal, supervision is faced as a learning-teaching relationship that occurs when a less experienced therapist presents clinical material to a more experienced one (Ferro, 2011). We can also say that it has an affective-cognitive nature and that it resembles the analytic situation, although remains different because it must not induce regression (Neto, 2000). Among its objectives is creating the opportunity for the supervisee to comprehend the essence of the therapeutic process as it is understood by the supervisor and therefore recreate it in the current psychotherapeutic framework of his or her own group (Moro, 2007). It should be noted that in this process, many conscious and unconscious phenomena arise from the supervisor, from the supervisee and from their intersubjective relation, likely the "analytic third" Ogden mentions (Ogden, 1994).

From the supervisees:

a   The supervisees' own groupanalytic process and their comparison with their therapist, confronting their own analysis with the one they are initiating in a different position.

b   Their own selection of patients which is both consciously and unconsciously predetermined.
c   The way they will be able to disclose their own emotions and overall counter-transference.
d   Their confidence in their own theoretical knowledge.
e   Their more or less worked through narcissistic needs and blind spots that may be overcome in their personal groupanalysis.

From the supervisor:

a   The supervisor's countertransference with the supervisee's group and with the supervisee and the supervision group as a whole.
b   Their affects regarding their own training process and their relation to the organization they represent.
c   Their relationship with power and leadership.
d   Their relationship with the supervisee's groupanalyst.

From the intersubjective area created between supervisor and supervisee and the rest of the supervision group:

a   The way everyone faces competition, rivalry, envy, admiration, and gratitude, i.e., how thoroughly character traits were approached and worked through in their own analysis.

Although this division may seem artificial as all of these items are related, we believe that it helps us to explore our points of view.

The three main areas of training are not independent. We find difficult to consider that someone should obtain success in leading a group and presenting in supervision, being understood and supported by colleagues and supervisor, if they haven't really gone through a recognition of their own psychic functioning, their main defence mechanisms and their self-object identifications. Probably this person will spend supervision time measuring words; they will have many problems writing down *verbatim* sessions; they will have difficulty acknowledging their possibly aggressive or unsupportive feelings towards some group members; and ultimately they will not understand other supervisees' perspectives about their patients, maintaining their rigidity towards them, leading finally to drop-outs or groups where everyone is hiding conflicts and where everyone is arduously trying to leave the "bad ones" outside.

Difficult or uncomfortable feelings such as aggressiveness, sexual desire, envy, jealousy, and shame, are required to be observed in a groupanalytic group (see Chapter 8); their systematic absence in an analyst's sessions report may point to the therapist resistance to acknowledge them. Verbatim session reports are clearer and more truthful than indirect narratives and avoid the perhaps painful process of confrontation with the analyst's belief about what went on in that particular session.

As already mentioned, in order for an analyst to really understand their psychic functioning, de-idealization of their own groupanalyst is mandatory. This has to do with the process of becoming a leader of a group instead of a group member that Moro (2007, p. 182) describes:

> When a trainee begins supervision, his/her group that he/she leads is no longer just the imagination that he/she has in his/her experience group; rather that group truly exists. These two important groups (being a group member and being a group leader) acquire a transfer link in the minds of trainees.

Moro (2007. p. 182) asserts that the trainee should

> [...] adhere to 'technical' group leadership to begin listening to what the members of the group convey rather than thinking about what to say during supervision.

We believe that this is much more "lived" than "learned". The groupanalyst still sits in a group as a member and not as its leader (supervision group); although this group is not an analytical group and its task is to use analytical tools to achieve a broader comprehension of the mental processes present in the relationship between the groupanalyst and his group and of the members of that group and their different matrices. Nevertheless, in a supervision group, transferential and countertransferential processes also occur and may have to be acknowledged and verbalized, not with a primary therapeutic purpose, but with the aim of achieving a better understanding of the group that isn't there physically and of maintaining the supervision group focused and cohesive over the task. This view brings supervision groups to a pivotal point between their path through personal groupanalysis and their path as a groupanalyst.

Moreover, supervisors should find an empathic way to communicate the mistakes/inadequate interventions noticed in the supervision; they ought to suggest that the supervisees speak about those issues in their personal groupanalysis so that those issues may be better worked through and eventually overcome. If the supervisee has already finished their personal groupanalysis, the supervisors ought to suggest a more reflexive attitude towards the issue noticed as a kind of blind spot. Teaching and explaining clearly what is being thought and understood are learning tools belonging in our opinion to the ongoing feature of any analytic process.

Group supervision

Preferring group supervision to individual supervision, in our opinion, tends to protect everyone (groupanalyst, group, and supervisor) from unconscious collusions that subvert the purpose of supervision. This has to do with Bion's work regarding different vertices and two concepts already discussed in Chapter 6: the group as a space of optional doubt (Silva, 1994) and as an empathic resonance box (Dinis, 2001). When embracing an analytic task, although not with a therapeutic objective, each of us mobilize defences originated by our blind spots and narcissistic features. The group may easily detect and reflect these events without losing its containment capacity, allowing each of the members to work through each of their representations and mostly, the groupanalytic process, matrix, and pattern that are being analyzed.

Frequency and duration

Frequency and duration are two important issues to look at. Frequency is obviously an advantage in supervision: as the groupanalyst conducts their group, they maintain this safe net that supervision performs and gain progressive confidence in their own skills as a groupanalyst. Nevertheless, both supervisor and supervisee must evolve from a more dependent situation to a symmetric relationship.

The long duration that supervision takes might, in our opinion, be slightly inflated. Candidates have to maintain supervision for at least six years or until they deliver the written work that allows advancement to full member status. Candidates must have two different supervisors, not concurrently but consecutively throughout the training path. Recently, some changes are being studied to reformulate these requirements and adapt them to the demands of modern society. For some years now, supervisors have not had to be training analysts.

Another component in supervision is the opportunity for candidates to evaluate their supervisors and vice versa. It is clear for us that supervisors should assume the responsibility to efficiently and formally evaluate the groupanalysts. This seems to be difficult, at least in Portugal. This might be because supervision is not "institutional", although mandatory: supervisors welcome candidates into their homes or offices and perform supervision without direct interference of the institute/society. There are obvious advantages and disadvantages in this procedure.

Moreover, the narcissism of the supervisor or even the groupanalyst may be at stake if a candidate should fail or at least be under-evaluated. This may create unconscious collusions that prevent authentic evaluations from taking place.

The pyramidal character typical of psychoanalytic (and group-analytic, as far as we can see) associations is maintained because of the persistence of poor democratic processes. Everyone, including training analysts and supervisors, involved in an analytic society may—off the record—speak about the incorrect or even unethical behaviour of colleagues. But rarely are such things deemed official; merely speaking about an issue without concrete action achieves nothing. How much better would it be to start off with the basics, and promote and support ways for candidates to evaluate supervisors?

The group analyst as a patient

The analyst's mental health—is this an issue?

We believe that it is widely accepted that one's mental health is the most important tool to becoming an analytic psychotherapist. Our own unconscious is always "on demand" in every relationship, and that is obvious in the psychotherapeutic relationship. Therefore, the use we make of it may be extremely helpful in creating empathy, providing a holding environment to support anxiety or interpreting primitive object relations failures, for example; as it is potentially disastrous if colluding with patients' maniac defences, supporting sadistic character traits, or sustaining pathological dependent analytic relations. This course cannot be left to chance and the analyst tries to be capable at all times (and not only in supervision) of perceiving their counter-transference. If we consider that groupanalysis has the advantage over dyadic psychoanalytic settings of easily revealing narcissistic character traits and rigid defence mechanisms and that it is the best setting to understand and elaborate any unconscious pathological collusions between analyst and patient, then we may defend that it is the most suitable setting to train groupanalysts. Such a setting does not carry the danger of leaving untouched narcissistic clusters that would probably be acted out while working with groups in groupanalysis and that supervision might not be capable of dealing with.

Training in mixed groups

Other training programmes accept that the trainee's analysis is mostly undertaken in a dual setting, with a complementary experience in group; some accept the experience in a group featuring only trainees or even the frequency of very short-term experiential groups such as small groups at congresses; the other's personal group analysis is taken in blocks, perhaps four times per year, with a huge number of sessions in one week, alternating with a theoretical programme, and so on. Some of these alternatives imply that the groups are composed of trainees, with very similar professional backgrounds and objectives, besides the relation with the institute which has accepted them.

Hilpert (1995) writes an article that is very critical about block training in the Heidelberg Institute of Group Analysis. His major conclusion is that personal group therapy taken in blocks, under the strong interference of the institute, leads to transferential phenomena that give rise to significant difficulties for the analysts, thereby compromising an authentic emotional process occurring in the group. In reference to block training, he states: "I have the impression that little attention has been given to the position of the group conductor in this form of training" (Hilpert, 1995). Besides this observation and its consequences, our attention is drawn to other issues such as the fact that the training occurs among candidates only and that there has not been a previous alliance with the therapist. Therapists do not choose the candidates; neither do they know anything about them, all of which has implications in the analyst's counter-transference. The other criticism noted in this article (Hilpert, 1995, p. 306) is a deeper one regarding how analytic institutes and candidates in general perceive their personal analysis: there seems to be a split between resorting to psychotherapy for training purposes and doing so as a means to seek to comprehend their own mental suffering.

> In group-analytic and psychoanalytic training, however, one must always presuppose that the desire for training is accompanied by, or arise[s] from, psychotherapeutic needs. It cannot be a matter of training versus therapy, as though they were mutually exclusive. There can be no learning and training in groupanalysis without the subjective experience of an emotional process as a member of a group (Hilpert, 1995, p. 306).

We think that these experiences are valuable and, as stated earlier, sometimes the only chance groupanalysis has to evolve in some larger countries. Nevertheless, this type of training is not sufficient if there are personality clusters that not only need to be acknowledged, but also need to change. From the Portuguese point of view, only the working-through of these traits will build capacities in the future groupanalyst. We see the candidate who has the potential to become a groupanalyst as someone who begins analysis with curiosity about their psychic processes, but who may also be dealing with ego syntonic or dystonic symptomatology and dysfunctional object relations just as much as any other human being; and therefore, needs to go deep in their mind and retrieve the tools to deal with their mental/relational suffering prior to beginning to treat others. This acceptance of one's humanity is, as we see it, a prerequisite to becoming a good therapist.

The need to train in groups of trainees may hide the need to deviate from the confrontation with the candidate's own symptoms or simple difficulties, which would obviously be flagrant in a mixed group, where other patients would participate because they are seeking a "cure" and not undergoing training. Rationalization among future colleagues can be a tempting resource.

The frequency and length of the groupanalyst's analysis

Frequency and length are two distinct aspects, but they come together if we consider time as an important variable of the analytic process. We cannot talk about the importance of time in a rigid way, merely forgetting real demands in people's lives, making training absolutely unbearable. Nevertheless, time is crucial for transference to set, be analyzed and solved. Time is also very important if we face groupanalysis (as any analytically based psychotherapy) from a corrective emotional experience point of view (Christian, Safran & Muran, 2012). Relational phenomena highly unconsciously motivated take time to be understood, become conscious and be worked through. This justifies the frequency—at least twice a week—and length—usually from 4 to 11 years—that personal groupanalysis lasts.

Nowadays, economic and professional demands tend to inhibit people from accessing groupanalysis. The need to try new technologies such as video conferencing in a group-analytic setting must not be considered as out of the question as long as the groupanalyst is not absent and that this is the exception and not the rule. Shortening analysis by concentrating sessions in a period of time seems to be complex: it may fail to catch a glimpse on different life events over time, becoming too intellectualized or detached from everyday life; on the other hand, the change accommodation process also requires support from the group and groupanalyst to succeed and that may not be effective when the periods of absence are too long. How can the mutual recognition among training institutes from different countries be achieved if we avoid acknowledging the existing differences and similarities between training programmes?

This topic needs to be discussed further among analytic societies, namely within EGATIN. Nevertheless, we would like to stress that we are not referring to a common patient that needs help in a certain issue and has time, money or availability restraints; in those cases, after a thorough analysis of the patient's possible resistances and other unconscious motivations and the group's reactions to it, flexibility clearly should apply. We are stating that these requirements should be mandatory for the trainees since they will be treating people in the future.

What does it have to do with the pattern?

From our perspective, it has already become clear how these training requirements relate to the Portuguese conceptualization of groupanalysis, especially with the concept of pattern. By defending that the concept of pattern implies a relational approach of psychoanalytically based psychotherapies, we are stressing the huge importance that the groupanalyst's personality and mental health, and therefore his or her personal analysis, has in his or her patient's transformation processes. The concept of pattern makes the groupanalyst (or the individual analytic therapist) the major responsible member of the groupanalytic process, as Cortesão put it "a conveyor, a transmitter, [...] a catalyst" (Cortesão, 1989, p. 115). Because it is "through the groupanalytic pattern that the groupanalyst propagates in the group's matrix a special imprint, defined through latent rules and specific attitudes" (Cortesão, 1989, p. 115). This importance of the groupanalyst's own analysis rests on the fact that he or she needs to recognize and eventually transform primitive defences, narcissistic traits, or even character issues in order to avoid acting them out in the future therapies he or she will offer, under the risk of severely harming his or her patients.

Concluding remarks

From our discussion, it will have become clear that we believe that the more or less therapeutic conceptualization of group analysis roots the design of the training programme of each society. We have not come to a consensus about what group analysis is, what its aims are or what the future holds in store for these type of psychotherapies, time consuming, and expensive as they are. Nevertheless, we believe they are the ones that prove to be truly effective in the long run. That is the main reason we think that it is inadvisable to relinquish the demanding training programmes currently in place in Portugal. That would lead to a decrease in the number of criteria involved in becoming an analyst and, arguably, to a poorer outcome of the efficacy of such therapies.

Hilpert (1995) states, regarding the Heidelberg Institute, that it is his experience "that quite a few candidates opting for group-analytic training would have preferred psychoanalytic training if they had had the formal qualifications" (p. 304). This is not strange to the Portuguese way of thinking. Although many groupanalysts/group analysts also have psychoanalytic training and the two psychotherapies proceed from the same theoretical basis, we still have to deal with a certain prejudice when comparing the two. Perhaps it is a hangover from former times, when psychoanalysis was striving to succeed. We see groupanalysis as a psychoanalytic psychotherapy with a common theoretical basis with psychoanalysis and a different technical procedure, as its setting includes a multiplicity of mental apparatuses and not only two, as in the dual setting. Moreover, in psychoanalysis we have been witnessing what are hopefully fruitful questions about classical technique and various proposals to modify it, thereby integrating new and recovered paradigms and scientific discoveries.

Hopper (2009) poses several questions about group-analytic identity, saying that "attempts to define professional identity in terms of what various sub-groups and counter-groups are *not*, rather than in terms of what they are, leads to continuous massification and scapegoating, and, hence, to fatal purification" (p 422).

In Portugal, as perhaps in other parts of the world, defining groupanalysis as "not psychoanalysis" is out of the question. We do struggle with some kind of bastard child statute regarding psychoanalysis. However, we can stand up to the challenge of healing narcissistic wounds created by this general (and often self) perception. What we should not embrace is the idea that our common roots, i.e., psychoanalytic theory, diminishes our identity. As Hopper writes, "whereas psychoanalysis does not appreciate the sociality of human nature, group analysis without psychoanalysis is an empty glove" (2009, p. 408).

The Portuguese training programme still has much room for improvement, in our opinion, but the future path cannot lose sight of our identity and of what we believe to be an effective way to treat individuals—and that is within a group using the framework conceptualized by Cortesão as practised by the Portuguese school of groupanalysis.

References

Abreu-Afonso, J. de (2004) Sonhos e Grupanálise [Dreams and groupanalysis]. *Grupanálise* [Groupanalysis], 2004: 45–56.

Abreu-Afonso, J. de (2010) *Transferência e Contratransferência – Particularidades da Situação Grupanalítica* [Transference and Countertransference – Special Features of the Groupanalytic Situation]. Paper presented at the XI National Conference in Groupanalysis. 12–13 November, Lisbon, Portugal.

Abreu-Afonso, J. A. de, Dinis, C. V., Ferreira, G., Ferro, S., Marques, P. M., Melo, J. C., Neto, I. M. & Rodrigues, T. B. (2015) Group analysis: other sights of the conscious and the unconscious. *Psychology Research*, 5(**1**): 10–22.

Ancona, L. (1992) Matrix et Pattern en Analyse de Groupe ou Groupanalyse [Matrix and pattern in group analysis or groupanalysis]. *Grupanálise* [Groupanalysis] 4: 23–37.

Anzieu, D. (1976) L'enveloppe sonore du Soi [The sound image of the self]. In J. B. Pontalis, (ed.) *Nouvelle Revue de Psychanalyse* [New Psychoanalytical Review], 13 (**Narcisses**): 161–180.

Ashuach, S. (2012) Am I my brother's keeper? The analytic group as a space for re-enacting and treating sibling trauma. *Group Analysis*, 45(**2**): 155–167.

Badaracco, J. G. (1986) Identification and its vicissitudes in the psychosis; the importance of the concept of the "maddening object". *International Journal of Psychoanalysis*, 67 :133–146.

Badaracco, J. G. (2000) *Psicoanálisis multifamiliar. Los otros en nosotros y el descubrimiento del sí mismo* [Multifamily Psychoanalysis. The Others in Us and the Discovery of the Self]. Buenos Aires: Paidós.

Baker, M. N. (1993) Self psychology and group psychotherapy. In H. I. Kaplan and B. J. Sadock (eds.) *Comprehensive Group Psychotherapy* (3rd edition). Baltimore, MD: Williams & Wilkins, pp. 176–185.

Balint, M. (1968) *The Basic Fault: Therapeutic Aspects of Regression*. London: Tavistock.

Baranger, W. et al. (1980) *Aportaciones al concepto de objeto en psicoanálisis* [Contributions to the Concept of Object in Psychoanalysis]. Buenos Aires: Amorrortu. 306–321.

Battegay, R. (1986) Specific differences and reciprocal influences of individual and group psychotherapy. *Group Analysis*, 19(**4**): 341–346.

References

Behr, H. (2008) Education about group analysis is as important as research: response to 'From Freud to Foulkes to the future: the development of group analysis and its continual Evolution' by Az Hakeem. *Group Analysis*, 41(**1**): 53–59.
Behr, H. (2011) Why is the past important in group analysis? *Group Analysis*, 44(**4**): 454–465.
Behr, H. & Hearst, L. (2005) The group in action. *Group-Analytic Psychotherapy - A Meeting of Minds*. London: Whurr Publishers, pp. 102–120.
Berger, M. (2013) Vengefulness as a discredited emotion. In I. Urlic, M. Berger and A. Berman (eds.) *Victimhood, Vengefulness, and the Culture of Forgiveness*. New York, NY: Nova Science Publishers, pp. 65–88.
Berger, M. (2014) The vocabulary of vengefulness: its function in the analytic group and beyond. *Group Analysis*, 47(**3**): 227–241.
Billow, R. M. (2003) The authority of the group therapist's psychology. In R. M. Billow (ed.) *Relational Group Psychotherapy - From Basic Assumptions to Passion*. London and New York, NY: Jessica Kingsley, pp. 33–44.
Bion, W. R. (1961a) *Experiences in Groups and Other Papers*. London: Tavistock.
Bion, W. R. (1961b) Experiences in groups: IV. In W. R. Bion (ed.) *Experiences in Groups and Other Papers*. London: Routledge, pp. 77–92. (Original work published 1949).
Bion, W. R. (1961c) Experiences in groups: VI. In W. R. Bion (ed.) *Experiences in Groups and Other Papers*. London: Routledge, pp. 115–126. (Original work published 1950).
Bion, W. R. (1961d) Experiences in groups: VII. In W. R. Bion (ed.) *Experiences in Groups and Other Papers*. London: Routledge, pp. 127–137. (Original work published 1951).
Bion, W. R. (1961e) Re-View: group dynamics. In W. R. Bion (ed.) *Experiences in Groups and Other Papers*. London: Tavistock, pp. 139–191. (Original work published 1952).
Bion, W. R. (1962) *Learning from Experience*. London: Heineman.
Bion, W. R. (1965) *Transformations. Change from Learning To Growth*. London: Heinemann.
Bion, W. R. (1967a) *Second Thoughts*. London: Heinemann.
Bion, W. R. (1967b) Notes on memory and desire. *Psycho-analytic Forum*, II-3: 271–280.
Bion, W. R. (1976) THREE. The Roland Harris Educational Trust, *Four discussions with W. R. Bion*. Perthshire: Clunie Press, pp. 25–45.
Bion, W. R. (1978) *Four Discussions with W.R. Bion*. Perthshire, Scotland: The Clunie Press. (Reprinted in Clinical Seminars and Other Works. London: Karnac, 1994).
Blackmore, C., Tantam, D., Parry, G. & Chambers, E. (2012) Report on a systematic review of the efficacy and clinical effectiveness of group analysis and Analytic/Dynamic group psychotherapy. *Group Analysis*, 45(**1**): 46–69.
Bleichmar, H. (1997) *Avances en psicoterapia psicoanalitica. Hacia una técnica de intervenciones específicas* [Advances in Psychoanalytic Psychotherapy. Towards a Technique of Specific Interventions]. Madrid: Paidós.
Bleichmar, H. (2004) Making conscious the unconscious in order to modify unconscious processing. *International Journal of Psychoanalysis*, 85: 379–400.
Bollas, C. (1987) *The Shadow of the Object: Psychoanalysis of the Unthought Known*. London: Free Association Books.

Brito, M. E. (1992) O padrão grupanalítico [The groupanalytic pattern]. *Grupanálise* [Groupanalysis], 4: 7–21.
Brown, D. (1985) Bion and Foulkes basic assumptions and beyond. In M. Pines (ed.) *Bion and Group Psychotherapy*. London: Routledge and Kegan Paul, pp. 208–231.
Brown, D. (2006a) Self development through subjective interaction. A fresh look at "Ego training in action". In J. Maratos (ed.) *Resonance and Reciprocity - Selected Papers by Dennis Brown*. London and New York, NY: Routledge, pp. 107–123
Brown, D. (2006b) Bion and Foulkes. Basic assumptions and beyond. In J. Maratos (ed.) *Resonance and Reciprocity - Selected papers by Dennis Brown*. London and New York, NY: Routledge, pp. 208–231.
Burrow, T. (1949). *Neurosis of Man*. London: Routledge and Kegan Paul.
Burrow, T. (2013a) Psychoanalysis and life. In E. G. Pertegato and G. O. Pertegato (eds.) *From Psychoanalysis to Group Analysis: The Pioneering Work of Trigant Burrow*. London: Karnac, pp. 7–16. (Original work published 1913).
Burrow, T. (2013b) The laboratory method in psychoanalysis: its inception and development. In E. G. Pertegato and G. O. Pertegato (eds.) *From Psychoanalysis to Group Analysis: The Pioneering Work of Trigant Burrow*. London: Karnac, pp. 145–155. (Original work published 1926).
Campbell, J. (2005) Chopping up the rainbow: quality assurance and the challenge to group-analytic training. *Group Analysis*, 39(**3**): 341–355.
Campos, J. (1992) Beyond dichotomy: the orientation of Trigant Burrow. Lifwynn Correspondence 2/2, pp. 2–9. Presented at the 11th Congress of IAGP, Montreal, 22–28 August.
Canestri, J. (2017) Looking at the future of the European Psychoanalytical Federation (Letter from the President of the European Psychoanalytic Federation). *International Journal of Psychoanalysis*, 98: 7–13.
Carvalho, J. M. (2009) O conceito de circunstância em Ortega y Gasset [The concept of circumstance in Ortega y Gasset]. *Revista de Ciências Humanas, Florianópolis, EDUFSC* [Human Sciences Journal Florianópolis, EDUFSC], 43(**2**) **Outubro** [October]: 331–345.
Carvalho, P., Galamba, G. & Neto, I. M. (2008) *Training Challenges. Portuguese Experience and Contribution*. Survey presented at the EGATIN Study Days, Oslo, 25–26 April.
Centeno, M. J., Fialho, T. & Godinho, P. (2014). Growing with groups: 57 years making science with art. Poster presented at the 16th European GASi Symposium in Group Analysis. Lisbon, 29 July–1 August.
Christian, C., Safran, J. D. & Muran, J. C. (2012) The corrective emotional experience: a relational perspective and critique. In L. G. Castonguay and C. E. Hill (eds.) *Transformation in Psychotherapy*. Washington, DC: APA Books.
Coderch, J. (2010) *La práctica de la psicoterapia relacional - el modelo interactivo en el campo del psicoanálisis* [The Practice of Relational Psychotherapy - the Interactive Model in the Field of Psychoanalysis] (2nd edition). Madrid: Ágora Relacional.
Constitution of the European Federation for Psychoanalytic Psychotherapy in Health and Related Public Services EFPP. (2017). Adopted on 10th March 1991, Amended on 26th March 1993, 24th March 1995, 5th March 1999, 30th March 2001, 13th March 2009, 1st March 2013, 3rd March 2017. [Viewed 20 August 2019]. <https://efpp.org/uploads/join-efpp/Constitution.pdf>.

Cortesão, E. L. (1967a) Based on the practice and theory of group-analytic psychotherapy: some further thoughts on the concept of group matrix. *Group Analysis*, 1 :29–36. Available from: doi: 10.1177/053331646700100106

Cortesão, E. L. (1967b) *Termo da Grupanálise* [The end of a Groupanalysis]. Lecture presented in the Theoretical Course on Group Analysis, 3rd year - 1966/67 of the Portuguese Society of Groupanalysis.

Cortesão, E. L. (1971) On interpretation in group-analysis. *Group Analysis*, 4: 39–53.

Cortesão, E. L. (1977/2004) Uma tarde em Golders Green [One afternoon at Golders Green]. *Grupanálise* [Groupanalysis], 1.

Cortesão, E. L. (1989) *Grupanálise – Teoria e Técnica* [Groupanalysis – Theory and Technique]. Lisbon: Fundação Calouste Gulbenkian. (Reprinted 2008. Lisbon: SPG).

Cortesão, E. L. (1991) Group analysis and aesthetic equilibrium. *Group Analysis*, 24, 271–277.

Cortesão, E. L. (2004) Politicoterapia [Politico-therapy]. In E. L. Cortesão (ed.) *Um Psiquiatra na Revolução* [A Psychiatrist in the Revolution] (2nd edition). Lisbon: Climepsi Editores, pp. 119–121. (First published in 'Semanário Opção' 20 October 1977).

Cozolino, L. (2014). *The Neuroscience of Human Relationships: Attachment and the Developing Social Brain* (2nd edition). New York, NY: W.W. Norton & Company.

Damásio, A. (1994) *Descartes' Error. Emotion, Reason and the Human Brain*. New York, NY: Putnam.

Damásio, A. (1995) *O erro de descartes* [Descartes' Error]. Lisbon: P.E.X.

Damásio, A. (2010) *O Livro da Consciência: A Construção do Cérebro Consciente* [The Book of Consciousness: The Construction of the Conscious Brain]. Lisbon: Círculo de Leitores.

Damásio, A. (2019) *Sem inteligência afectiva nunca teria havido vida*. [Without affective intelligence there would never have been life]. In 'Expresso' 8 de Junho de 2019, Primeiro caderno, Sociedade, pp. 22–23. [Viewed 20 August 2019]. [Expresso, 8 June 2019. First supplement. Society. 22-23]. <https://leitor.expresso.pt/semanario/semanario2432/html/primeiro-caderno/sociedade/sem-inteligencia-afetiva-nunca-teria-havido-vida>.

Davis, J. T. (2001) Revising psychoanalytic interpretations of the past. *International Journal of Psychoanalysis*, 82: 449–462.

Dias, C. A. (2005) *Freud para além de Freud* [Freud Beyond Freud]. Lisbon: Climepsi.

Dinis, C. V. (1994) Algumas Reflexões a Propósito da Neurose de Transferência em Grupanálise [Some reflections on transference neurosis in groupanalysis]. *Grupanálise* [Groupanalysis], 5: 7–18.

Dinis, C. V. (2000a) Desejo e Perda na Contratransferência [Desire and loss in countertransference]. *Revista Portuguesa de Grupanálise* [Portuguese Journal of Groupanalysis], 1: 51–58.

Dinis, C. V. (2000b) Da Comunicação À Interpretação Em Grupanálise [From communication to interpretation]. *Revista Portuguesa de Grupanálise* [Portuguese Journal of Groupanalysis], 2: 23–30.

Dinis, C. V. (2001) Existir na Net e ser na matriz grupanalítica [Existing on the net and being in the groupanalytic matrix]. *Revista Portuguesa de Grupanálise* [Portuguese Journal of Groupanalysis], 3: 15–26.

Dinis, C. V. (2002) A neutralidade possível ou a pessoalidade resgatada [Possible neutrality or the rescued personality]. *Revista Portuguesa de Grupanálise* [Portuguese Journal of Groupanalysis], 4: 7–15.

Dinis, C. V. (2003) O Tempo e a Mudança. *Revista Portuguesa de Grupanálise*, 5: 28–37.

Dinis, C. V. (2004) Grupanálise: compatibilização de protagonismos [Groupanalysis: compatibilizing protagonisms]. *Revista Portuguesa de Grupanálise* [Portuguese Journal of Groupanalysis], 2004: 9–16.

Dinis, C. V. (2005) "Um Entre Outros" ou "Primus Inter Pares"? ['One among Many' or 'Primus Inter Pares'?]. *Revista Portuguesa de Grupanálise* [Portuguese Journal of Groupanalysis], 2005: 9–16.

Dinis, C. V. (2006) Le Temps et le Changement [Time and change]. In L. Michel and J. N. Despland (eds.) *Temps et Psychothérapie* [Time and Psychotherapy]. Paris: Editions In Press, pp. 27–37.

Dinis, C. V. (2016) *Pessoas como nós* [People like us]. Conference presented at the XVI Congresso da SPGPAG [Conference presented at the XVI National Congress of Groupanalysis and Analytic Group Psychotherapy], Lisbon, 7–8 October.

Engelbrecht, H. (1997). Report of the ad hoc committee on the crisis of psychoanalysis: challenges and perspectives - welcome to the crisis. IPA Newsletter 6, 53–59. *International Journal of Psychoanalysis*, 85(**5**): 1257–1260.

Etchegoyen, R. H. (2002) *Os fundamentos da Técnica Psicanalítica* [The Basis of Psychoanalytic Technique] (2nd edition). Porto Alegre: Artes Medicas.

Fairbairn, W. R. D. (1954) *An Object Relations Theory of the Personality*. New York, NY: Basic Books.

Fernandes, W. J., Svartman, B. & Fernandes, B. S. (2003) *Grupos e Configurações Vinculares* [Groups and Vincular Confiigurations]. São Paulo: Artmed Editora, S.A.

Ferreira, A. G. (1969) Grupo Comunitário no Hospital de dia [Community group at the day Hospital]. *Jornal do Médico* [Doctor's Journal], Vol. LXIX, Abril de 1969: 71–86.

Ferreira, A. G. (1988) Transference and transference neurosis in group-analysis. *Group Analysis*, 2: 93–99.

Ferreira, G. (1989) Psicoterapias de Grupo e Grupanálise: suas especificidades e relações [Group psychotherapies and groupanalysis: their specificities and relationships]. *Análise Psicológica* [Psychological Analysis], VII: 265–276.

Ferreira, G. (1990) Terapia de grupo e Grupanálise: sua evolução e perspectivas de futuro em Portugal e no contexto internacional [Group therapy and groupanalysis: its evolution and future prospects in Portugal and in the international context]. *Grupanálise* [Groupanalysis], 2: 7–20.

Ferreira, A. G. (1992) A matriz grupanalítica [The groupanalytic matrix]. *Grupanálise* [Groupanalysis], 3: 45–56.

Ferreira, A. G. (2004) O problema e a procura de uma metateoria em grupanálise [The problem and the search for a metatheory in groupanalysis]. *Revista Portuguesa de Grupanálise* [Portuguese Journal of Groupanalysis], 2004: 17–30.

Ferreira, A. G. (2005) A interpretação em grupanálise [Interpretation in groupanalysis]. *Revista Portuguesa de Grupanálise* [Portuguese Journal of Groupanalysis], 2005: 70–79.

Ferreira, A. G. (2006) *The importance of S.H. Foulkes in Group analysis and group psychotherapy in Portugal*. Paper presented at the virtual Congress of Psychiatry – Round table The complete works of S. H. Foulkes, organized by J. Campos Avilar.

Ferreira, A. G. (2015a) *As noções de matriz e padrão grupanalítico e a construção de uma metateoria em grupanálise e sua importância* [The notions of matrix and groupanalytic pattern and the construction of a metatheory in groupanalysis and its importance]. Comunicação apresentada no XII Encontro Luso-Brasileiro de Grupanálise e Psicoterapia Analítica de Grupo e XV Congresso Nacional de Grupanálise e Psicoterapia Analítica de Grupo [Paper presented at the XII Luso-Brazilian Conference on Groupanalysis and Analytic Group Psychotherapy and the XV National Congress of Groupanalysis and Analytic Group Psychotherapy], October, Lisbon, Portugal.

Ferreira, A. G. (2015b) Group analysis and the different approaches: the Portuguese contribution. A Tribute to E. L., Cortesão. *Group Analysis*, 48(**4**): 465–486.

Ferro, S. (1997) Experiência de Psicoterapia de Grupo de base Analítica em Meio Hospitalar. In M. R. M. Leal (ed.) *Grupanálise: processo dinâmico de aprendizagem* [Groupanalysis: A Dynamic Learning Process]. Lisbon: Fim de Século, pp. 73–83.

Ferro, S. (2010) A Identidade Grupanalítica em Questão [Groupanalytic identity as stake]. *Revista Portuguesa de Grupanálise* [Portuguese Journal of Groupanalysis], 2010: 11–20.

Ferro, S. (2011) A Supervisão em Grupanálise [Supervision in Groupanalysis]. Grupanáliseonline – Nova Série, 2. [Viewed 20 August 2019]. https://grupanalise.pt/wp-content/uploads/2015/12/Texto_Revisto_Superviso_em_Grupanlise_Sara_Ferro_2011.pdf

Ferro, S. (2012) A Acção Terapêutica em Grupanálise. Interpretação e outros elementos de mudança [Therapeutic action in groupanalysis. Interpretation and other changing factors]. *Revista Portuguesa de Grupanálise* [Portuguese Journal of Groupanalysis], 2012: 19–26.

Ferro, S., Abreu-Afonso, J. de, Marques, P. M. & Neto, I. M. (2014) *The Portuguese School of Group Analysis - Bridging the Gaps: From Foulkes, Bion and Cortesão to Many Others*. Panel of papers presented at the 16th European GASi Symposium in Group Analysis. Lisbon, 29 July–1 August.

Filipe, E. Cruz (1992) Padrão grupanalítico [The groupanalytic pattern]. *Grupanálise* [Groupanalysis], 4: 23–37.

Filipe, E. Cruz (2000a) Perlaboração da Neurose de Transferência [Perlaboration of transference neurosis]. *Revista Portuguesa de Grupanálise* [Portuguese Journal of Groupanalysis], 1: 43–50.

Filipe, E. Cruz (2000b) *Reflexões Pontuais sobre Grupanálise, Psicanálise e Música* [Selected Reflections on Groupanalysis, Psychoanalysis and Music]. Self-published.

Fonagy, P. (1999) Memory and therapeutic action. *International Journal of Psychoanalysis*, 80: 215–223.

Fosshage, J. (1994) Toward a reconsideration of transference. *International Journal of Psychoanalysis*, 75: 275–280.

Fosshage, J. (2005) The explicit and implicit domains in psychoanalytic change. *Psychoanalytic Inquiry*, 25: 516–539.

Foulkes, E. (ed.) (1990) S.H. Foulkes *Selected Papers. Psychoanalysis and Group Analysis*. London: Karnac.

Foulkes, S. H. (1964a/2002) *Therapeutic Group Analysis*. London: George Allen and Unwin.

Foulkes, S. H. (1964b) Outline and development of group analysis. *Therapeutic Group Analysis*. London: George Allen & Unwin Ltd, pp. 66–82. (Reprinted London: Karnac, 1984)

Foulkes, S. H. (1964c) *Personal Encounters with S. H. Foulkes*. (DVD). Presented by Luisa Brunori & Werner Knauss. Preface by Elizabeth Foulkes. Introduction by Dr. Malcolm Pines. Copyright Group Analytic Society 1999–2008.

Foulkes, S. H. (1971) Access to unconscious processes in the group-analytic group. *Group Analysis*, 4: 4–14.

Foulkes, S. H. (1975a) *Group-Analytic Psychotherapy: Methods and Principles*. London: Gordon & Breach.

Foulkes, S. H. (1975b) *Group Analytic Psychotherapy. Method and Principles*. London: Maresfield Library.

Foulkes, S. H. (1990a) Access to unconscious processes in the group-analytic group. In E. Foulkes (ed.) S. H. Foulkes *Selected Papers. Psychoanalysis and Group Analysis*. London: Karnac, pp. 209–221. (Original work 1970).

Foulkes, S. H. (1990b) The leader in the group. In E. Foulkes (ed.) S. H. Foulkes *Selected Papers. Psychoanalysis and Group Analysis*. London: Karnac, pp. 285–296 (First published in 1975).

Foulkes, S. H. (2002). *Therapeutic Group Analysis*. London: Karnac. (Original work published in 1964).

Foulkes, S. H. (2004). The group as a matrix of the individual's mental life. In E. Foulkes (ed.) *Selected Papers of S. H. Foulkes: Psychoanalysis and Group Analysis*. London: Karnac, pp. 223–233. (Reprint of Chapter in L. R. Wolberg and E. K. Schwartz (eds.) *Group Therapy 1973 - An Overview*. New York, NY: Intercontinental Medical Book Corporation, 1973).

Foulkes, S. H. (2005) *Introduction to Group Analytic Psychotherapy*. London: Karnac. (Original work published 1948).

Foulkes, S. H. & Anthony, E. J. (1957a) *Group Psychotherapy: The Psychoanalytic Approach*. (1st edition – 1957; 2nd edition 1965). London: Karnac.

Foulkes, S. H. & Anthony, E. J. (1957b) *Group Psychotherapy – The Psychoanalytic Approach*. London: Penguin Books.

Foulkes, S. H. & Anthony, E. J. (1957c) *Group-Psychotherapy – The Psychoanalytic Approach*. London: Karnac (reprinted London: Karnac, 1984).

Foulkes, S. H. & Anthony, E. J. (2014) *Group Psychotherapy: The Psycho-Analytic Approach*. London: Karnac. (Original work published 1957).

Foulkes, S. H. & Foulkes, E. (1971) The symposium in retrospect: an introduction to the discussion in G A I P A C. *Group Analysis*, 4(**1**): 61–63.

Freud, S. (1921) *Group Psychology and Analysis of the Ego*. S. E., 18: 65–144. London: Hogarth Press.

Freud, S. (1950) *Project for a Scientific Psychology*. S. E., 1. London: Hogarth Press. (Originally written in 1895).

Gans, J. S. (2010) *Difficult Topics in Group Psychotherapy: My Journey from Shame to Courage*. London: Karnac.

Garland, C. (ed.) (2010a) The groups book. *Psychoanalytic Group Therapy: Principles and Practice Including The Groups Manual: a Treatment Manual, With Clinical Vignettes*. London: Karnac.

Garland, C. (2010b) How does a psychoanalytic group work? In Caroline Garland (ed.) *The Groups Book - Psychoanalytic Group Therapy: Principles and Practice Including the Groups Manual*. London: Karnac, pp. 37–59.

Garza-Guerrero, C. (2002a) The crisis in psychoanalysis: what crisis are we talking about? *International Journal of Psychoanalysis*, 83: 57–83.

Garza-Guerrero, C. (2002b) Organisational and educational internal impediments of psychoanalysis: contemporary challenges. *International Journal of Psychoanalysis*, 83: 1407–1433.

Graham, F. W. (1984) Psychoanalysis and group psychotherapy. *Group Analysis*, 18(1): 12–16.

Green, A. (2005) *Key Ideas for a Contemporary Psychoanalysis - Misrecognition and Recognition of the Unconscious*. London and New York, NY: Routledge.

Greenberg, J. R. (1986) Theoretical models and the analyst's neutrality. *Contemporary Psychoanalysis*, 22: 87–106.

Grinberg, L., Langer, M. & Rodrigué, E. (1957) *Psicoterapia de grupo - enfoque psicanalítico* [Group Psychotherapy: A Psychoanalytic Approach] Translation by Maria Helena Raffard Fleury and Vera Maria de Mello Cardoso. Rio de Janeiro: Forense Universitária, 1957/1976.

Guntrip, H. (1975) My experience of analysis with Fairbairn and Winnicott - how complete a result does psychoanalytic therapy achieve? *International Review of Psychoanalysis*, 2:145–156.

Hilpert, H. R. (1995) The place of the training group analyst and the problem of personal group analysis in block training. *Group Analysis*, 28 :301–311.

Hopper, E. (1982) Group-analysis: the problem of context. *Group Analysis*, XV(**2**): 136–157.

Hopper, E. (2003) On the Nature of Hope in Psychoanalysis and Group Analysis. In E. Hopper (ed.) *The Social Unconscious - Selected Papers*. London: Jessica Kingsley, pp. 189–214.

Hopper, E. (2006) Theoretical and conceptual notes concerning transference and countertransference. Processes in groups and by groups, and the social unconscious: part I. *Group Analysis*, 39(**4**): 549–559.

Hopper, E. (2007) Theoretical and conceptual notes concerning transference and countertransference processes in groups and by groups and the social unconscious: part 2. *Group Analysis*, 40: 29–42.

Hopper, E. (2008) Response 'From Freud to Foulkes to the future: the development of group analysis and its continual evolution' by Az Hakeem. *Group Analysis*, 41(**1**): 60–62.

Hopper, E. (2009) Building Bridges between psychoanalysis and group analysis in theory and clinical practice. *Group Analysis*, 42(**4**): 406–425.

Hume, P. (2010) Bion and group psychotherapy: bion and foulkes at the Tavistock. In C. Garland (ed.) *The Groups Book - Psychoanalytic Group Therapy: Principles and Practice Including the Groups Manual*. London: Karnac, pp. 101–128.

Hutchinson, S. (2010) *Is all group analysis applied group analysis? Can group analysis and training adapt to changing times and contemporary clinical challenges?* Paper presented at EGATIN Study Days 16–17 April, Vienna.

Kadis, A., Krasner, J., Winick, C. & Foulkes, S. (1963) *A Practicum of Group Psychotherapy*. New York, NY: Harper & Row.

Kaës, R. (2003) *As Teorias Psicanalíticas do Grupo* [The Psychoanalytic Theories of the Group]. Lisbon: Climepsi Editores. (First published in 1999).

Kahn, M. (2014) The intransience of the sibling bond: a relational and family systems view. In K. Skrzypek, B. Maciejewska-Sobczak and Z. Stadnicka-Dimitriew (eds.) *Siblings: Envy and Rivalry, Coexistence and Concern*. London: Karnac, pp. 41–56.

Karterud, S. (2015a) On structure and leadership in mentalization-based group therapy and group analysis. *Group Analysis*, 48(**2**): 137–149.
Karterud, S. (2015b) *Mentalization-Based Group Therapy (MBT-G): A Theoretical, Clinical, and Research Manual*. Oxford, UK: Oxford University Press.
Kernberg, O. (1976) *Object Relations Theory and Clinical Psychoanalysis*. New York, NY: Aronson.
Kernberg, O. (1979) Some implications of object relations theory for psychoanalytic technique. *Journal of the American Psychoanalytic Association*, 27: 207–239.
Kernberg, O. (1996) Thirty methods to destroy the creativity of psychoanalytic candidates. *International Journal of Psycho-Analysis*, 77: 1031–1040.
Kernberg, O. (2003) Sanctioned social violence: a psychoanalytic view. Part I. *International Journal of Psychoanalysis*, 84:683–698.
Kibel, H. D. (1993) Object relations theory and group psychotherapy. In H. I. Kaplan and B. J. Sadock (eds.) *Comprehensive Group Psychotherapy* (3rd edition). Baltimore, MD: Williams and Wilkins.
Kibel, D. & Stein, A. (1981) The group-as-a-whole approach: an appraisal. *International Journal of Group Psychotherapy*, 31(**4**): 409–427.
Kirsner, D. (2000) *Unfree Associations*. London: Process Press.
Klein, M. (1952) *Contributions to Psychoanalysis*. London: Hogarth Press.
Kohut, H. (1971) *The Analysis of the Self*. New York, NY: I. U. P.
Kohut, H. (1972) *The Restoration of the Self*. New York, NY: I. U. P.
Kohut, H. (1984) In A. Goldberg and P. Stepansky (eds.) *How Does Analysis Cure?* Chicago and London: The University of Chicago Press.
Kutter, P. (1982) *Basic Aspects of Psychoanalytic Group Therapy*. London: Routledge & Kegan Paul.
Lavie, J. (2005) The lost roots of the theory of group analysis: taking interrelational individuals seriously! *Group Analysis*, 38: 519–535.
Leal, M. R. M. (1968) Transference neurosis in group analytic treatment. *Group Analysis*, 1(**2**): 99–109.
Leal, M. R. M. (1970) Le Transfert analytique dans l'analyse de Groupe [Analytical transfer in group analysis]. *Bulletin de Psychologie de l'Université de Paris* [Psychology Bulletin of the University of Paris], 285 **XXIII, 13–16**: 760–764.
Leal, M. R. M. (1975) Addendum. *Group Analysi*s, 8: 199–200.
Leal, M. R. M. (1981) Resistances and the group-analytic process. *Group Analysis*, 15 (**2**): 97–110.
Leal, M. R. M. (1994a) *Grupanálise: um percurso (1963–1993)* [Groupanalysis: A Journey (1963–93)]. Lisbon: Sociedade Portuguesa de Grupanálise.
Leal, M. R. M. (1994b) Aspectos Comunicacionais da emoção de transferência. [Communicational aspects of the emotion of transference]. In M. R. M. Leal (ed.) *Grupanálise: um percurso (1963–1993)* [Groupanalysis: A Journey (1963–93)]. Lisbon: Sociedade Portuguesa de Grupanálise, pp. 13–30.
Leal, M. R. M. (1994c). A "neurose de transferência" no tratamento grupanalítico [Transference neurosis in group analytic treatment]. In M. R. M. Leal (ed.) *Grupanálise: um percurso (1963–1993)* [Groupanalysis: A Journey (1963–93)]. Lisbon: Sociedade Portuguesa de Grupanálise, pp. 77–89.
Leal, M. R. M. (1997) Comunicação, Interpretação e Mudança. In M. R. M. Leal (ed.) *A Grupanálise: processo dinâmico de aprendizagem* [Groupanalysis: A Dynamic Learning Process]. Lisbon: Fim de Século, pp. 119–128.

Leal, M. R. M. (2010) *Passos na construção do Eu* [Steps in the Construction of the Ego]. Lisbon: Fim de Século.
Leffert. M. (2013) Some particular issues concerning therapeutic action. In M. Leffert (ed.) *The Therapeutic Situation in the 21st Century*. New York and London: Routledge, Taylor & Francis, pp. 188–228.
Locke, N. (1961) *Group Psychoanalysis: Theory and Technique*. New York, NY: I.U.P.
Lorentzen, S. (2010) Some ideas on how group analysis can survive: response to lecture by jane campbell. *Groupanalysis*, 43(**4**): 450–464.
Lorentzen, S. (2011) One group analysis or many? Does a 'main-stream group analysis' exist? (Introduction to a workshop at the London symposium in group analysis, August 30th). *Context, December 2011*, 54: 43–44.
Lorentzen, S. (2014). *Group Analytic Psychotherapy: Working with Affective, Anxiety and Personality Disorders*. London and New York, NY: Routledge.
Lorentzen, S. (2016) Comments on Karterud's 'On structure and leadership in mentalization-based group therapy and group analysis. *Group Analysis*. 49(**1**): 70–77.
Marques, P. M. (2015) *O Conceito de Matriz Grupanalítica na Escola Portuguesa de Grupanálise* [The Concept of the Groupanalytical Matrix in the Portuguese School of Group Analysis]. Dissertação de doutoramento em psicologia [Doctoral Dissertation]. ISPA-Instituto Universitário, Lisbon.
Marten, R. F. (1999) Power, institution and group-analytic training. *Group Analysis*, 32(**2**): 207–215.
Martins, C., Perestrelo, C. V. & Neto, I. M. (2018) *Groupanálise/Psicoterapia Analítica de Grupo à distância: vantagens e inconvenientes* [Groupanalysis/Analytic Group Psychotherapy online: advantages and inconveniences]. Paper presented at the XVIII National Conference in Groupanalysis, 19–20 October, Lisbon.
Meltzer, D., Bremner, J., Hoxter, S., Weddell, D. & Wittenberg, I. (1980) *Explorations dans le monde de l'autisme* [Explorations in Autism: A Psycho-Analytical Study]. Paris: Payot.
Miller, I. (2016) Expressions of vernacular psychoanalysis. *International Forum of Psychoanalysis*, 24(**4**): 225–229.
Mollon, P. (2002) *Shame and Jealousy – The Hidden Turmoils*. London: Karnac.
Molnos, A. (1986) Anger that destroys and anger that heals: handling hostility in group analysis and in dynamic brief psychotherapy. *Group Analysis*, 19(**3**): 207–221.
Money-Kyrle, R. (1956) Normal countertransference and some of its deviations. *International Journal of Psychoanalysis*, 37: 360–365.
Moreno, J. L. (1997) *Psicodrama* [Psychodrama]. São Paulo: Editora Cultrix. (First published 1946).
Moreno, J. L. & Moreno, F. B. (1944) Spontaneity theory of child development. *Psychodrama monographs*, 8: 1–48.
Morin, E. (2008) *Introdução ao Pensamento Complexo* [An Introduction to Complex Thought]. Lisbon: Piaget.
Moro, L. (2007) The role of supervision in training psychotherapists. *Group Analysis*, 40(**2**): 178–188. [Viewed 20 August 2019]. Available from: doi: 10.1177/0533316407077074.
Nava, A. S. (2003). *O cérebro apanhado em flagrante* [The Brain Caught in the Act]. Lisbon: Climepsi.
Nava, A. S. (2007) Empathy and group analysis: an integrative approach. *Group Analysis*, 40(**1**): 13–28.

Neto, I. M. (1993) *Agressividade e Narcisismo* [Aggressiveness and Narcissism]. Paper presented at the II Encontro Luso-Brasileiro de Grupanálise e Psicoterapia Analítica de Grupo [II Luso-Brazilian Conference on Groupanalysis and Analytic Group *Psychotherapy*], 11 November, Lisbon.

Neto, I. M. (1999) *The Freedom and the Capacity to say NO and its Healing potential*. Paper presented at the EFPP II European Conference on Group Analytic Psychotherapy, 28–30 May, Barcelona.

Neto, I. M. (1999a) *Selection in Groupanalysis. Similarities and Differences. Some risks we take in Group Analysis*. Paper presented at the 11th GAS Symposium in Group Analysis, Budapest, August 1999.

Neto, I. M. (1999b) *O padrão: A importância do grupanalista na grupanálise*. Paper presented at the X Congresso Brasileiro de Psicoterapia Analítica de Grupo e V Encontro Luso-Brasileiro de Grupanálise e Psicoterapia Analítica de Grupo, [X Brazilian Congress of Analytic Group Psychotherapy and the V Luso-Brazilian Conference on Groupanalysis and Analytic Group Psychotherapy], 12–14 November, Rio de Janeiro, Brasil.

Neto, I. M. (2000) A Supervisão - outra visão sobre os pacientes, o grupanalista e o supervisor - um caminho para o inconsciente [Supervision – another view of patients, the groupanalyst and the supervisor – a way to the unconscious]. *Revista Portuguesa de Grupanálise* [Portuguese Journal of Groupanalysis], 2: 92–106.

Neto, I. M. (2001) *Não basta parecer: o analista tem de ser…autêntico* [Appearances are not enough: the analyst must BE authentic]. Paper presented at the VI Congresso Luso-Brasileiro de Grupanálise e Psicoterapia Analítica de Grupo e IV Congresso Nacional da Sociedade Portuguesa de Grupanálise [Paper presented at the VI Luso-Brazilian Conference on Groupanalysis and Analytic Group Psychotherapy and the IV National Congress of Groupanalysis], 8–10 November, Lisbon, Portugal.

Neto, I. M. (2002) *To see and be seen: an added value in Group Analysis*. Paper presented at the 12th GAS European Symposium in Group Analysis, 26–31 August, Bologna, Italy.

Neto, I. M. (2003) Estabelecendo elos entre a realidade interna e a realidade externa: os membros do grupo como encenação da realidade interna do analista [Establishing links between internal reality and external reality: the members of the group as a staging of the internal reality of the analyst]. *Grupanaliseonline*, 1(**1**): 24–28. Retrieved from <https://grupanalise.pt/wp-content/uploads/2015/07/revistaonline1.pdf>

Neto, I. M. (2006) *Clinical Applications of Dreams*. Presented at the II Mestrado em Ciências do Sono [Master's degree in Sleep Science]. Lisbon: ISPA.

Neto, I. M. (2009/2010) Grupppenanalytische Identität – Klinische und ausbildungsrelevante Bedeutung [Group Analytic Identity - Clinical and Training Impact]. *Jahrbuch für Gruppenanalyse* [Group Analysis Yearbook], **Band 15/16**: 99–109 (original Lecture at the 4th EFPP Group Section Conference, Prague, 28–31 May 2009).

Neto, I. M. (2010a) *A Bússola do Grupanalista* [The Groupanalyst's Compass]. Paper presented at the XI Congresso Nacional de Groupanálise da SPGPAG [XI National Congress in Groupanalysis], 12–13 November, Lisbon, Portugal.

Neto, I. M. (2010b) Moving groupwork into the day hospital setting. In J. Radcliffe, K. Hajek, J. Carson and O. Manor (eds.) *Psychological Groupwork with Acute Psychiatric Inpatients*. London: Whiting & Birch, pp. 325–342.

Neto, I. M. (2012) Ver e ser visto: um «valor acrescentado» em Grupanálise [To see and be seen: an "added value" in groupanalysis]. *Revista Portuguesa de Grupanálise* [Portuguese Journal of Groupanalysis], 2012: 77–86.

Neto, I. M. (2014) Psicopatologia relacional. Os grupos grupanalíticos como situações de eleição para o seu diagnóstico e elaboração [Relational psychopathology. Groupanalytic groups as an adequated setting for its diagnosis and elaboration]. *Revista Portuguesa. de Grupanálise* [Portuguese Journal of Groupanalysis], 2014: 69–76.

Neto, I. M. (2015) *Compreensão psicanalítica de conceitos grupanalíticos* [Psychoanalytic understanding of groupanalytic concepts]. Paper presented at the meeting Trabajando en Grupo: Nuevas perspectivas, 27–28 November, Palma de Maiorca, Spain.

Neto, I. M. (2017) Multi family group analysis – (MFGA). *Current Psychiatry Reviews*, 13 (3): 165–170. [Viewed 21 August 2019]. Available from: doi: 10.2174/157340051 3666170503113353.

Neto, I. M. & Babo, T. (2000) O termo de uma Grupanálise e a elaboração estética do conflito [Ending groupanalysis and the aesthetic elaboration of the conflict]. *Revista Portuguesa de Grupanálise* [Portuguese Journal of Groupanalysis], 1: 59–73.

Neto, I. M. & Centeno, M. J. (2003) *Crossing generations. Through an institutional psychoanalytical group – A multifamily group psychotherapy*. Paper presented at the IAGP 15th International Congress - Crossroads of culture: Where groups converge. 25–29 August, Istanbul, Turkey.

Neto, I. M. & Centeno, M. J. (2005) *Is There a Crisis in Psychoanalysis and Group Analysis? Essence and Preconception*. Presented at the 34th GAS Winter Workshop, Lisbon, 12–15 January.

Neto, I. M. & Centeno, M. J. (2014) Psicoanálisis Multifamiliar ≈ Multifamily Psychoanalysis. Poster presented at the16th GASi Symposium, Lisbon, 18 July–1 August.

Neto, I. M. & David, M. (2017) Dealing with conflicts, rage, anger, and aggression in group analysis. In G. Ofer (ed.) *Bridge Over Troubled Water*. London: Karnac for the European Federation for Psychoanalytic Psychotherapy, pp. 91–105.

Neto, I. & Dinis, C. (1994) Patologia limítrofe. Organização Borderline da personalidade. Personalidade Borderline. Estados limite, ou os Trabalhos de Hércules dos Psiquiatras [Borderline pathology. borderline personality organisation. borderline personality. Boundary states, or the psychiatrists' labours of hercules]. *Revista Portuguesa de Pedopsiquiatria* [Portuguese Journal of Child Psychiatry], 6: 45–61.

Neto, I. & Dinis, F. V. (2010) O Mal, a Maldade, Violência e Terrorismo [Malice, evil, violence and terrorism]. *Revista Portuguesa de Grupanálise* [Portuguese Journal of Groupanalysis], 2010: 87–101.

Neto, I. M.; Fialho, T.; Godinho, P. & Centeno, M. J. (2010a) Treating and training: a 30 year experience of a team with a group-analytic framework: part I. *Group Analysis*, 43(1): 50–64.

Neto, I. M.; Fialho, T.; Godinho, P. & Centeno, M. J. (2010b) Treating and training: a 30 year experience of a team with a group-analytic framework: part II. *Group Analysis*, 43(2): 107–126.

Nitsun, M. (1991) The anti-group: destructive forces in the group and their therapeutic potential. *Group Analysis*, 24(1): 7–20.

Nitsun, M. (1996) *The Anti-Group – Destructive Forces in the Group and Their Creative Potential*. London and New York, NY: Routledge.
Nitsun, M. (2006) *The Group as an Object of Desire. Exploring Sexuality in Group Therapy*. London and New York, NY: Routledge, Taylor & Francis.
Nitsun, M. (2009) Authority and revolt: the challenges of group leadership. *Group Analysis*, 42(**4**): 325–348.
Nitsun, M. (2015) *Beyond the Anti-Group - Survival and -Transformation*. London and New York, NY: Routledge Taylor & Francis.
Nitzgen, D. (1999) From demand to desire: what do we offer when we offer group analytic training? *Group Analysis*, 32: 227–239.
Ogden, T. H. (1992) *Projective Identification and Psychotherapeutic Technique*. London: Karnac.
Ogden, T. H. (1994) The analytic third: working with intersubjective clinical facts. *International Journal of Psycho-Analysis*, 75: 3–20.
Osório, L. C. (2007) *Grupoterapias – Abordagens Atuais*. [Group Therapies – Current Approaches] Brazil, Porto Alegre: Artmed Editora S.A.
Panksepp, J. & Biven, L. (2012) *The Archaeology of Mind: Neuro-Evolutionary Origins of Human Emotions*. New York, NY: W. W. Norton & Company.
Paparo, F. & Nebbiosi, G. (1998) How does psychotherapy cure? A reconceptualization of the group process: from self psychology to the intersubjective perspective. In I. Harwood and M. Pines (eds.) *Experiences in Group - Intersubjective and Self Psychological Pathways to Human Understanding*. London and Philadelphia, PA: Jessica Kingsley, pp. 70–82.
Pertegato, E. G. (2014) Foulkes's roots in Trigant Burrow's writings. *Group Analysis*, 47: 312–328.
Pichon-Rivière, E. (1965) *Teoria del vínculo* ['The Link and the Theory of the Three Ds (Depositant, Depository, and Deposited): Role and Status']. Buenos Aires: Nueva Vision.
Pichon-Rivière, E. (1988). *Del Psicoanálisis a la Psicologia Social* [On Psychoanalysis and Social Psychology]. Buenos Aires: Nueva Visión.
Pichon-Rivière, E. (2000a) *O processo grupal* [The Group Process]. São Paulo: Martins Fontes. (First published in 1983).
Pichon-Rivière, E. (2000b) *Teoria do Vínculo* ['The Link and the Theory of the Three Ds (Depositant, Depository, and Deposited): Role and Status']. São Paulo: Martins Fontes. (First published 1982).
Pigott, C. (1990) *Introduction à lá Psychanalyse Groupale*. Paris: Apsygée.
Pines, M. (1994) The group-as-a-whole. In D. Brown and L. Zinkin (eds.) *The Psyche and the Social World - Developments in Group-Analytic Theory*. London and New York, NY: Routledge, pp. 47–59.
Pines, M. (1997) *Circular Reflections: Selected Papers on Group Analysis and Psychoanalysis*. London and Philadelphia, PA: Jessica Kingsley Publishers.
Pines, M. (1998) *Circular Reflections - Selected Papers on Group Analysis and Psychoanalysis*. London and Philadelphia, PA: Jessica Kingsley.
Pines, M. (2000) The contribution of S. H. Foulkes to group psychotherapy. In M. Pines (ed.) *The Evolution of Group Analysis*. London and Philadelphia, PA: Jessica Kingsley, pp. 265–285. (First published in 1983).
Pines, M. (2009) The matrix of group analysis: an historical perspective. *Group Analysis*, 42: 5–15.

Pinto, T. S. & Salgado, F. (2001) História da Grupanálise em Portugal [The history of groupanalysis in Portugal]. *Revista Portuguesa de Grupanálise* [Portuguese Journal of Groupanalysis], 3 **(Outubro)**: 52–57.

Pinto, T. S. & Salgado, F. (2002) História da Grupanálise em Portugal [The History of Groupanalysis in Portugal], 4 **(Verão)**: 54–65.

Potthoff, P. & Moini-Afchari, U. (2014) Mentalization-based treatment in groups—a paradigm shift or old wine in new skin? *Group Analysis*, 47(**1**): 3–16. Available from: doi: 10.1177/0533316413518488.

Ribeiro, J. P. (1994) *Gestalt-terapia: O Processo Grupal. Uma abordagem fenomenológica da teoria do campo e holística* [Gestalt Therapy: The Group Process. A Phenomenological Approach to Field and Holistic Theory] (4th edition). São Paulo: Summus Editorial.

Ribeiro, J. P. (2007) O conceito de resistência na psicoterapia grupo-analítica: repensando um caminho [The concept of resistance in groupanalytic psychotherapy: rethinking the path]. *Psicologia: Teoria e Pesquisa* [Psychology: Theory and Research], 23 (special issue): 65–71.

Rickman, J. (1950) The factor of number in individual and group-dynamics. *The Journal of Mental Science*, 96(**404**): 770–773.

Roth, B. E. (1993) Freud: the group psychologist and group leader. In H. I. Kaplan and B. J. Sadock (eds.) *Comprehensive Group Psychotherapy* (3rd edition). Baltimore, MD: Williams and Wilkins, pp. 10–20.

Rouchy, J. C. (1982) Archaic processes and transference in group analysis. *Group Analysis*, 15: 235–260.

Ruesch, J. & Bateson, G. (1951) *Communication: The Social Matrix of Psychiatry*. New York, NY: W. W. Norton & Comp, Inc.

Ruesch, J. & Bateson, G. (1987) *Communication: The Social Matrix of Psychiatry*. New York, NY: W. W. Norton & Comp, Inc. (Original work published 1951) Retrieved from http://www.archive.org/details/communicationsoc00inrues

Rutan, J. S. & Stone, W. N. (1993) *Psychodynamic Group Psychotherapy* (2nd edition). London: The Guilford Press.

Salgado, F. & Silva Pinto, T. (2000) Rivalidade fraterna em grupanálise [Sibling rivalry in groupanalysis]. *Revista Portuguesa de Grupanálise* [Portuguese Journal of Groupanalysis], 2: 46–58.

Sandison, R. (1987) Agents for healing in the small group. *Group Analysis*, 20(**4**): 343–349.

Santos, M. & Zaslavsky, J. (2007) Pesquisando conceitos e tendências em psicoterapia e psicanálise [Researching concepts and trends in psychotherapy and psychoanalysis]. *Revista Brasileira de Psicanálise* [Brazilian Journal of Psychoanalysis], 41(2): 115–124.

Schain-West, J. (1998) Infant research and intersubjective responsiveness. In I. N. H. Harwood and M. Pines (eds.) *Self Experiences in Group, Intersubjective and Self Psychological Pathways to Human Understanding*. London and Philadelphia, PA: Jessica Kingsley, pp. 99–108.

Shedler, J. (2010) The efficacy of psychodynamic psychotherapy. *American Psychologist*, 65(**2**): 98–109.

Silva, A. V. da (2012) *Considerações acerca do conceito de identificação projectiva (IDP)* [Considerations on the Concept of Projective Identification]. Comunicação apresentada no *Seminário Eduardo Luís Cortesão* da Sociedade Portuguesa de

Grupanálise [Paper presented at the E.L.Cortesão Seminar hosted by the Portuguese Society of Groupanalysis]. Lisbon. Portugal.

Silva, J. A. (1971) Reflexions Sur L'Abordage De L'Inconscient Et Sur L'Interpretation Dans Le Groupe Groupe-Analytique [Reflections on the approach to the unconscious and on interpretation in the group-analytical group]. *Group Analysis*, 4(**1**): 15–22. [Date viewed 20 August 2019]. Available from: doi: 10.1177/053331647100400103.

Silva, J. A. (1994) Comunicação metadramática e Interpretação Grupanalítica [Metadramatic communication and groupanalytic interpretation]. *Grupanálise*. [Groupanalysis], 5: 49–64.

Souza, R. F. de (2011) George Herbert Mead: Contribuições para a história da psicologia social [Contributions to the history of social psychology]. *Psicologia & Sociedade (online)* [Psychology and Society], 23(**2**): 369–378. [Viewed 20 August 2019]. Available from: doi: 10.1590/S0102-71822011000020001].

Stern, D. (1977) *The First Relationship: The Infant and the Mother*. Cambridge, MA: Harvard University Press.

Stern, D. (1998) *The Interpersonal World of the Infant. A View from Psychoanalysis and Developmental Psychology*. New York, NY: Basic Books.

Stern, D. N. (2004a) *The Present Moment in Psychotherapy and Everyday Life*. New York, NY: W.W. Norton & Company.

Stern, D. N. (2004b) Therapeutic change: a summary and some general clinical implications. In *The Present Moment in Psychotherapy and Everyday Life*. New York, London: W. W. Norton & Company. 219–227.

Stern, D. N., Sander, L. W., Nahum, J. P., Harrison, A. M., Lyons-Ruth, K., Morgan, A. C., Bruschweilerstern, N. & Tronick, E. Z. (1998) Non-interpretive mechanisms in psychoanalytic therapy: the 'Something More' than interpretation. *International Journal of Psycho-Analysis*, 79: 903–921.

Stone, W. (2009) *Contributions of Self Psychology to Group Psychotherapy – Selected Papers*. London: Karnac.

Thomae, H. (1991) Idee und Wirklichkeit der Lehrenanalyse. Ein Pladoyer fur Reformen. *Psyche*, 5: 385–433; *Psyche*, 6: 481–505.

Torres, N. (2010) Protomentality. In R. Morgan-Jones (ed.) *The Body of the Organisation and Its Health*. London: Karnac, pp. 53–79.

Tubert-Oaklander, J. (2019) Beyond psychoanalysis and group analysis. The urgent need for a new paradigm of the human being. 43rd Foulkes Lecture. 17 May 2019. Senate House, University of London (Available at https://doi.org/10.1177/0533316419863037)

Tubert-Oklander, J. & de Tubert, R. H. (2004) Operative groups. *The Latin- American Approach to Group Analysis*. London: Jessica Kingsley, Pub. Ltd.

Tubert-Oklander, J. & Hernández-Tubert, R. (2014) The social unconscious and the large group part I: the British and the Latin American traditions. *Group Analysis*, 47(**2**): 99–112 [Viewed 21 August 2019]. Available from: doi: 10.1177/0533316414523209.

Valbak, K. (2015) Clinical wisdom. *Group Analysis*, 48(**4**): 515–534.

Vaughan, S., Spitzer, R., Davies, M. & Roose, S. (1997) The definition and assessment of analytic process: can analysts agree? *International Journal of Psychoanalysis*, 78(**5**): 959–973.

Wallerstein, R. (1995) The outcomes of psychoanalysis and psychotherapy at termination and at follow-up. *The Talking Cures - The Psychoanalysis and the Psychotherapies*. New Haven and London: Yale University Press, pp. 480–506.

Wallerstein, R. S. (2005) Will psychoanalytic pluralism be an enduring state of our discipline? *International Journal of Psychoanalysis*, 86(**3**): 623–626.

Wampold, B. E. (2011). Qualities and actions of effective therapists. American Psychological Association Education Directorate. Retrieved from http://www.apa.org/education/ce/effective-therapists.pdf

Weinberg, H. (2014) *The Paradox of Internet Groups: Alone in the Presence of Virtual Others*. London: Karnac.

Weinberg, H. (2016) Impossible groups that flourish in leaking containers – challenging group analytic theory? *Group Analysis*, 49(**4**): 330–349.

Weinberg, H. (2020) Online group psychotherapy. Challenges and possibilities during COVID-19 – A practice review. *Group Dynamics: Theory, Research and Practice*, 24(**3**): 201–211.

Wellendorf, F. (2014) Sibling rivalry: psychoanalytic aspects and institutional implications. In K. Skrzypek, K. B. Maciejewska-Sobczak and Z. Stadnicka-Dimitriew (eds.) *Siblings: Envy and Rivalry, Coexistence and Concern*. London: Karnac (for the European Federation for Psychoanalytic Psychotherapy), pp. 3–11.

Wilke, G. (2018) *The Art of Group Analysis in Organisations: The Use of Intuitive and Experiential Knowledge*. New York, NY: Routledge.

Winnicott, D. W. (1958) *Collected Papers*. London: Tavistock.

Young, D. (2006) How does group analysis work? *Group Analysis*, 39(**4**): 477–493.

Zender, J. (1991) Projective identification in group psychotherapy. *Group Analysis*, 24(**2**): 116–129.

Zimerman, D. (1993a) A Formação de um Grupo Terapêutico de base Analítica. In *Fundamentos Básicos das Grupoterapias*. Porto Alegre: Artes Médicas Sul, pp. 64–69.

Zimerman, D. (1993b) Insight. Elaboração. Cura. In *Fundamentos Básicos das Grupoterapias*. Porto Alegre: Artes Médicas, pp. 139–147.

Zimerman, D. (1999) *Fundamentos Psicanalíticos. Teoria, Técnica e Clínica – Uma Abordagem Didática* [Psychoanalytical Fundamentals. Theory, Technique and Clinic - A Didactic Approach]. Brazil: Editora Artes Médicas Sul.

Zimerman, D. (2000) *Fundamentos Básicos das Grupoterapias* [Basic Fundamentals of Group Therapies]. Porto Alegre: Artes Médicas.

Zimerman, D. (2001) *Vocabulário Contemporâneo de Psicanálise* [Contemporary Vocabulary of Psychoanalysis]. Brazil, Porto Alegre: Artmed.

Zimerman, D. (2003) Psicanálise Individual e Grupanálise: Semelhanças e Diferenças [Individual psychoanalysis and groupanalysis: similarities and differences]. *Grupanálise Online* [Groupanalysis Online], 1(**1**): 4–8.

Zimerman, D. E., Osório, L. C. et al. (1997) *Como trabalhamos com grupos* [How We Work with Groups]. Brazil, Porto Alegre: Artes Médicas.

Zinkin, L. (1983) Malignant mirroring. *Group Analysis*, 16(**2**): 113–129.

Bibliography

Adler, A. (1929) *The Practice and Theory of Individual Psychology*. New York, NY: Harcourt, Brace & Company, Inc.
Bach, G. (1954) *Intensive Group Psychotherapy*. New York, NY: Ronald Press.
Bacon, F. (1600) Novum Organum. In: Comprins α Onset (eds.) *The Philosophers of Science*: 1947. New York, NY: Random House, pp. 78–157.
Benedict, R. (1934) *Patterns of Culture*. Boston, MA: Houghton Mifflin Company.
Bergson, M. (1907) *L'évolution créatrice* [Creative Evolutions]. Paris: PUF. (1981).
Berne, E. (1961) *Transactional Analysis in Psychotherapy*. New York, NY: Grove Press.
Bertalanffy, B. von (1956) General system theory. In B. von Bertalanffy and A. Rapoport (eds.) *General Systems: Yearbook of the Society for the Advancement of General Systems Theory*, **Vol**. 1.
Bowlby, J. (1988) *A Secure Base: Clinical Applications of Attachment Theory*. London: Brunner-Routledge.
Comte, A. (1842) Système de philosophie positive. Préliminaires généraux et conclusions (1830–1842) [System of positive philosophy. General preliminary remarks and conclusions (1830–1842)] *Archives Positivistes* [Positivist Archives]**1 vol.** 1942. Paris: Maison d'Auguste Comte, 1942.
Derrida, J. (1967) *L'écriture et la différence* [Writing and Difference]. Paris: Seuil.
Descartes, R. (1639 *Discours de la méthode* [Discourse on the Method]. Paris: Garnier.
Devereux, G. (1977) *Essais d'ethnopsychiatrie générale* [Essays on General Ethnopsychiatry] (3rd edition). Paris: Gallimard.
Durkheim, E. (1901) *Suicide*. Paris: P.U.F. (1967).
Erikson, E. H. (1950) *Childhood and Society*. New York, NY: Norton.
Foucault, M. (1961) *Folie et Déraison: Histoire de la folie à l'âge classique* [A History of Insanity in the Age of Reason]. Paris: Plon.
Foucault, M. (1963) *Naissance de la Clinique* [The Birth of the Clinic]. Paris: P.U.F.
Frank, L. K. (1948) Society as the *Patient: Essays* on *Culture* and *Personality.* New Jersey: Rutgers University Press.
Freud, S. (1913) *Totem and Taboo*. S. E., 13. London: Hogarth Press.
Freud, S. (1939) *Moses and the Monotheism*. S. E., 23. London: Hogarth Press.
Gergely, G. & Watson, J. S. (1996) The social biofeedback theory of parental affect-mirroring: the development of emotional self-awareness and self-control in infancy. *International Journal of Psychoanalysis*, 77: 1181–1212.
Greenson, R. (1967) *The Technique and Practice of Psychoanalysis*, Vol. I. London: Hogarth Press.

Hartmann, H. (1969) *Essays on Ego Psychology*. New York, NY: I.U.P.
Hegel, G. W. F. (1809) *Logique métaphysique* [The Science of Logic]. Paris: Gallimard.
Husserl, E. (1964) *Leçons pour une phénopanologie de la conscience interne du temps* [On the Phenomenologie of the Consciousness of Internal Tiwme]. Paris: P.U.F.
Jaspers, K. (1963) *General Psychology*. Manchester: Manchester University Press.
Kant, I. (1781-90) *Oeuvres completes* [Complete Works]. Paris: Bibliothèque de la Pléiade, Gallimard.
Klapman, J. K. (1946) *Group Psychotherapy, Theory and Practice*. New York, NY: Grune & Stratton.
Kreeger, L. (ed.) (1973) *The Large Group: Dynamics and Theory*. London: Constable.
Lacan, J. (1966) *Écrits* [Writings]. Paris: Éditions du Seuil.
Lévi-Strauss, C. (1974) *Anthropologie Structurale* [Structural Anthropology]. Paris: Plon.
Lewin, K. (1951) *Field Theory in Social Science*. New York, NY: Harper & Row.
Merleau-Ponty, M. (1945) *Phénoménologie de la perception* [Phenomenology of Perception]. Paris: Gallimard.
Pines, M. (1993) Group-analysis. In H. I. Kaplan and B. J. Sadock (eds.) *Comprehensive Group Psychotherapy* (3rd edition). Baltimore, MD: Williams and Wilkins.
Popper, K. (1959) *The Logic of Scientific Discovery*. London: Hutchison & Co.
Racker, H. (1988) *Estudos sobre Técnica Psicanalítica* [Studies on Psychoanalytical Technique] (3rd edition). Porto Alegre: Artes Médicas.
Rapaport, D. (1959) The structure of psychoanalytic theory. In Koch (ed.) *Psychology: A Study of Science*, 3. New York, NY: McGraw-Hill, pp. 55–103.
Russell, B. (1962) Our knowledge of the internal world. In W. Barrett and H. D. Aiken (eds.) *Philosophy in the Twentieth Century*. New York, NY: Random House, 1, pp. 646–665.
Schilder, P. (1959) Psychotherapy. New York, NY: Norton.
Slavson, N. R. (1958) *Analytic Group Psychotherapy*. New York, NY: Columbia University Press.
Thornton, C. (2010) Group and team coaching. *The Essential Guide*. London and New York, NY: Routledge.
Wallerstein, R. (1988) One psychoanalysis or many? *International Journal of Psychoanalysis*, 69: 5–21.
Winnicott, D. (1965) *The Maturational Processes and the Facilitating Environment*. New York, NY: I.U.P.
Wittgenstein, L. (1922). *Tractatus Logico-Philosophicus*. Translated by D. F. Pears and B. F. McGuinness. First published in 1961 by Routledge & Kegan Paul. Revised edition 1974. London and New York, NY: Routledge.
Wittgenstein, L. (1953) *Philosophical Investigations*. In P. M. S. Hacker and J. Schulte, (eds.) (4th edition). Hoboken, NJ: John Wiley & Sons, 2010.
Wolf, A & Schwartz, E. K. (1962). *Psychoanalysis in Groups*. New York, NY: Grune & Stratton.
Yalom, I. D. (1995) *The Theory and Practice of Group Psychotherapy* (3rd edition). New York, NY: Basic Books.
Zimerman, D. E. & Osório, L. C. (1999) Classificação Geral dos Grupos [General classification of groups]. In Zimerman, D. E. and Osório, L. C. et al. (eds.) *Como Trabalhamos com Grupos*. Brasil, Porto Alegre: Artmed, pp. 75–81.

Index

Page numbers in **bold** indicate **tables**.

Abraham, K. 15
actings-out 142
Adler, A. 12, 13, 15
aesthetic equilibrium 24, 34, 59–60
aggressiveness/aggression 64–67, 101, 130, 139–145, 148, 150, 152, 162
AGPA, *see* American Group Psychotherapy Association (AGPA)
Almeida, A. F. de 21
American Declaration of Independence (1776) 9
American Group Psychotherapy Association (AGPA) 39
analytic field conceptualization 64
analytic group psychotherapy 21, 133–134
analytic labour 59, 65
analytic societies, crisis in 155–157
Anarcho-Syndicalist International 9
Ancona, L. 23, 24
anger 139–144; *see also* destructivity/destructiveness
Anthony, E. J. 32, 76, 78
anti-group 26, 67, 97
Aristotle 139
Ashuach, S. 149
associative experience 121
autocratic monarchies 9
autonomy 5, 8, 14, 43–51, 56, 60, 64, 99, 110, 118, 141, 146, 154 Azevedo e Silva, J. 25, 26, 61, 62, 84, 124, 125

Bach, G. 15, 16
Bacon, F. 9
Badaracco, J. G. 26, 160
Balint groups 5, 40, **51**
Balint, M. 13, 22, 65, 119

Baranger, W. 64
basic fault 13, 65
Bateson, G. 18, 75
Battegay, R. 21, 100
Behr, H. 4, 29, 32, 36, 104
Benedict, R. 11
Berger, M. 139–140, 145
Bergson, M. 10
Berne, E. 16
Bertalanffy, L. von 12
"Beyond the Pleasure Principle" (Freud) 12
Billow, R. 103, 105
Bion, W. R. 6, 7, 13, 16–19, 25, 32, 33, 36, 62, 64, 75, 93, 103, 138, 164
Bivar, A. 87, 137–154
Biven, L. 138
Bokeman, F. 18
Bollas, C. 69
Boston Change Process Study Group 107, 132
Boston Study Group 64
Bowlby, J. 25
British Middle Group 13, 22
British Psychoanalytic Society 53
British Society of Psychoanalysis (BSPA) 92, 93
Brito, M. E. de 23, 86
Brown, D. 19, 32, 103, 105, 109
Brunori, L. 21
BSPA *see* British Society of Psychoanalysis (BSPA)
Burrow, T. 15–18, 32, 74, 76

Campbell, J. 34–35
Campos, J. 17, 24
Canestri, J. 30–31
Capisano, F. H. 24

Index

Carvalho, P. 21
Centeno, M. J. 7, 26, 28–52, 155–157
Coderch, J. 107
Cogito ergo sum 10
collective unconscious 13, 78
communication 84, 85, 134; disorder 81; group matrix 79; levels of 120–122; *see also* levels of experience/communication; and mental illness 75; metadramatic 8, 60–62, 124–125; non-verbal 65, 78, 85, 88, 102, 106, 116, 146; symbolic 65; theory of 20, 74–75; verbal 78, 84, 85, 88, 101, 102, 125, 146
Communist Manifesto (Marx and Engels) 9
commutative interpretation 58–59, 122
Comte, A. 10
conductors 2, 4–6, 23, 34–37, 41, 42, **43–51**, 62, 70, 91–94, 102–105, 110, 113, 116, 127, 166; *see also* groupanalysts/group analysts
Cortesão, E. L. 1, 5, 17, 24–25, 53, 61, 64, 65, 82, 113–125, 159–161, 168, 169; group analysis 21–24, 34, 137–154; groupanalysis *versus* Foulkes group analysis: designation 113; duration and frequency 114; influences 114; subject in the group *versus* group as a whole 115–116; theoretical foundations 114–115; therapeutic factors 116; transference neurosis 116–117; groupanalytic matrix 77–80; groupanalytic process 117–120; on hostile transference 149; legacy of group analysis: group transference neurosis 19, 23, 24, 25, 54, 57–62, 79, 80, 85, 119, 123, 126–133; interpretation 57–60; pattern 8, 54–56, 90–112; process 56–57; working-through 57–60
countertransference 6, 17, 54, 55, 62, 85, 126–136, 158 disclosure 162; in group-analytic psychotherapy 150–151
continuity 38, **43–51**
co-therapy **43–51**
counter transference **43–51**, 55, 165–166
Cozolino, L. 138, 139
creativity interpretation 122
crisis, in psychoanalysis and group analysis 30–31
"Critique of Practical Reason" (Kant) 10
"Critique of Pure Reason" (Kant) 10
CT awareness **43–51**
culturalists 12–13

Dalal, F. 29
Damásio, A. 3, 10, 138
David, M. 21
Davies, M. 37
defence mechanisms 18, 57, 62, 98, 109, 140, 147, 162, 165
delays in payment 142 de Abreu-Afonso, J. 126–136
demo groups 39–40, **50**
Dennis Brown Essay Prize 4
Derrida, J. 11
Descartes, R. 10
destructivity/destructiveness 101, 130, 140–145
developmental interpretation 122
Devereux, G. 12
Dias, C. A. 160
Dinis, C. V. 8, 25, 26, 55, 58, 62–65, 83, 85–86, 90–112, 122–124, 126–136, 137–154
"Discourse on the Method" (Descartes) 10
"double" axis theory 13
dreams 17, 19, 67–68, 111–112, 159
drop-outs 142, 145, 146, 152, 162
dual analytic psychotherapy 119
dual neurotic relationship 75
Dürkheim, E. 11
dystonic and syntonic, ego 59, 98, 110, 133, 146, 148, 166

economic context 9–12
Effective Therapists (ETs) 96–97
EFPP *see* European Federation for Psychoanalytic Psychotherapy (EFPP)
EGATIN *see* European Group Analytic Training Institutions Network (EGATIN)
ego 12, 13, 19, 69, 71
"Ego and the Id, The" (Freud) 12
"Ego and the Mechanisms of Defence" (Freud) 12
ego-dystonic changes **43–51**, 59, 110, 133
ego ideal 16
ego psychology, as a school of thought 14, 18
ego-syntonic changes **43–51**, 146, 148
'ego training in action' 19, 41, **43–51**, 59, 62, 80, 81, 93, 109, 116, 134
Elias, N. 18, 76
emotional corrective experience 105
emotional transformative experiences **43–51**

empathic resonance box 8, 25, 62–64, 85–86, 122–125, 131, 132, 138, 164
empathic symmetry 63
empathy 14, 42, **43–51**, 61, 64, 66, 69, 85, 97, 101, 102, 107, 109, 133, 138, 139, 148, 153, 154, 165
Engels, F.: Communist Manifesto 9
English School 80
Erikson, E. 12, 20, 76
erotic transference 143, 151–152
ETs *see* Effective Therapists (ETs)
Europe, industrial revolutions in 9
European Federation for Psychoanalytic Psychotherapy (EFPP) 30–31, 38; Group Section 6, 21
European Group Analytic Training Institutions Network (EGATIN) 6, 21, 38, 98, 155, 156, 167
experiential groups 40, **50**, 165
Ezriel, H. 17, 19

Fairbairn, W. R. D. 13, 22, 82, 97, 119, 142
family therapy 15
Ferenczi, S. 13, 15, 67
Fernandes, W. J. 24, 33, 160
Ferreira, A. G. 7, 9–27, 56, 58, 60, 61, 78, 82
Ferro, S. 7, 26, 53–72, 74, 138
field theory 76, 79, 114
figure-ground perception 76
Filipe, E. C. 23, 83–84
First European Symposium of Group Analysis (1970) 32
Fliess, W. 12
Fonagy, P. 2, 131
"Formulations on the Two Principles of Mental Functioning" (Freud) 12
43rd International Psychoanalytical Association Congress: "Psychoanalysis—Method and Application" 3
Fosshage, J. 69
Foucault, M. 11
Foulkes, E. 32, 160; group analysis *versus* Cortesão groupanalysis: designation 113; duration and frequency 114; influences 114; subject in the group *versus* group as a whole 115–116; theoretical foundations 114–115; therapeutic factors 116; transference neurosis 116–117

Foulkes, S. H. 1, 6, 7, 16, 17, 18–20, 23, 25, 26, 32, 34, 36, 53, 55, 62, 67, 76, 78, 80, 93, 109, 113–125; on conductor/therapist/group analysts 91–92; on pattern 91
Foulkes Day 20
França, M. 1, 7, 8, 53–72, 155–169
França de Sousa, J. 26, 138
Frank, L. K. 17
free-floating-discussion **43–51**
French Revolution (1789) 9
French Society of Psychoanalysis 93
Freud, A. 12
Freud, S. 12, 14–17, 22, 67, 74, 92–93, 118, 159
Friedman, R. 21

Galt, A. 17
Gans, J. S. 150–151
GAP *see* group-analytic/groupanalytic psychotherapy (GAP)
Garland, C. 6, 32, 35, 36, 94, 103, 105
Garza-Guerrero, C. 30, 155
GASi *see* Group Analytic Society International (GASi)
GAS *see* Group Analytic Society, London (GAS)
"General Psychology" (Jaspers) 10
general systems theory 79, 109, 114
genetic determinism 68–69
genetic reconstruction **43–51**
Gestalt theory 79
Goldstein, K. 19, 76, 78, 79, 114
Gomes, A. A. 27
good enough mother 13, 62, 66
Graham, F. W. 100
Green, A. 3, 30
Greenson, R. 14
gregariousness 92
Grinberg, L. 115
group analysis/groupanalysis 1–9, 18–27, 43–51, **44**, 137–154; British group 20–21; characteristics of 42; cluster identity of 28–52; controversies and ambiguities within 32–40; Cortesão 21–24; crisis in 30–31; definition of 32, 34–36, 41; distinguished from group-analytic psychotherapy 32; Foulkes 18–20; Foulkes *versus* Cortesão: designation 113; duration and frequency 114; influences 114; subject in the group *versus* group as a

whole 115–116; theoretical foundations 114–115; therapeutic factors 116; transference neurosis 116–117; multifamily 39; Portuguese school of 24–27, 53–72, 77, 80, 90, 94–112; transference-countertransference interaction in 133–134; *see also* group psychotherapy
groupanalysts/group analysts 2–6, 20, 21, 22, 24, 30, 31, 36, 37, 39–42, 80, 91–94, 97, 98, 101–103, 106, 110, 124, 127, 132, 135, 141; empathic symmetry of 63; frequency and length of analysis 167–168; groupanalyst pattern 106, 135, 167–168; long lasting idealization of 143; mental health 165; narcissism of 63–64; as a patient 155–169; patient's selection 26, 63, 95, 100–102; personhood of 63; responsibility of 63–64; training in mixed groups 165–166; *see also* conductors
group-analytic cluster 40–41; brand 41–42
Group Analytic Coaching 5, 40, 42, **49**
group-analytic/groupanalytic 7, 22–24, 26, 36, 41, 42, 55–57, 65, 68, 71, 73, 78–80, 82, 86–90, 95, 98, 102, 107, 108, 114, 117–121, 123, 125–127, 129, 137–154, 164, 168; *see also* training
groupanalytic matrix 23, 77–79; clinical practice of 86–88; culture in 84–85; definition of 77, 78; developments on 86–88; historic and evolutive perspectives of 73–76
groupanalytic pattern 22–24, 26, 79, 80, 86, 88, 110, 126
groupanalytic process 7, 22–24, 26, 36, 41, 42, 55–57, 65, 68, 71, 73, 78–80, 82, 86–90, 95, 98, 102, 107, 108, 114, 117–121, 123, 125–127, 129, 143, 145, 152, 164, 168; theoretical framework of 118–119
group-analytic/groupanalytic psychotherapy (GAP) 5–6, 29, 34, 37, 45, 103, 113, 133–134, 137–154; countertransference 150–151; distinguished from group analysis 32; Individual and relational psychopathology 146–148; meaning of 140–145; paradoxical group features 145–146; phenomenology of 140–145; transference 148–150; triggers of 145–151
"Group Analytic Psychotherapy: Method and Principles" (Foulkes) 19

Group Analytic Society, London (GAS) 4, 20, 21, 27, 29, 33, 93; Management Committee 21, 25
Group Analytic Society International (GASi) 6, 21, 29, 35, 41
Group Analytic Society Winter Workshop: "Group Analysis today: Concepts and Preconceptions" 2
group-analytic spectrum 5
group-analytic technique 119
group-analytic training: challenges 156; component 6; conductor's 42; within groupanalytic societies and institutes 155; Heidelberg Institute 168; influence in institutional interventions 27; institutions responsible for 34; organizations 8; in Portugal 119–120; training criteria within 37; unifying 21; *see also* training
group as a whole 6, 17, 55, 58, 66, 72, 74, 75, 79, 82, 84, 102–104, 123, 127, 132, 141, 149, 160, 162; vs individual interpretation 103, 124, 130–131; interpretation 43–51, 103, 132, 160; vs subject in the group 115–116
group designation **43**
group-object relation 97
group process 19, 27, 32, 36, 38, **43–51**, 81, 91, 93, 103–104
"Group Psychology and the Analysis of the Ego" (Freud) 92, 93
group psychotherapy 6, 15–18; basic principles of 17–18; *see also* group analysis
"Group Psychology and the Analysis of the Ego" (Freud) 15–16
"Group Psychotherapy: The Psychoanalytic Approach" (Foulkes) 26
group supervision 163–164
group transference neurosis 19, 23, 24, 25, 54, 57–62, 79, 80, 85, 87, 119, 123, 129, 130; complexity of 126–129
Grunbaum, A. 11
Grupanálise 77
"Grupanálise—Teoria e Técnica" (Groupanalysis—Theory and Technique) (Cortesão) 1
Guntrip, H. 13, 22, 97, 119

Hadden 21
Hartmann, H. 13, 14, 22, 82

Hearst, L. 32, 104
Hegel, G. W. F. 10
here-and-now vs. there-and-then **43–51**, 102, 104, 105, 110, 151
Hernández-Tubert, R. 33
Hilpert, H. R. 165–166, 168
historical context 9–12
"History of Western Philosophy, A" (Russell) 10
Hopper, E. 6, 20, 21, 25, 26, 34, 100, 105, 168, 169
horizontal transference 127
Horkheimer, M. 18
Horney, K. 12, 13
hostility 140, 141, 150–151
HSM *see* Santa Maria Hospital (HSM)
"Human Knowledge: Its Scope and Limits" (Russell) 10
Husserl, E. 10
Hutchinson, S. 29
Huxley, T. H. 76

ideal of the self 74
IGA see Institute of Group Analysis, London (IGA)
implicit mental model 69
implicit relational knowledge 69, 131
indirect therapeutic benefits 33, **43–51**
individual interpretation **43–51**
Individual psychopathology 146–148
individual relationship matrix *see* personal group matrix
individual subjective experience 120
inner space of optional doubt 62, 124–125
insight 1, 20, 24, 35, 54, 56, 57, 59, 64, 66, 95, 109, 110, 116, 121, 122, 124, 130, 153, 154
Institute of Group Analysis, London (IGA) 29, 33, 36, 103
institutional groups 40, **45**
internal interpersonal network *see* personal group matrix
internal relational matrix *see* personal group matrix
International Association for Group Psychotherapy 25
International Psychoanalytic Association (IPA) 92, 93
International Society of Group Psychotherapy 21
Internet groups 5, 40, **48**
interpersonalist 11–12

interpretation 20, 54, 64, 66, 102, 107, 57–60; dream interpretation 68; group as a whole vs individual interpretation 103, 124, 130–131; interpretative activity 56, 66, 67, 95, 110; meaning 122; mutative interpretation 54, 58, 59; transference neurosis interpretation 57–59, 85, 106; *see also* levels of interpretation
"Interpretation of Dreams, The" (Freud) 12
intersubjective 38, 39, 64, 69, 71, 83, 88, 90, 93, 99, 106, 109, 110, 119, 161, 162
intersubjectivism, 63
IPA *see* International Psychoanalytic Association (IPA)

Jacobson, E. 18
Jane Abercombie Prize 27
Jaspers, K. 10
Julio de Matos Hospital 26
Jung, C. 17

Kaës, R. 76, 82
Kant, I. 10
Kardiner, A. 12, 13
Kernberg, O. 22, 65–67, 97, 99
Kibel, H. 18
Kirsner, D. 156
Klapman, J. K. 16
Klein, M. 13
Kleinian group 13, 33
Knauss, W. 21
knowledge, theory of 10
Koch, S. 11
Kohut, H. 13–14, 18, 65–67, 82, 109, 119, 160
König, K. 24
Kreeger, L. 18

Lacan, J. 14
Lacanian group 20
language 61
large group 5, 18, 91, 158
Lavie, J. 80
Laxenaire, M. 14, 20
Leal, M. R. 15, 19, 23, 25, 60–61, 73, 83, 115; personal group matrix/internal relational matrix 7, 25, 26, 60–62, 73–76, 80–83, 87, 105, 126, 140, 146
learning 33, 42, **43–51**, 74–75, 99, 157, 160–161, 163, 166

Le Bon, G. 11, 92
Leffert, M. 108, 143
levels of experience/communication 120–121; *see also* communication, levels of
levels of interpretation 54, 57, 58, 115, 119, 121–122; commutative interpretation 54, 58, 119, 122; creativity interpretation 122; developmental interpretation 122; genetic-evolutionary interpretation 122; meaning interpretation 122; multiple subjective experience 121; transference interpretation 56, 58, 122
Lévy-Strauss, C. 12
Lewin, K. 12, 74, 76, 114
Linton, R. 11
Lisbon Group Analytic Society 5
Locke, N. 16, 17
"Logic of Scientific Discovery, The" (Popper) 11
Lorentzen, S. 6, 28, 32, 35, 38, 62, 94, 105, 156
Lorenz, K. 25

Mahler, M. 18
Main, T. 32
malignant mirroring 147, 148
Malinowski, B. 12
Mara Selvini Palazzoli School 15
Maré, P. de 18
Marques, P. M. 7, 8, 73–89, 113-125
Marten, R. 156
Marx, K.: Communist Manifesto 9
Marxism 9, 10
Mauss, M. 12
MBT-G *see* Mentalization-Based Group Therapy (MBT-G)
McDougall, W. 11, 92
Mead, G. 82
Mead, M. 11
Medina, F. 26
meeting moments 64, 132
Melo, J. C. 7, 8, 73–89, 113-125
Meltzer, D. 13
memory 69
Mentalization-Based Group Therapy (MBT-G) 38, 39, **47**
Mentalization-Based Treatment 42
mentalization capacities **43–51**
Merleau-Ponty, M. 10
metadramatic communication 8, 60–62, 124–125

metapsychology 12–13, 14, 71, 79, 90, 114, 118, 119
Meyer, A. 17
MFGA *see* multifamily groupanalysis (MFGA)
microculture 84
Miguel Bombarda Hospital 26
Miller, I. 38
Miller, J. G. 12
mirroring 25, 41, 60–62, 64, 66, 79, 81, 93; distorted mirroring 141, 146, 148; malignant mirroring 26, 146–148, 151, 153
mirror reaction 115; *see also* mirroring
Mollon, P. 139, 144
Molnos, A. 139
Money-Kyrle, R. 13
Moreno, F. 75
Moreno, J. L. 15, 21, 74–75
Moro, L. 163
"Moses and Monotheism" (Freud) 16
multifamily groupanalysis (MFGA) 5, 7, 26, 39, 46, 160
multiple subjective experience 121
Muñoz, M. 24
mutative interpretation 54, 58

narcissism 13–14, 22, 37, 60, 63–64, 63–67, 70, 86, 97, 101, 133, 138, 142–144, 152, 153, 156, 159, 162, 164, 165, 168, 169
Nava, A. S. 67
Nebbiosi, G. 106
negative therapeutic reaction (NTR) 142
Neto, I. M. 1, 7, 8, 21, 25, 27, 28–52, 65, 67–68, 86, 90–112, 138, 155–169
neuronal network 78, 79
neuropsychoanalysis 67
neuroscience 68–69
Nitsun, M. 26, 32, 34, 67, 94, 97, 100, 145
Nitzgen, D. 158
non-invasive conduction **43–51**
non-repressed unconscious 69
NTR *see* negative therapeutic reaction (NTR)

object relations theory (ORT) 13, 18, 22, 60, 62, 63, 71, 79, 85, 114, 118, 119, 160
Oedipus complex 58, 149, 160
Ogden, T. H. 161
Olsen, A. 29
"One Group Analysis or many?" (2017 GASi Symposium, Berlin) 29

on the group 16–17, 32–33, **43–51**, 85, 99, 114–115, 127
on the individual 33, **43–51**, 57, 74
"Open Society and Its Enemies, The" (Popper) 11
operative groups 32–34, **44–45**, **51**
organismic theory 19, 79, 114
organizational and educational syncretism 30
Ormont, L. 132
ORT *see* object relations theory (ORT)
Osório, L. C. 5, 33
"Outline of Psycho-Analysis, An" (Freud) 12

Paiva, L. M.; de 24
Palo Alto Group 15
Panksepp, J. 138
Paparo, F. 106
"Papers on Metapsychology" (Freud) 12
paradoxical group features 145–146
parents groups 5, 40, **46**
patient's selection 26, 63, 95, 100–102
pattern 5, 8, 11, 22–24, 26, 37, 39, 41, 42, 54–64, 69, 71, 77–79, 80, 86, 88, 90–113, 115, 119, 126, 130, 134, 135, 139, 140, 142, 146, 147, 150, 153, 160, 161, 164, 167–168; analytic interventions and interpretations of 102–107; attitudes 102; controversies of 91–94; debate of 91–94; definition of 94–112; function 100–107; history of 91–94; nature 96–100; objectives 107–112; rules of 101; selection 100–101; setting 101–102; in 21st century 112
personal groupanalysis 8, 26, 70, 90, 95, 98, 99, 110, 119, 156–159, 162, 163, 165, 167
personal group matrix/internal relational matrix 7, 25, 26, 60–62, 73–76, 80–82, 87, 105, 126, 140, 146; historic and evolutive perspectives of 73–76
personality 96–98
personhood 64
Pertegato, E. G. 74
philosophical context 9–12
"Philosophical Investigations" (Wittgenstein) 10
Pichon-Rivière, E. 16, 33, 60, 82
Pigott, C. 25, 32
Pines, M. 19–21, 24, 25, 32, 62, 76, 105, 109
Póci, N. 24

political leadership, personality features of 97
Popper, K. 11
Portuguese Groupanalytic Society 54; Statutes of the 114
Portuguese school of groupanalysis 1, 2, 7, 8, 21, 24–27, 32, 38, 53–72, 77, 80, 90, 98, 102–103, 109, 110, 146, 150, 155–158; empathic resonance box 8, 25, 62–64, 85–86, 122–125, 131, 132, 138, 164; group transference neurosis 57–60; inner space of optional doubt 62; metadramatic communication 60–62; neuroscience 68–69; pattern 5, 8, 11, 22–24, 26, 37, 39, 41, 42, 54–64, 69, 71, 77–79, 80, 86, 88, 90–113, 115, 119, 126, 130, 134, 135, 139, 140, 142, 146, 147, 150, 153, 160, 161, 164, 167–168; personal group matrix/internal relational matrix 7, 25, 26, 60–62, 73–76, 80–82, 87, 105, 126, 140, 146; preliminary considerations for 53–54; specificities in 64–68; working-through 17, 22, 23, 25, 54, 57–60, 68, 95, 99, 107, 109, 116–119, 124, 129, 130, 132, 154, 166
Portuguese Society of Neurology and Psychiatry, Groupanalytic Section 1
Portuguese Society of Psychoanalysis 93
Potthoff, P. 39
"Poverty of Historicism, The" (Popper) 11
Pratt, J. H. 15
"Principia Mathematica" (Russell) 10
"Project for a Scientific Psychology, The" (Freud) 12
"Psicoanálisis Multifamiliar" (Multifamily Psychoanalysis) 7
psychic groupality 82
psychoanalysis 2–3, 6; crisis in 30–31; as hermeneutics 3
psychoanalytic group psychotherapy *see* group psychotherapy
psychoanalytic group therapy: definition of 35
psychoanalytic theory: evolution of 12–15; new developments in 14–15
psychology, ego 14, 18, 22, 66, 71, 114
"Psychology. A Study of Science" (Koch) 11
punctuality 42, **43–51**, 101

Rank, O. 13, 15
Rapaport, D. 14, 22, 82
regression 19, **43–51**, 54–56, 58, 71, 80, 82, 95, 114–115, 117–118, 123, 126, 130, 134–135, 161
Reich, W. 13
relational paradigms 1, 63, 64, 71
relational psychopathology 146–148
repetition-compulsion 57, 142
repressed unconscious 69
resonance 8, 19, 25, 41, 62–64, 67, 79, 81, 82, 85–86, 93, 122–125, 131, 132, 138, 164
reverie 62, 66
Ribeiro, N. A. 20, 24, 26, 76
Rickman, J. 32, 75
Róheim, G. 12
Roose, S. 37
Ruesch, J. 18, 75
Russell, B. 10

Sandison, R. 100
Santa Maria Hospital (HSM) 26; Psychiatric Day Hospital 39
Santos, M. 118
Saussure, F. de 14
scapegoating 140–143
Schilder, P. 15, 76
Schützemberger, A. 24
Schwartz, E. K. 16
scientific context 9–12
self-disintegration 66
self-disorganization 66
self-knowledge/insight 24, 35, 42, **43–51**, 54, 56, 57, 59, 64, 66, 107, 110, 116, 121–122, 124, 130, 133, 153–154
self psychology 13–14, 18, 22, 63, 66, 71, 109, 114, 144, 160
setting 1, 4–8, 15, 19, 28, 37–41, 54, 56–58, 61, 62, 64–67, 69, 70, 71, 91, 94, 98, 100–102, 106, 108, 110, 123, 125–127, 132–134, 137–154, 157, 159, 165, 167, 168; duration 101; frequency 101; selection 100
shame 139, 144
Shedler, J. 108
Sheffield University 29
sibling rivalry 149
Silva, J. A. 24
Silva, R. da 27
16th European Symposium of GASi, Lisbon (2014) 7

Slavson, N. R. 16
social atom 75
Socialist Internationals 9
social leadership, personality features of 97
'Sociedade Portuguesa de Grupanálise e Psicoterapia Analítica de Grupo' (SPGPAG, Portuguese Society of Groupanalysis and Analytic Group Psychotherapy) *see* Portuguese school of groupanalysis
socio-political context 9–12
Souza, R. F. de 82
specificities, in groupanalysis 64–68
SPGPAG *see* 'Sociedade Portuguesa de Grupanálise e Psicoterapia Analítica de Grupo' (SPGPAG, Portuguese Society of Groupanalysis and Analytic Group Psychotherapy)
SPG *see* Portuguese Society of Groupanalysis (SPG)
Spitzer, R. 37
"Spontaneity Theory of Child Development" (Moreno & Moreno) 75
Statutes of the Portuguese Groupanalytic Society 114
Stekel, W. 15
Stern, D. 64, 69, 131–132
Stone, W. 144, 150
Strachey, J. 57, 58
structuralism 12
Sullivan, H. S. 12, 13
Sulloway, F. 11
super-ego 18, 19
supervision 70, 71, 99, 120, 157–158; duration of 164–165; frequency of 164–165; group 163–164; importance of 161–165
supervision groups 33, **51**, 162–163
Sutherland, J. D. 17
symbolic communication 65
symptomatic release **43–51**
"Systematic Review of the Efficacy and Clinical Effectiveness of Group Analysis and Analytic/Dynamic Group Psychotherapy, A" (Group Analytic Society, University of Sheffield) 4

Tarde, G. 11
task-centred groups 5, 33, 40, **51**
Tavistock group 17, 36, 103

team work groups 40, **51**
therapeutic action, evolution of 23
therapeutic alliance **43–51**
therapeutic factors 38, 116, 134–136
"Therapeutic Group Analysis" (Foulkes) 19
therapeutic groupanalysis 2, 5, 8, 28, 30, 33, 39, 44, 151–154
therapeutic objectives 3, 33, 120, 164; analytic cure/psychoanalytic cure **43–51**, 56, 157, 161; objectives **43–51**; results **43–51**
Thomae, H. 156
to see/to be seen 64–65, 69, 106, 124, 139, 156
"Totem and Taboo" (Freud) 15
"Tractatus Logico-Philosophicus" (Wittgenstein) 10
training 2, 5–8, 18, 20, 21, 24, 27, 30, 33, 34, 36–38, 42, 55, 59, 62, 69–72, 76, 80, 90, 93, 98–100, 109, 110, 116–120, 125, 130, 134, 137, 155–169; block training 38, 155, 161, 165, 166; 'ego training in action' 19, 41, 59, 62, 80, 81, 93, 109, 116, 134; group-analytic 119–120, 155; in mixed groups 165–166; personal groupanalysis 8, 26, 70, 90, 95, 98, 99, 110, 119, 156–159, 162, 163, 165, 167; programme 27, 38, 71, 98, 137, 155–157, 159, 160, 165, 167–169; programme structure 157–158; supervision 5, 8, 30, 33, 37, 70, 71, 95, 99, 101, 110, 120, 121, 130, 155–157, 158, 161–165; theoretical programme 158–161
transference 6, 19, 64, 69, 126–136, 158; erotic 143, 151–152; in group-analytic psychotherapy 148–150; in group-analytic treatment 134–136; group transference neurosis 19, 23, 24, 25, 54, 57–62, 79, 80, 85, 87, 119, 123, 126–133; horizontal 127; hostile 149; interpretation 122; lateral 127–128; neurosis 116–117; simultaneous 127
transference interpretation 43–51, 56, 58, 122; *see also* interpretation

transgenerational inheritance 6
treatment-groups (T-groups) 40, **50**
Trotter, W. 11, 92
Tsegos, Y. 21
Tubert, R. H. 32, 33
Tubert-Oklander, J. 3, 32, 33

unconscious processes 17, 36, 55, 67, 84, 127, 141
Urturbey, L. de 135

Valbak, K. 29
Valente da Silva, A. 86
Vaughan, S. 37
vernacular psychoanalysis 38
Vienna Group 15

Wallerstein, R. S. 3, 30, 108
Wampold, B. 96
WASP *see* World Association of Social Psychiatry (WASP)
Watson, J. S. 25
Weinberg, H. 32, 39–40
Wender, L. 15
Wernicke, C. 20
Wilke, G. 32
Winnicott, D. W. 13, 22, 62, 66, 67, 97, 119
Winther, G. 21
Wittgenstein, L. 10
Wolf, A. 16, 17
working-through 17, 22, 23, 26, 54, 57–60, 68, 95, 99, 107, 109, 116–119, 124, 129, 130, 132, 154, 166
World Association of Social Psychiatry (WASP) 27

Yalom, I. D. 18, 40
year-round course 161
Young, D. 4

Zaslavsky, J. 118
Zender, J. 100
Zimerman, D. 5, 16, 25, 30, 33, 100, 105, 108–109, 128, 146, 160
Zinkin, L. 26, 147